DATE DUE

PRIMITIVE MUSIC

Da Capo Press Music Reprint Series

GENERAL EDITOR

FREDERICK FREEDMAN

VASSAR COLLEGE

PRIMITIVE MUSIC

*An Inquiry Into the Origin and Development
of Music, Songs, Instruments, Dances and
Pantomimes of Savage Races*

By Richard Wallaschek

DA CAPO PRESS · NEW YORK · 1970

A Da Capo Press Reprint Edition

This Da Capo Press edition of
Primitive Music
is an unabridged republication of
the first edition published in
London in 1893.

Library of Congress Catalog Card Number 72-125062

SBN 306-70028-X

Published by Da Capo Press
A Division of Plenum Publishing Corporation
227 West 17th Street
New York, N.Y. 10011

PRIMITIVE MUSIC

ABERDEEN UNIVERSITY PRESS

PRIMITIVE MUSIC

AN INQUIRY INTO THE ORIGIN AND DEVELOPMENT OF
MUSIC, SONGS, INSTRUMENTS, DANCES, AND
PANTOMIMES OF SAVAGE RACES

BY

RICHARD WALLASCHEK

WITH MUSICAL EXAMPLES

LONDON
LONGMANS, GREEN, AND CO.
AND NEW YORK: 15 EAST 16TH STREET
1893

PREFACE.

IT was a suggestion of my friend Dr. Edward Wester-marck that my original essays on primitive music should be revised and amplified so as to form a fairly serviceable treatise on the subject. While engaged in this work I have met with so much assistance and encouragement that I can only quite inadequately acknowledge my deep gratitude to Mrs. Plimmer, Prof. and Mrs. Sully for all the help and advice (scientific and other) they have given me from the beginning of my labours. I have also to express my thanks to Mr. R. H. Legge for his aid in preparing this English version of the work for the press, to Prof. Rhys Davids and Mr. James Sime for giving me the benefit of their knowledge and experience, and to Dr. H. R. Mill for his kind revision of the proof-sheets and for his most valuable suggestions in so many geographical and ethnological details.

As to the importance of ethnology for the science of art I need hardly say many words, it being a generally accepted fact. In the present work it has been my aim to deal with the music of savage races only, while the music of ancient civilisation has merely been glanced at whenever it was necessary to indicate the connecting links between the most primitive and the comparatively advanced culture.

With regard to technical particulars I may mention that on Dr. Mill's advice the names of savage tribes are spelt according to the new system proposed in 1891 by the London Geographical Society. The mode of quoting adopted in this book is that I refer with *l. c.* to the book mentioned in the list of authorities at the end of this work.

RICHARD WALLASCHEK.

LONDON, *April*, 1893.

LIST OF CONTENTS.

CHAPTER I.

General Character of the Music of Primitive People.

CHAPTER II.

SINGERS AND COMPOSERS IN PRIMITIVE TIMES.

CHAPTER III.

INSTRUMENTS.

CHAPTER VII.

Dance and Music.

CHAPTER VIII.

Primitive Drama and Pantomime.

CHAPTER IX.

Origin of Music.

CHAPTER X.

Heredity and Development.

CHAPTER I.

GENERAL CHARACTER OF THE MUSIC OF PRIMITIVE PEOPLE.

1. AFRICA.

It is with music as with language : however far we might descend in the order of primitive people, we should probably find no race which did not exhibit at least some trace of musical aptitude, and sufficient understanding to turn it to account. In fact it would appear that among races of the very lowest order of civilisation there are frequently to be found some which have more musical capacity than many of a higher order. This is undoubtedly the case with the *Bushmen*.

The Bushman sings while he dances, swaying his body about in strict time with the music; nor does he cease until, tired out, he sinks to the ground and once more takes breath. Then he sings again, still keeping time to the music, and, raising himself quickly, begins to dance with renewed vigour. When dancing in his hut he leans upon two sticks, the lowness of the roof not admitting of his standing upright, while the hut itself is so small that it is only in the middle of a narrow circle that there is sufficient room for even a single dancer.[1] Notwithstanding this apparently tiring amusement, the Bushman takes manifest delight in the dance, and the more weary he becomes the happier he is.[2]

[1] Burchell, *l. c.*, ii. p. 63.
[2] Wood, *Nat. Hist. of Man*, i. p. 292.

It may well be imagined what the atmosphere of the hut is, and what the effect of a Bushman dance. It is indeed similar to that of a Turkish bath, and travellers state that an European could scarcely exist in it. This may be, but, at the same time, I am of opinion that it would not fare better with a Bushman were he to enter a ball-room in a small country village of Germany. He would find that the bodily exertion is not less severe than that of the savages, while the fumes of gas, tobacco, food and drink are not much of an improvement upon those of a Bushman's hut.

Burchell gives two examples of dance melodies[1] [Mus. Ex. 20], and he is quite correct in asserting that they contain very strange combinations of sound. Other travellers, too, who have heard them have spoken of them in terms of high praise, Burchell even going so far as to declare that mere words were insufficient to describe their beauties. "They must be heard; they must be participated in." From these dances he derived as much pleasure as did the natives, so quiet and orderly were they. No rude laughter, no noisy shouting, no coarse, drunken, ribald wit was there; throughout it was a modest, sociable amusement. For this reason Burchell wished that these poor creatures might be more justly judged than is usually their lot, and, as a matter of fact, had he not had further experience of them, he would not have hesitated to declare the Bushmen the happiest of mortals. "Music softened all their passions, and thus they lulled themselves into that mild and tranquil state in which no evil thoughts approach the mind. The soft and delicate voices of the girls, instinctively accordant to those of the women and the men, the gentle clapping of the hands, the rattles of the dancers, and the mellow sound of the water-drum, all harmoniously attuned and keeping time

[1] *L. c.*, pp. 66-87.

together, the peaceful happy countenances of the party, and the cheerful light of the fire—were circumstances so combined and fitted to produce the most soothing effects on the senses, that I sat as if the hut had been my home, and felt as though I had been one of them." [1]

Whether this effect is to be entirely attributed to the music or not is an open question. I think that in all probability it was partly due to the romantic scenery, to the unusual appearance of the natives, to the unvarying monotony of the three constantly repeated bars of melody. Whatever may be the capabilities of their music, the Bushmen understand to some extent how "tune" is made, and undoubtedly this is an artistic beginning.

The *Hottentots* are great whistlers, and for this purpose they draw their lips to one side and whistle between their teeth.[2] Burchell asserts that dance music is the most congenial to the Hottentots, "at least among all the musicians who were at different times in his service, none ever played any other kind, nor did Burchell ever hear a Hottentot performing a slow air, or singing to his own performance ".[3] Many of the natives cannot discriminate between a regular tune and a mere noise, and Burchell's flute had no effect whatever upon them.

On his journey to Kafirland, Burchell, at Litakun, met with tribes which found a great source of delight in European music. In the evening a whole army of boys would come to his hut and listen with manifest pleasure to the tones of his violin, and would repeat the melodies he played with surprising accuracy.[4] The neighbouring Kafir races, however, do not appear to share this gift; they have, in fact, a very singular conception of music. "Their notion of melody is but very slight, while their timing is perfection itself, and the very fact that several hundred men will sing the various war-songs as if they

---

[1] *L. c.*, ii. p. 66.   [2] Thunberg, *l. c.*, p. 37.
[3] Burchell, *l. c.*, ii. p. 396.   [4] *Ibid.*, *l. c.*, ii. p. 438.

were animated with a single spirit shows that they must
all keep the most exact time." [1]   During the song they
remain seated, making very violent movements the while,
and by striking their elbows against their ribs with all
their power drive out the air from their lungs.   Shooter
gives a few musical examples. [2]   [Mus. Ex. I.]   The
natives sing in a kind of falsetto, suddenly dropping
into a gruff bass, and they seem to think that a song is
no song unless it be sung with the whole power of the
lungs.   The same is the case, I am afraid, in much more
cultured countries.   Of harmony there is absolutely no
trace; they care only for unison singing.

Stevens heard a round sung by the Batlapi Kafirs
in which the moon was compared to a heartless, loveless
hound which wandered alone, cold and insensible, through
the sky.   The Batlapi reminded Weber of Venetian
Gondoliers, or of the Lazzaroni in Naples.   One would
improvise a stanza which others would immediately sing
in chorus to a charming melody.   Each in turn impro-
vises thus so that all have an opportunity of exhibiting
their talents for poetry and wit.   The fact that all words
ended in a vowel-sound simplified the extemporisation of
verses which were not invariably accurate as regards
rhythm.   The general singing of these stanzas seemed to
afford the greatest amusement to the singers as they sat
in a circle round the camp fire.   Weber adds that the
Hottentots and Bushmen have no songs at all, and the
Eastern Kafirs only their ear-splitting war-songs. [3]   The
Kafirs who travelled with Weber were not in the least
impressed with the Prayer from " Norma," or with that
from " Les Huguenots," but the Radetzki march and a
Spanish song attracted them.   One Bechuana man had
constructed an instrument for himself after the manner
of a European piano, by stretching steel wires over

[1] Wood, *Nat. Hist. of Man*, i. p. 229.   [2] Shooter, *l. c.*, p. 237.
[3] Weber, *l. c.*, i. p. 221.

hollow water-melons; these wires were played by means of small reed hammers.[1]

The reports concerning Bechuana music are for the most part unfavourable. In Shoshong (the residence of the Bechuana chief Matcheen), a village of some 30,000 inhabitants, the traveller Mohr seems to have had few opportunities of hearing interesting music. The noise of drums, dancing and howling was kept up uninterruptedly day and night; "it was just the time when the young women who had reached maturity had to undergo singular treatment and ceremonies". Numbers of these dusky damsels are as it were chaperoned by old women, who, armed with branches of a prickly thorn, pounce upon every man who attempts anything against the girls. The latter are tormented by excessive watching, and are inured to hard work in order that they may be prepared for the duties of a housewife.[2]

Music is not very much better with the *Damaras*. Their highest idea of a musical performance merely consists in the imitation of the galloping or trotting of various animals.[3] Thus it appears that rhythmical movements are considered the main point. The Damaras are great lovers of animals, notably of oxen and sheep, of which they possess enormous herds; but so slight is their intelligence that they are utterly unable to count their number. Nevertheless, they never lose an animal: they recognise the face of every head of cattle which they have once seen! These things considered it can readily be understood that cattle form the chief subjects of their poetry. The Damaras rarely dance; in fact, only on extraordinary occasions; and they sing just as rarely *together*,[4] although fond of solo-singing, the words for which they extemporise while the refrains are taken up by a chorus. Their dances are for the most part war-

[1] Weber, *l. c.*, i. p. 140.　　[2] Mohr, *l. c.*, i. p. 160.
[3] Galton, *Travels, etc.*, p. 117.　　[4] *Ibid.*

dances, but occasionally they give expression to ordinary feelings by dancing. So says Galton, at any rate, when speaking of a dance which they performed after having slain two men whom they had falsely accused of cattle-stealing.[1] Possibly the occurrence of a robbery gave rise to such excitement in the tribe as could only be quieted down by an abnormal effort.

But the Damaras are not the only tribe in whose art-system cattle play the most important part. The *Makololo* dance and sing with even greater tumultuous excitement and consequent fatigue. Livingstone, who once witnessed such a dance, wondered how such exertions could give pleasure. "It is very hard work," replied the dancer, "but it is very nice, and Sekeletu (their chief) will give us an ox for dancing for him."[2] This reply may surprise us, yet how often may one see in European concert-rooms an artist worn out by exertions which have only demonstrated the strength and endurance that have enabled him to overcome every technical difficulty and nothing more. He deems the playing with all the strength of his arm to be the only right method, and when at length he quits the hall, weary and dishevelled, he, too, seems to say: "It's hard work, but Sekeletu will give me an ox for playing for him". Undoubtedly in this naïve expression of the savages we can see a good thing—our own, hitherto veiled Psychology. Is it indeed remarkable that the Kafir in his poetry only recognises a threefold subject: war, cattle and excessive adulation of his ruler?[3] The hymns to the chief are for the most part written by himself! How comic this seems to us, and yet every day just such things occur in civilised countries, the only difference being that in the latter, people are more ceremonious. However this may be, the fact which we must not lose sight of now is that

[1] Galton, *Travels, etc.*, p. 55.   [2] Livingstone, *l. c.*, p. 225.
[3] Waitz, ii. p. 387.

the subject of primitive Art is very simple, and has little bearing upon the higher emotion of Love.

Proceeding from Kafir- and Damara-land into the heart of Africa we come to the *Congo* people. The tribes of the Lower Congo are usually described as indolent.[1] Who knows if this be correct? To judge from Tuckey's account they are dreamers rather. Of the men of Inga it is said that they devote themselves to a kind of art-decoration. If one of them receive a few vari-coloured beads, he relinquishes his work in the fields to his wife, while he remains at home stringing the beads together in all manner of combinations until he discover an arrangement which pleases his fancy. In spite of this "indolence" the Ingese, like all the people of the Congo, take great delight in a species of dancing, which consists of different gesticulations and movements of the arms not always the most artistic. Their song, of which they are particularly fond, is merely a monotonous howl, not exactly adapted to gratify the ear.[2]

A similar report is given by Schweinfurth of the *Bongo* tribes. Their orgies always impressed him with the idea that the natives were merely attempting to surpass in violence the fury of the elements![3] It is strange that he likens their music to a bubbling recitative in which the words, as it were, stumble upon each other. "At one time it suggests the yelping of dogs, at another the lowing of a cow." This may be, but as a rule such is not the character of our recitative. He may be correct, however, in associating music with our imitative instincts. It is but a question of what is imitated, and this is clear enough in the case of primitive music.

There still remains a long list of minor races all of whom in their different ways have a characteristic conception of music. In Guinea all music is at an end

[1] Tuckey, *l. c.*, p. 198. [2] *Ibid.*, *l. c.*, p. 373.
[3] Schweinfurth, *l. c.*, i. p. 130.

during periods of mourning.[1] In the kingdom of Benin, on the other hand, such occasions are made use of for the expression of lamentations and funeral songs, which are at the same time accompanied by the music of their instruments. These instruments cease at stated intervals of time, during which the entire assembly gives itself up to drink.[2] These Benin-negroes are an original people; they play willingly enough, but never for money, only for beans.[3]

The *Abongo* people, a race of dwarfs in West Africa, have no musical instruments, and content themselves by striking two pieces of wood together while they improvise songs which consist of nothing but lengthy repetitions of words describing certain circumstances, as "The white man is a good man and gives the Abongo salt," etc. Notwithstanding this fondness of the negroes for singing, Lenz never found a single song amongst any of the tribes he visited which had been handed down from generation to generation; everywhere they were merely a verse or two improvised to describe some passing event.[4]

Mungo Park gives a description of a strange custom which was introduced with song and dance. If a Kafir or negro is unable to keep his wives in order, a festival is held to settle the quarrel, and all the inhabitants of the village are invited to take part. At midnight there is a sudden stillness during which Mumbo Jumbo appears bearing a club as his insignia of office, seizes the quarrelsome wife, who is naked, binds her to a stake, and amid the shouts of laughter of the audience, gives her a sound drubbing.[5]

Mbira-music of the *Makalaka*, which is by no means unpleasant to listen to, usually consists of a phrase of

[1] *Astley Collect.*, iii. p. 22.   [2] *Ibid.*, p. 97e.
[3] *Ibid.*, p. 96.   [4] Lenz, *l. c.*, p. 111.
[5] Schauenburg, *l. c.*, p. 92; ill. Wood, i. 675.

eight bars repeated *ad infinitum;* to it are sung improvised verses with a refrain.[1]

The *Inenga* are given up to drink : they especially like
rum, the arrival of which in a village is always a cause of
festivity, of obscene dances and of much brawling. I
cannot let this pass without stating that this particular
form of entertainment has probably the influence of civilisation to thank for its origin.[2]

The Hottentot *Korana* appear to be very gifted ; they
are described as " docile, good-tempered, and were not only
willing but impatiently desirous of gaining knowledge of
a missionary who visited them ; they invariably asked
that he would teach them the alphabet with music, and
many a night's rest was interrupted by their inordinate
desire for instruction ".[3]

The *Karagwe* tribes have small, plaintive songs which
were easily remembered and repeated, " they were so
sweet and pleasing to the ear ".[4] Among the *Mittu* tribes
music is held in high esteem : they appreciate a genuine
melody better than any other African tribe, while the
majority of negroes—as Schweinfurth asserts in opposition to the statements of other travellers—only recognise
alliterations and recitatives. He once heard a chorus
sung by a hundred Mittus, male and female, old and
young, who kept admirable time, and succeeded by a
gradual cadence in producing some very effective variations
of a well-sustained air.[5]

Much less poetical apparently are the *Wanyori* in so
far as we can determine from the utterances of their king.
His ideal is the musical-box. " One does not require to
study it, and it can be set going at night to play you to
sleep when you are too drunk to play it yourself." [6]

Who, however, would think of making a tribe answer-

[1] Mauch, *l. c.*, p. 43. [2] Lenz, *l. c.*, p. 57.
[3] Wood, *l. c.*, p. 303. [4] Grant, *l. c.*, p. 182.
[5] Schweinfurth, *l. c.*, p. 198. [6] Baker, S. W., *Ismailïa*, p. 355.

able for the statements of a not very gifted king?
Elson though says of the people themselves that a
London organ-grinder could march through Central Africa
always accompanied by a horde of enthusiastic and
admiring followers.[1] It is said, too, that a musical-box
created a great sensation among the *Aduma* (West Africa),
and that hundreds of curious negroes listened devoutly
to the strains of " Czar und Zimmermann," and the
" Marseillaise ". Lenz frequently made use of the
wonderful effect of the instrument when he wished to
accomplish some hazardous enterprise.[2] Renoki, King of
the Inenga (West Africa), derived great pleasure from a
beautiful musical-box, and was never tired of listening to
the melodies of "Madame Angot".[3] But from the descriptions I am of opinion that it was not only the music
but the works of the instrument which drew forth so
much admiration ; the wheels and cylinders astonished
him greatly, and the majority of savages wished to *see*
the box.

Many tribes use their musical ear for other than
artistic purposes. The *Maruns* (Sierra Leone), for
example, have intercourse with each other at great
distances with the help of a horn, and they can recognise
the note when ordinary individuals can scarcely hear the
sound. On this horn they have a fixed "call" (a species
of Leitmotiv) for each one, so that they are enabled to
summon whom they please.[4] For this it is obviously
necessary to have a definite sense of melody.

Now, however, if we turn to a group concentrated in
East Africa we find comparatively favourable reports.
Stanley, at any rate, speaks in terms of high praise of
East African music. In mentioning the phalanx dance
of Mazamboni's warriors, he says : " There are solos and
duets, but there must always be a chorus, the grander

[1] Elson, *l. c.*, p. 274.   [2] Lenz, *l. c.*, pp. 286-7.
[3] *Ibid.*, *l. c.*, p. 62.   [4] Dallas, *l. c.*, i. p. 89.

the better, and when the men, women and children lift
their voices high above the drums and the chatter and
murmur of the crowd, I must confess to having enjoyed
it immensely, especially when the Wanyamwezi are the
performers, who are by far the best singers on the African
continent. The Zanzibaris, Zulus, Waian, Wasegara,
Waseguhha and Wagindo are in the main very much
alike in method and execution, though they have each
minor dances and songs, which vary considerably, but
they are either dreadfully melancholic or stupidly barbarous."[1] Stanley believes that only Wanyamwezi music
would gratify an English audience. For this reason
possibly Burton's verdict was so unfavourable, for he
wrote that music in East Africa was at a very low ebb.
It is nevertheless marvellous how the East Africans keep
time, although they are no melodists, while their instruments are imported from Madagascar and the coast.[2] They
delight in singing, yet they have no metrical songs and
their recitative usually ends with "Ah, ha".[3] A simple
and largely-used musical exercise is that which Behr
describes: "One musical negro takes a drum, strikes it,
and is accompanied by the lookers-on with singing and
time-beating. Dancers surround the drummer, and move
backwards and forwards according to the rhythm of the
songs."[4] More striking is the cultivation of the rhythmic
sense described by Grant, whose people when cleaning
rice were always supported by singers who accompanied
the workers with hand-clapping and foot-stamping. This
was kept up until the rice was almost ground to powder.[5]

If we now once more go to the West and examine
the music of tribes which have been in contact with
Europeans for years we find among the *Ashantis* music
in a high state of cultivation. Both here and in Dahomey

---

[1] *In Darkest Africa*, i. p. 412.　　[2] Burton, *Lake Reg.*, ii. p. 291.
[3] *Ibid.*, p. 338.　　[4] Behr, *l. c.*, p. 243.
[5] Grant, *l. c.*, p. 62.

there is harmony in the music, which by some is considered the best in Africa,[1] although so delicate a question
as this can only be decided by one who has had experience
of the harmony of all African tribes, which is the case
with no scientific writer. A few of the Ashanti songs
are in the form of dialogues and the *rôles* are sung by
both sexes, who step out in turn from the ranks of the
performers as they stand opposite to each other with their
Sankús and other instruments.[2] In Dahomey the king
himself dances and sings during the festivals which precede
human sacrifices and which are of common occurrence
there. His song is answered by a chorus which sounds
like laughter, but is in reality a song of mourning while
a melancholy accompaniment is made by means of a
cymbal. Then the king raises himself, holding his sceptre
on high, and prays to his father's spirit.[3] Quite opposed
to the praise lavished by Waitz upon the music of Dahomey
is the opinion of Bouche in speaking of its orchestras:
"Cette musique sauvage ne sourrait être riche qu'en
discords".[4] Song and tam-tam are the usual accompaniment of a rhapsodist.[5] Even at the festivities the songs
and dances are most wearying in their monotony. Young
girls engaged in the service of the fetishes constantly
repeat the prayers "Ah, Han!" in two different tones,
this only occasionally being varied by the cry "Kyrie,"
which suggests at once the influence of Christianity.[6]

Further West still in Fort St. Louis the natives sing

---

[1] Waitz, *l. c.*, ii. p. 238.   [2] Beecham, *l. c.*, pp. 167-8.
[3] Burton, *Mission to Gelele*, i. p. 365. Concerning these human sacrifices, which will disgust many Europeans, I cannot refrain from quoting a
very apt statement of Burton's. Only malefactors and prisoners of war
are slain. "In the year of grace 1864 four murderers were hanged in
Liverpool in view of 160,000 people. The last but one of our Christian
kings caused a starving mother of seventeen, with her child at her breast, to
be put to death because she had stolen a yard of linen from a shop."
Other lands can tell similar stories.
[4] Bouche, *l. c.*, p. 95.   [5] *Ibid.*, *l. c.*, p. 92.   [6] *Ibid.*, *l. c.*, p. 97.

some war-songs in praise of their princes and generals, and into these songs they never fail to introduce compliments, but unfortunately they do it in their own interests.[1] Other parts of Africa are now so much in touch with civilisation as to have little importance for us; at the same time a few examples of, as it were, semi-civilisation will be of interest. The natives of Abyssinia accompany their religious ceremonies with music, beating the earth with sticks and emphasising the strokes with suitable bodily movements. When they become warm the beating ceases, and they begin to dance and jump, clapping their hands and shouting at the top of their voices until at length all idea of melody and metre is lost, and it becomes a riotous rather than a religious assembly.[2] Nevertheless they consider themselves to be the true Christians.

Again, European influence may be remarked in *Angola*, where the negroes whistle and sing every tune which they have once heard from a European.[3] The *Moors*, too, in *Morocco* are musical and have some sustained songs, melancholy in their monotony, while those in a quick *tempo* are both simple and pretty.[4] The *Bedouins* of *Juf* are renowned for their poetical and musical talents. Their singers from time to time visit the *Aenezes* and sing for a small *pour boire* before the tents of the Sheikty.[5] The Arabs, however, do not seem to possess great inventive powers, for the songs of their women (Asámer) and those of the men (Hojeing) are always sung to the same melody.[6] Music in *Morocco* is in a truly pitiable condition. In days gone by there dwelt there people who could sing the Alkoran in the original verse-metre in spite

---

[1] Brüe, *l. c.*, p. 48.   [2] Lobo, *l. c.*, p. 27.

[3] Soyaux (*l. c.*, ii. p. 178) quotes in music three Angola songs and six Mbalundu.

[4] Lempriere, *l. c.*, p. 773.   [5] Burckhardt, *l. c.*, p. 43.

[6] Arab. and Moor. instr. and mus. ex.: Shaw, *l. c.*, p. 270 *seq.*; Brown, *l. c.*, pp. 183-213.

of the difficulty of reducing the Alkoran language into regular periods.[1] Musicians never appear to be embarrassed by this difficulty. The natives have both vocal and instrumental music which is pedantic and commonplace, everything fresh being avoided.[2] Much more musical are the *Ethiopians*. Stanley describes their *Canto Trionfale*, in which the high voices of the women and children, harmonising with the deep voices of the men, sounded like the shrill whistling of the wind through the rigging of a ship during the roar of a mighty storm.[3]

Before quitting Africa let us glance at *Madagascar*. The Malagasy are passionately fond of music, and several of their songs have been highly praised by travellers for their beauty. Strangely enough the language of the natives and their *poetry* have produced no single rhythmical work.[4] On the other hand, their *music is* rhythmical. The constant, regular clapping of hands which gives the measure to the music is quite affecting to Europeans.[5] In addition to this rhythmical music they also have a sort of alternating recitative. The subject of the song is usually declared in the first line, which also gives it its name; it is begun by a chorus and answered by the leader until the chorus once more begins, and so on.[6] Madame Ida Pfeiffer's report is less favourable; this clever and resolute lady was the first of her sex to undertake these long journeys in order to see, study and understand the world. At a national festival the natives sang and danced for her, but all was dull and uninteresting. A few girls struck a small stick with all their might against a bamboo post, while others sang, or rather

[1] Addison, *l. c.*, pp. 422-5.   [2] *Ibid.*, *l. c.*, p. 439.

[3] Stanley, *Coomassie*, p. 489; *Egypt. Instr.* by Lenoir de la Fage, *l. c.;* Comettant, *l. c.*, pp. 574-6.

[4] J. Richardson, *l. c.*, p. 23, etc.; Sibree, *l. c.*, p. 97.

[5] Ellis, *Hist. of Mad.*, i. p. 274.

[6] *Ibid.*, p. 275.

howled, at the top of their voices, and the uproar was truly horrible.[1]

The general character of African music, then, is the preference for rhythm over melody (when this is not the sole consideration); the union of song and dance; the simplicity, not to say the humbleness, of the subjects chosen; the great imitative talent in connection with the music and the physical exertion and psychical excitement from which it arises and to which it appears so appropriate.

2. ASIA.

Asia, the "cradle of mankind," is for the ethnologist a less profitable study than are other parts of the globe. The lasting memorials of the most ancient civilisation are, indeed, a warning to him to proceed with the greatest caution. To hope to find to-day important traces of primitive, original music in Asia would be, in the face of the antiquity of civilisation and of the lasting European influence of centuries, a most sanguine condition of mind. Nevertheless, let us betake ourselves to this continent and search for the little that is to be found, so that the thread of our researches in primitive culture may not be broken at the earliest period, and that the further study of the music of semi-civilisation may be facilitated.

It may still be possible to find a few traces of the

[1] Ida Pfeiffer, *Madag.*, pp. 185-6. For those who are interested in this noble woman I would recommend her biography (the Introduction to the above work). Her sad life, fate and her unbounded energy are deserving of every sympathy and admiration. The mere fact that she was a woman lends additional attraction to her works, for she observed much that was passed over by men, or was carefully concealed from a male traveller. Even the expeditions of Mrs. and Miss Tinne and Miss Capellen, which were on too large a scale to be entirely successful, were for a short time crowned by a success which whole English armies never obtained. The slave-trader Mohammed Ches was so much afraid of the ladies, whom he took for daughters of the Sultan, as to offer to proclaim one of them Queen of the Sudan (Heuglin, *Tinnesche Exp.*, pp. vi.-vii.).

most ancient music in China, for which we have to thank
that spirit of conservatism which causes this unhappy
people always to run unwearyingly in one and the same
groove.   It seems as though the immense physical power
of the people for work had led them by some false path
to an eternal mountain in which they were to be for ever
buried without hope of salvation.   The marvellous depth
and thoroughness of the Chinese spirit admitted of music
being dealt with as a splendid science which had been
diligently studied in the schools and brilliantly taught, and
which was found in abundance in the learned treatises in
libraries.   One thing only does the Chinaman lack—
life, *i.e.*, everything.   The Imperial Library, however,
contains 130 scientific works (according to Billert 482),
collected in 1710, which have been carefully stored up.[1]
These are diligently studied, examinations are held, the
strictness of which costs some youths their lives, while
they give to others an invaluable testimony, possessing
which they are at once deemed great composers.   Thus
everything is ordered, everything properly regulated.   All
the other nations understand nothing of this, for the
Chinese—a great nation encompassed by perishing peoples
—are alone musical, and the music of the others is not
worth discussing.

Endowed with such excellent principles, the Chinese
have preserved from time immemorial an Ancient Hymn
[Mus. Ex. 2], whose regular melody, written within the
pentatonic scale (or within the natural tones of wind
instruments), offers a pleasing picture to the *eye*.[2]   The
well-known Chinese melody in Weber's " Turandot "

---

[1] Williams, *l. c.*, i. p. 673 ; Symes, *l. c.*, p. 508 ; Billert, *l. c.*, i. p. 395.

[2] Further ex. by Amiot, *l. c.*, with illust. of the scene at the singing of
the hymn ; Dr. Wagener, *l. c.*, pp. 42-61 ; Ernest Faber in Chin., Rev. i., ii. ;
Ausland, 1867, p. 887 ; Aalst, *Chin. Music ;* Williams, *l. c.*, ii. pp. 93-98,
90-104 ; Instr. illus. by Anderson, *l. c.*, pp. 134, 142 ; *Astley Collect.*, iv. p. 179 ;
Hipkins, *l. c.*, plate xlvii. ; Lenoir de la Fage, *l. c. ;* Brown, *l. c.*, pp. 28-59.

overture is similarly constructed. The majority of travellers vie with each other in eulogising Chinese music,
while Symes designates it a "horrible noise".[1] Berlioz
speaks in the follcwing manner: "The Chinese sing
like dogs howling, like a cat screeching when it has
swallowed a toad,"[2] and their instruments are veritable
instruments of torture. Ida Pfeiffer compares the good
Chinese in their music practices to savages: "They
scrape, scratch, strike their instruments in such a manner
as to produce merely a terrific noise".[3] All this comes
from the "High Musical Council" whose duty is to study
music, to compose, and, when a fitting opportunity arises,
to perform it.[4] Mr. Billert asserts that the rules which
govern the rhythm of their dances were not derived
from their speech, and everything we know of primitive
musical rhythm confirms this assertion.

This perfect, exact, scientific system of music does not
come under our consideration, nor does that of the
Japanese, whose notions are very similar to those of the
Chinese. It is extremely difficult to learn much about
this, for the Japanese musician is very uncultivated—like
the European—and he does not willingly speak of his
music.[5] I have frequently remarked that the genuine
schoolmaster spirit does not voluntarily betray what it
makes believe that it knows: so Nature herself prevents
the spread of intellectual weeds. What there was to
learn in the matter Müller has communicated, and I do
not doubt that the study of this system would afford any
student a merry hour.

[1] *L. c.*, p. 485.   [2] *A travers chants.*

[3] Pfeiffer, *First Voyage*, p. 119.

[4] Williams, *The Middle Kingdom*, i. p. 424.

[5] Dr. Müller (*l. c.*, pp. 13-32), further ex. and illus. of instr. of Japan in
Zeidwitz, *l. c.*; Kraus, *l. c.* The examples given by Fétis (*l. c.*, i. p. 80) are,
according to a Japanese (Mendel Reissmann, v. p. 367), incorrect, as probably is the whole *Sieboldt Collect.* (*q. v.*) from which they are taken.

It must be stated that Japanese ambassadors used to sing their speeches at audiences in European courts.[1] As a matter of fact they had a sort of " Song-speech ". It would be vain, however, to seek for primitive music upon which culture has had no influence among this, comparatively speaking, highly cultured people.[2]

Similar negative results are yielded also in *India*. It is indeed a fact that the Art and Life of India are still as they were in remote antiquity, so that the descriptions in Arnold's *Light of Asia* may still claim to be considered correct,[3] but this does not seem to apply to music. In India one often hears of very ancient melodies which are called Rangs or Rangenes. The first five of the six Rangs were originated by the god Mahades, who evolved them from his lovely head.[4] Their performance had the most varied consequences : night, rain, seething floods, destruction by fire, etc. ; but it is all a wonderful tale with no tangible facts. In India, too, song formed the chief part of the dance or drama, though in the latter speech took the place of song at a later date. (Not the reverse !)[5] These and similar sayings and traditions suggested to Wm. Jones to examine the matter and to investigate primitive Indian music. He tells us : " When I first read the songs of Jayadeva, I had hopes of procuring the original music ; but the Pandits of the South referred me to those of the West, and the Bráhmens of the West would have sent me to those of the North ; while they, I mean those of Népál and Cashmir, declared that they had no ancient music, but imagined that the notes to the Gítagóvínda must exist, if anywhere, in one of the southern provinces where the poet was born ".[6]

---

[1] Billert, *l. c.*, v. p. 368.

[2] *Mus. Instr.* with illus. by Hipkins, *l. c.*, xlviii. ; Brown, *l. c.*, pp. 69-79.

[3] Birdwood, *l. c.*, i. p. 128.   [4] Ouseley, *l. c.*, p. 72.

[5] Lassen, *l. c.*, ii. pp. 503-4.

[6] William Jones, *l. c.*, p. 205, and vol. vi. of his *Works*.

From this Jones decided that ancient Indian music
was lost, although there still *may* remain a few remnants
in the pastoral songs of Mat'hurà concerning the love and
life of the Indian Apollo.   Further, he relates that in
ancient India certain tunes were always connected with
certain hours and seasons, that the Hindus knew nothing
of harmony, although they could discriminate between
consonance and dissonance.   But the few musical
examples that exist are so modern as to be worthless
for our purpose.[1]

In India, in the southern part of the peninsula, a
few wild races in the *Nilgiri* Hills and in the Blue
Mountains of Coimbatore have attracted the notice of
ethnologists, particularly as their origin is involved in
obscurity.   They sing to the music of a Tabor.[2]   During
their funeral ceremonies the sonorous voices of the men,
and the gentle, flexible tones of the women, are alternately raised as they lament the wandering spirit of the
departed.[3]   The *Todas* of the same race have such
uneuphonious tones in their songs as are fit rather to
frighten wild animals away than to lull a man to sleep,
for which latter purpose their music is, however, intended.[4]
Among the Todas and Badagas the Kurumba tribes are
usually employed as musicians, in which capacity they
officiate at all festivities.   Their flute-playing and manage-
ment of the tom-tom arouses the wonder of the Todas,

[1] So especially the airs in Bird's *Collect.*, by Ouseley, *l. c.*, p. 72; *Indian
Instr.*, by Brown, *l. c.*, pp. 106-131.   Instr. are famous for their beauty:
comp. Birdwood (edit. 1880), ii. p. 67; Lenoir de la Fage, *l. c.; Indian
Drums*, illustr. by Meyer, *l. c.*, vol. iv. tab. 17.   Remarks on the ear-breaking
music of the Hindus of Népál by Francis Hamilton, *l. c.*, p. 111.   I do
not think that we shall ever get examples of the most primitive music (as
Mr. Chrysander hoped, *l. c.*, p. 28) by examining the art of India.   All that
could be obtained (primitive and modern) is laid down in an excellent book,
unique in its kind, by Captain Day (*l. c.*).

[2] Harkness, *l. c.*, p. 157.

[3] *Ibid.*, *l. c.*, p. 169.

[4] Metz, *l. c.*, p. 30.

but beyond this they regard all other races with fear,
and are in terror of their witchcraft.[1]

In *Siam* singing is the ruling passion of the people;
the audiences their king grants to ambassadors are carried
on in singing; the people go to the temples singing, and
sing during all their festivals.   Children shout for joy
when they hear a drum or oboe, and every one is his
own instrument maker.   This passion is so strong that
missionaries deemed it prudent to teach, with the aid of
music, the first rules of Latin Grammar to the natives.[2]
Poor Siamese!   Siamese songs do not lack a certain
melancholic expression, and are full of repetitions.   Their
subjects are usually historic, warlike or amorous, the
latter being often rude and even lascivious.[3]   The soft, melodious tones of their music offer a pleasing contrast to the
monotonous noise of the Chinese, and hence, as Bowring
declares, comes their preference for pleasure and poly-
gamy.[4]   The natives learn to play the organ (of which
they are particularly fond) entirely by ear.[5]   Among the
Sinhalese of *Ceylon* music also takes an important place:
in some books in the Pali tongue are to be found pieces
of music;[6] of course this is not *primitive* writing, for the
existence of books proves a certain state of civilisation;
neither are they musical symbols, the notes being
described by means of letters.   And so Joinville's remark,
" music in regular notes," is incorrect.   It is impossible
to write music down without signs of metre, and nobody
can recognise a melody without such signs.   So it has
come about that the ancient music is almost entirely
forgotten.   Even to-day there is nothing less gratifying

---

[1] Shortt, *l. c.*, p. 277.   [2] Turpin, *l. c.*, p. 596.
[3] Bowring, *l. c.*, i. p. 149.   [4] *Ibid.*, p. 150.
[5] Turpin, *l. c.*, p. 597; *Siamese Instrum.*, by Clément, *l. c.*, p. 137;
Hipkins, *l. c.*, xlix.; Bowring, *l. c.*, i. p. 147; Comettant, *l. c.*, pp. 556-
568; Brown, *l. c.*, pp. 131-140.
[6] Joinville, *l. c.*, p. 438.

than Sinhalese songs, although they themselves like them
and even listen willingly to strange melodies. A grandee
when travelling always has a singer in front of him and
another behind. They sing alternately religious songs in
honour of their gods, and historical ones in honour of
their king. These are invariably melancholy in character,
are never joyful, and are so irregular in metre as to be
extremely difficult to note down.[1] Yet there exists a
scale of seven notes which " possibly " corresponds with
our diatonic scale.

These remarks, however, must be received with
caution, for other travellers—Tennent, for example—
report less favourably of the native's science, and sometimes state the exact opposite. All the artistic efforts
of the Sinhalese have reference to the national faith, or
to their monuments and temples. Their music is derived
from the Hindus. It and the " eighteen sciences "[2] were
included in the education of their princes, while to-day
they are only studied by members of a lower caste.
There was no harmony : modulation and expression were
sacrificed to power and rhythmic effect.[3] The natives
themselves are uncommonly fond of their music, and even
prefer it to ours, which they say they do not understand.[4]
Every Sinhalese is more or less of a poet, but it is self-
interest and not love of Art which inspires him. His
poetry is always either sung or recited. The Sinhalese
have seven modes of modulation, that which they prefer
being called " horse trot " from its similarity to nature.
But we have no ground for derision, for many of the best

[1] Joinville, *l. c.*, p. 440.

[2] Mentioned by Upham, *l. c.*, ii. p. 90. Oratory, general knowledge,
grammar, poetry, languages, astronomy, knowledge of giving counsel, knowledge of obtaining Nirvana, ethics, shooting, knowledge of elephants,
discernment of thoughts, discerning of invisible beings, knowledge of words,
history, law, rhetoric, physics.

[3] Tennent, *l. c.*, p. 470.

[4] Davy, *l. c.*, p. 239 *seq.*

modern compositions are founded on the same principle
(*e.g.*, Walkürenritt).   Nell[1] is of opinion that it is impossible to write down the Sinhalese music in European
notation, principally because of the difference of the scales.
This contradicts the remark made above and is worthy of
note, because Nell distinguishes between Sinhalese and
Tamul music.   The latter alone is chiefly diatonic.   According to Virchow[2] this difference is correct.   The Sinhalese
is a mixed race of Veddas and immigrated Hindus and so
to be carefully distinguished from the Tamuls and Tanjore.

To-day even, the Sinhalese loves music and dancing.
Howling and singing he wanders through the streets in
the day-time, making no inconsiderable din with drums,
tom-toms, whistles and one-stringed instruments.[3]

In *Burma*, too, the natives are fond of music, especially
when at work.[4]   They sing willingly and loudly in imitation of Chinese music, and are in consequence much
influenced by civilisation.   This is made apparent by the
musical examples quoted by Low.[5]   Here also music is
a science, with which the Royal Library at Amarapura
is plentifully supplied : it is the language of the gods.[6]

Wherever we turn our footsteps in Asia we notice the
influence of ancient civilisation and little that is of use
to us for our present purpose.   Even the Buddhist
worship is so similar to that of Roman Catholics, the
music to Gregorian melodies, that the first Jesuit to go
there exclaimed involuntarily that some one must have
preceded him.[7]   To what extent the *Ostiaks* and *Samoyeds*
have progressed is shown by their instruments,[8] and in

---

[1] Nell, *l. c.*, p. 201.   [2] Virchow, *l. c.*, p. 484.

[3] Häckel, *Ind. Reisebr.*, p. 242 ; *Sinh. Inst.*, by Nell, *l. c.*, p. 201.

[4] Symes, *l. c.*, p. 485.

[5] *L. c.*, p. 47 ; illus. of inst., p. 49 : he quotes ten Siamese songs, one
Burmese air, and twenty-eight Malayan airs.   Bengal songs by Malcom,
l. c., ii. p. 38 ; inst. by Clément, *l. c.*, p. 137.

[6] Symes, *l. c.*, p. 508 ; inst. by Brown, *l. c.*, pp. 140-167.

[7] Graham, *l. c.*, p. 118.   [8] Finsch, *l. c.*, p. 519.

Russian Central Asia, according to the little we know, music appears to occupy an even higher position.[1] Mr. Palgrave thinks that where Mohammedans live their teaching has exercised an unfavourable influence on the study of music—at any rate in Asia. It is well known that Mohammed taught that music was an expedient of the evil one to ruin mankind.[2] Many examples, however, tend to prove that this doctrine was not accepted everywhere among Mohammedans. The Arabs consider themselves the natural successors of Orpheus; Turkish music undoubtedly influenced European; and the Persians as a rule possess good voices and a correct feeling for harmony.[3] The Mongols, too, have tolerably perfect instruments.[4] The most primitive musicians are probably the *Ainu*, who are very fond of singing at their Bear festivals, when travelling and carousing.[5] The words of their songs are very few, their melodies monotonous, melancholy and accompanied by hand-clapping. The Ostiaks have few and simple melodies, which the musicians play and sing according to their own fancy.[6] The songs of the Katshinzi Tatars, which are often merely a single word oftentimes repeated, "sound like violins, as the performers form the tones in their throats".[7]

All this however speaks most distinctly of the influence of an ancient and in many cases entirely novel civilisation, which it is unnecessary for us to consider further.

3. THE ISLANDS OF THE INDIAN ARCHIPELAGO AND PACIFIC OCEAN.

The races inhabiting the groups of islands in the Pacific Ocean are as different in character as in their

[1] Atkinson, *l. c.*, p. 63. [2] Palgrave, *l. c.*, i. p. 430.
[3] *Ibid.*, p. 310.
[4] Price, *l. c.*, illus. of a two-stringed violonc.
[5] Scheube, *l. c.*, p. 237. [6] Georgi, *l. c.*, p. 79.
[7] *Ibid.*, p. 238.

ideas of Art, and in their musical ability. If we now quit the Asiatic continent, we find in the *Andaman Islands* peculiar, and indeed original, musical practices. The songs of the natives refer to the presence of guests or of recently deceased persons whose merits are sung in oft-repeated verses. As a general rule only the men sing, the women contenting themselves with beating time. When greeting friends, they seat themselves round a fire, embrace each other and begin to cry out in a singing tone, the one group in high- the other in low-pitched tones. During this, which lasts some twenty to thirty minutes, a few shed tears.[1] The songs are all in unison, nevertheless the singers can discriminate exactly between the different modes of music, and they have derived much satisfaction and pleasure from the performances of a European military band. Mr. Man subjected a few natives to a most searching musical examination, which, however, yielded the very miserable result that they had not the remotest notion of pitch or of melody, so that in their own choruses the original was very difficult to find. The boys were far the best performers, but it required very energetic drill to " beat a few notes into their heads ".[2]

In *Java* the development of music has attained a very high standard,[3] but European influence is so unmistakable that the subject can hardly be considered to come under our notice. This music, which is not unlike old Scottish melodies, lacks the leading note,[4] and, as Raffles has said, the fourth and also the semitones; instead of the leading note they have the diminished seventh.

It is thus, obviously, music founded upon the penta-

---

[1] Jagor, *Andamanen*, p. 45.   [2] E. H. Man, *l. c.*, p. 392.
[3] Veth, *l. c.*, i. p. 451.
[4] Crawfurd, *l. c.*, i. p. 340; Raffles, *l. c.*, i. p. 470 (with mus. exampl. of a comparatively advanced order); instr. by Crawfurd, *l. c.*, pp. 332-339; Land, *l. c.* (with mus. exampl.).

tonic scale. The frequent repetitions of the same passages are artfully (almost contrapuntally) worked out, and the melodies are wild, wailing and interesting. In addition to this "pentatonic" music there is some in minor keys, as it were, but always minus the leading note.[1] Music-writing they naturally have not, but latterly they have been taught it by Europeans with a view to their being able to note down and preserve their original music. Land quotes several of their orchestral compositions, but grants that it is impossible to reproduce all their *fiorituri*.[2] This seems to be the fate of all "natural" music which happens to be reduced to writing in the modern notation; all the most important peculiarities are immediately lost.

Mr. Lay experienced this when travelling in China, for he noticed that all original tunes lost a great deal of their beauty when played on the violin,[3] and the same has been remarked by others.

Much more original is the music of the *Dyaks* in *Borneo*, who are passionate musicians,[4] but seem to have been at first neglected. Crawfurd says: "Borneo has made but little progress in Art,"[5] while Breitenstein declares that "dances (*i.e.*, war-dances of men and women) are the only representatives of the *beaux arts*".[6] This is however manifestly incorrect. Hein gives in the work quoted below such proofs of their ability for drawing and of their tasteful ornaments as to leave us no doubt of their possessing much artistic talent. Moreover, their deeply expressive poetry and mythology, their almost European "Münchauseniads," are well worthy of notice.[7] Mr. Boyle never succeeded in making a Dyak sing, although they own to a knowledge of both vocal and instrumental music; but they are as proud as a French

---

[1] Crawfurd, *l. c.*, i. pp. 32-339. [2] Land, *l. c.*, p. 19.
[3] Lay, *Chinese, as they are*, p. 81. [4] Hein, *l. c.*, p. 164.
[5] Crawfurd, *Borneo*, p. 86. [6] Breitenstein, *l. c.*, p. 253 (instrum.).
[7] H. Tromp, *l. c.*, p. 218.

Coryphée. Possibly, Boyle continues, they derived their music from the Malays, but this is fuller of mannerism and much more ponderous than that of any other Asiatic people.[1] Mr. Marryat[2] once witnessed a war-dance at which the awful war-cry and the dance movements increased in volume and power every moment, and eventually set the whole company in a tumult of excitement in which even the Europeans participated. The natives stretched their arms out like the wings of a bird and then struck one another with their hands, beating time to the music.

Of the music in *Celebes* we know little. Ida Pfeiffer heard it but once, and that when the Queen had some teeth filled—a grand event there. As soon as she entered the hall the music began, and after the ceremony a long hymn was chanted—howled would be more accurate —but the entire company behaved in a most exemplary manner, and during the actual operation remained perfectly quiet.[3]

On the island Salayer (South of Celebes) the natives have such highly ornamented bronze kettle-drums[4] that one cannot but suppose they are in reality much more artistic than is generally believed.

Mr. Zimmermann relates many interesting episodes of the island *Luzon* (one of the Philippines). In his honour the Alcade of Halahola gave a feast, and while the guests were at dinner, there suddenly arose so terrific a noise that Zimmermann feared there was an outbreak among the people. It was, however, merely "table music". Drums, whistles, ram-rods hung upon taut strings and beaten with sticks and stones, all helped to make a horrible din. The "music" "almost induced cramp in

---

[1] Boyle, *l. c.*, p. 220 *seq.*
[2] Marryat, *l. c.*, p. 85.
[3] Pfeiffer, *Second Voyage*, i. p. 443.
[4] A. B. Meyer, *l. c.*, vol. iv. tab. 16.

the stomach," and so shrill and piercing were the tones
that it is impossible to describe them in words.[1] What
was heard here of primitive music sounded much better.
It appears that the Spanish monks whose zealous efforts
succeeded in improving the race—so says Zimmermann[2]—
met with no such success as far as the music was concerned. On the island *Zebu* in the same group the
accuracy with which time was kept was so astounding
that the Europeans at once concluded that the knowledge
of music must have made considerable progress here.[3]

Of the Tagals, Philippine Islands, it is reported that
a chorus was performed in a truly charming manner by
twelve young native girls formed in a circle, one girl
standing in the middle to direct. The chorus was so
melodious and harmonious as to give rise to the opinion
that Spanish influence had been in some degree present,
but Zimmermann thinks this was not the case, for had it
been so, he says, the music would have been Spanish
and not native which it clearly was.[4] But this argument
is not quite sufficient, for, *e.g.*, Wagner influenced French
music, but nevertheless it has remained at bottom French.
How far such an idea can be adapted to the present case
I am naturally not able to decide.

Less of European influence, and, at the same time,
less developed music is remarked in the island Ceram
(*Molucca group*). The song of the natives is simple and
tedious, the same idea being repeated a hundred times.
The Ceramese laud the virtues of their heroes and mock
the voices of their neighbours in gay songs for hours at
a time. Drums, Triton shells and copper gongs, which
emit a tone like that of a deeply muffled bell, did duty
for instruments.[5] There Forrest heard the Moluccan boat-

---

[1] Zimmermann, *l. c.*, iii. p. 123.   [2] *Ibid.*, p. 122.
[3] Pigafetta, *l. c.*, p. 338.   [4] Zimmermann, *l. c.*, iii. p. 209.
[5] Schulze, *l. c.*, p. 118.

songs "which the weary rower uttered, each time with renewed vigour ".[1]

The inhabitants of *Papua* or *New Guinea* have no music which can be distinguished to advantage from that of the rest of Melanesia. Opinions on the subject do not entirely agree, and the reason of this may be found in the circumstances suggested by Mr. Turner, that in New Guinea there exist so many off-shoots from the aborigines that it is extremely difficult to sketch a uniform picture. Wood says of the Papuans in general that they accompany their national dances with music, and although the former are deserving of high praise, the latter is vastly inferior in merit. The *Motu* people as a rule dance "very orderly" and strictly in time, but without any undue haste, excitement or noise. They are extraordinarily lazy, and, "as if music were in some connection with exercise," are an unmusical race.[2] Of instruments they only possess the drum, *Kaba*, and a jews-harp, *Bibo*. Another judgment is that of D'Albertis: "Without doubt they love music and regard it with pleasure"; but they do not appear to have accomplished much. D'Albertis sang a few operatic arias to the natives who surrounded him to listen, and his success was immense, he being rapturously applauded and eventually compelled to repeat one or two songs. The women seemed particularly charmed. "I ought to confess, however, that I should not venture to sing in any other country than New Guinea," said D'Albertis.[3] I imagine the natives liked the unusual circumstance rather than the music.

The suspicion that for everything which the so-called "savages" possess they have to thank their contact with civilised people so frequently arises, that I think a remark of Wallace's concerning the wildness of the Papuans will

---

[1] Th. Forrest, *New Guinea*, p. 304 (mus. examp.).
[2] Turner, *Motu*, *l. c.*, p. 482.
[3] D'Albertis, *l. c.*, i. p. 346.

not be out of place.   Speaking of the inhabitants of Dorey
in New Guinea he says: "If these people are not savages,
where shall we find any?   Yet they have all a decided
love for the fine arts, and spend their leisure time in
executing works, whose good taste and elegance would
often be admired in our schools of design." [1]

In *New Britain* and in the *Admiralty Islands* European
music is much liked, and the natives themselves sing in
such a manner as to prove their great aptness and real
feeling for harmony and rhythm. [2]

We now come to one of the most important points
in the Pacific Ocean, the *Fiji Islands;* important because
" we can observe in the Fijian division something like a
school of arts for the other Pacific Islands ". [3]   The Fijians
are fond of dancing and poetry, and whoever understands how to teach them a new dance is sure to reap
an equitable reward. [4]   This artist's *honorarium* is called
votua, [5] and on account either of the great soul of the
artist or the small one of the public, this *votua* sometimes
falls short of expectation.   The Fiji poetry contains many
songs of lamentation of the badly-remunerated Art-
teachers.

But Fiji music still appears to have remained as it were
a "step-child".   Wilkes characterises it as infinitely ruder
than that of the other South Sea islanders with whom
he came in contact.   [Mus. Ex. 3.]   The men rarely have
any desire for music, [6] nor do they take pleasure in musical
sounds, while the women sing with shrill, penetrating
voices. [7]   The tones of the violin, accordion, flute and
musical-box, which gave so much pleasure to the other
islanders, had no charms for them.   Williams declares
that they are fond of music, but even he agrees that their

[1] A. R. Wallace, *Malay Arch.*, 10th ed., p. 389.
[2] Meinicke, *l. c.*, p. 147.   [3] D. Wilson, *l. c.*, i. p. 189.
[4] Wood, *Nat. Hist.*, *l. c.*, ii. p. 285.   [5] T. Williams, *l. c.*, p. 142.
[6] Wilkes, *l. c.*, iii. p. 247.   [7] Zimmermann, *l. c.*, i. p. 345 *seq.*

own efforts are very rude. In Lakemba, one of the Fiji Islands, a performance by a clown was accompanied by music and was received with rapturous applause by the audience. The musicians began a monotonous song on one note, "the bass alternating with the air; they then sounded one of the common chords in the bass clef without the alternation". Some of the performers clapped their hands and struck sticks together, while a few had two to three feet long bamboos open at one end into which they blew and from which they produced a tone similar to that emitted by a lightly stretched drum. "Although it could not be exactly called music, they kept good time."[1] This is confirmed by Williams.[2] At the close of each song they gave vent to a kind of war-whoop as they do in Polynesia. (The interval, *i.e.*, the distance between the first and last notes uttered in this cry, is said to be a tenth.)

The chief, Leonka, listened with rapt attention and pleasure to the music of drums and fifes, and, as it was night, a lantern was offered him to aid him in his investigations of the performing musicians. A youth who played a fife especially attracted his attention, and, quite overcome with astonishment, he held the lantern to the boy's mouth "in order to see if he really produced the sound".[3] Oddly enough many animals have a similar habit of hastening to the source whence the sound comes, and some of them will even leap on to the shoulders of the piper as if they really would examine the source.[4] Finally, the chief himself played a composition on the drum, being accompanied by one of his countrymen on the big drum. King Thakombau seems to be already civilised: he whistled "Gaudeamus igitur" with the greatest complacency.[5]   At Rotuma (north of Fiji and

[1] Wilkes, *l. c.*, iii. p. 189.   [2] Williams, *l. c.*, p. 142.
[3] Erskine, *l. c.*, i. p. 176.   [4] R. E. C. Stearns, *l. c.*
[5] Zimmermann, *l. c.*, i. p. 345.

now belonging thereto) Mr. Romilly made a great impression on the ladies by means of a banjo. If this was really caused by the music, the natives would seem to be more susceptible to its influence than those of the chief group.[1]

Music seems in a better condition on the *Tonga* or *Friendly Islands*. The natives usually sing while at work, and they also have dances accompanied by vocal and instrumental music as well as others without music at all. Their songs are divided into two classes, those similar to our recitative and others in regular measure and having a rhyming text.[2] The former are called *Hiva*, and are a sort of overture to the latter, which are called *Langi*,[3] and which begin immediately the *Hiva* cease. European music is also called *Hiva* here, because, as Mariner states, it is rarely accompanied by instruments or hand-clapping. The *Hiva* is constantly repeated, but when the *Langi* is to begin and the *Hiva* is nearly finished, it is generally ended with a sort of flourish difficult to describe, and stops abruptly as if significant of a sudden rush or assault. The texts of these songs are frequently in the Hamoa tongue, which the natives do not understand. When they sing in their own language the subject is generally a description of some scenery or a moral reflection.[4] Thus the Tonga islanders seem to be more intelligent than their neighbours. In Tongatabu, Mr. Labillardière heard a young girl sing a song the simple theme of which she repeated for half-an-hour.[5] She displayed such grace, however, in the movements with which she accompanied the song that Labillardière was really sorry she ceased so soon. On another occasion he attended a choral and orchestral performance, at which thirteen musicians

---

[1] Romilly, *l. c.*, p. 267.
[2] Mariner, *l. c.*, ii. p. 220; Meinicke, *l. c.*, ii. p. 88.
[3] Mariner, *l. c.*, ii. p. 220.
[4] *Ibid.*, *l. c.*, i. p. 244.
[5] Labillardière, *l. c.*, ii. p. 127.

assembled in the shade of a lofty breadfruit tree and sang in parts. Four of them held bamboos from one to one and a half metres long with which they struck the ground in order to beat time, the longest stick being used to mark all the divisions. The tone produced by these sticks somewhat resembled that of a tambourine, they being tuned thus : two sticks of medium length were in unison, the longest a minor third deeper, the shortest a fourth higher, *i.e.*, a chord of the sixth. The musician who sang the counter-tenor accompanied himself by striking a bamboo with two little sticks, while three performers who sat in front of him were occupied in explaining the subject of the song by means of suitable gestures. Everything had obviously been most carefully studied.[1]

Wilkes quotes a boat-song[2] which is sung entirely in two parts. He remarked that men and women were alike very musical, and that, to judge by the great desire they manifested for musical instruction, the subject could be taught them with the greatest success. They have indeed vocal schools, and their first teacher, Tengé, was also a celebrated composer, especially in the higher branches of music. Mariner declares that their music is of so unusual a character than a European could rarely retain more than a dozen notes.[3] Others again say that it is very European ; but on this point the opinion of the natives themselves is best worth having, and they believe that the music of a European drum surpasses all others. This characterises it better than any traveller has been able to do.

It is remarkable that in the Tonga Islands whistling is considered disrespectful to the gods.[4] This is very

---

[1] Labillardière, *l. c.*, ii. p. 139.
[2] Wilkes, *l. c.*, iii. p. 20.
[3] Mariner, *Quarterly Review*, No. 33, p. 35.
[4] *Ibid.*, *l. c.* (edit. 1818), ii. p. 131.

different from the idea of the Hottentots, with whom whistling is a harmless pleasure. Speaking of whistling it may not be out of the way to mention the different attitudes various savage tribes assume towards this habit. Arabs hate " El Sifr " or whistling, which they hold to be the chit-chat of the Jinns. Some say that the musician's mouth is not to be purified for forty days; others that Satan, touching a man's person, causes him to produce the offensive sound. The Hejazis objected to Mr. Burckhardt because he could not help " talking to devils," and walking about the room like an unquiet spirit. The Somali has no such prejudice. Like the Kafir of the Cape, he passes his day whistling to his flocks and herds; moreover, he makes signals by changing the note, and is skilful in imitating the song of birds.[1] With the *Koossa* (one of the Kafir tribes) whistling is the expression of astonishment.[2] Again, the Burmese are entirely ignorant of whistling. Mr. Malcom has seen them stare intently at a person who whistled, and heard them say to one another in surprise: " Why, he makes music with his mouth ".[3] In the Canary Islands whistling is so highly developed that people hold converse with each other whistling instead of speaking. The whistling language is composed of words, as it were, like any other language, so that the people can converse on all sorts of topics. The whistling noise is produced by placing two fingers inside the mouth. Mr. Layard, who observed this custom, declares that the language has great affinity with Spanish, being in fact a sort of whistling Spanish.

Among the Polynesians of *Samoa* music is, comparatively speaking, highly developed.[4] At *Tutuila* the inhabitants, after a great deal of persuasion, performed a

---

[1] Burton, R. F., *First Footstep*, p. 142.
[2] Lichtenstein, *l. c.*, ii. p. 519.
[3] Malcom, *l. c.*, i. p. 205.
[4] *Polyn. Instr.*, by Ratzel, *l. c.*, ii. p. 131.

number of their war-songs before the American Expedition. To the quoted example[1] [Mus. Ex. 4] they added
in perfectly correct harmony a sort of second part which
unfortunately is neither given nor accurately described.
How little they appreciate melody as such is made evident
by their singing something different at each repetition of
the song, so that a correct quotation is hardly possible,
and Mr. Wilkes thinks they have no special songs. They
also sing to dances performed, as a rule, by young girls:
some of those present sing a jovial text in two and three
parts whilst others add a sort of "deep grunt or guttural
noise". However, they always keep time well, which
here, as among all primitive people, is the chief point,
melody being quite a secondary consideration. As we
have so frequently heard this stated and shall hear it
again, I would lay stress upon it for further consideration;
it seems a fact that primitive music usually treats either
of mere keeping time without distinct tune or is merely
monotone, as there is no mention of modulation. In
Samoa, too, we can observe how the natives always
become more and more aroused during the performance
until thoroughly excited.

On *Pitcairn Island*, the lot of whose inhabitants has
been so strange,[2] it has been noticed that the natives were
rarely given to dancing, and it is worthy of note that they
had no especial taste for music. Their dance was little
more than a scraping of the feet, which they drag one
after the other. The modern violin did not give them the
pleasure which was anticipated, and they did not appreciate the value of harmony, but they enjoyed uncommonly
the rapid finger-movements of the player, and kept their

[1] Wilkes, *l. c.*, ii. pp. 77, 135, 145.
[2] The people are a mixture of Tahiti natives and English sailors. In
the year 1856 they were all transferred to Norfolk Island, from where many,
however, returned to Pitcairn. The history of the inhabitants is given by
Meinicke, *Pitcairn, l. c.;* Murray, B., *Pitcairn, l. c.,* p. 543.

eyes fixed upon the instrument as it was being played. (*Cf.* Ex., p. 30.) Later, a traveller heard that they preferred their own music to that of the violin.[1] It appears that they had not the very slightest musical ear, but he who stated this does not seem to have chosen his musical examples well. He wished to teach them the hundredth psalm, and was surprised to find that they exhibited neither talent nor inclination for it. He might have had similar experiences in France, Spain, Austria or Italy, notwithstanding that people there are musical; musical taste is everywhere different, and it is silly to approach a powerful race of savages with psalm music unless one is content with mechanical imitation, which many travellers appear to have been when they could only introduce a Church hymn.

In *Tahiti* (Society Islands) music is monotonous, melancholic and rarely in harmony.[2] Europeans have at times found pleasure in the pretty, plaintive songs of the children as they sit in groups on the sea-shore. Their voices sound well together, and though their songs are rather monotonous they detained them sitting upon the sandy beach till they could stop no longer.[3] In Tahiti the Hungarian violin virtuoso, Miska Hauser, once played Ernst's "Otello" fantasia and some variations by Paganini without making the smallest effect upon his native audience. He thereupon angrily tore three strings from his violin and played on the G string the "Carnival of Venice," which elicited a perfect storm of applause. From that moment he was the lion of the Tahiti season.[4] This remark looks to me like a satire upon European virtuosi, for similar occurrences take place among us too.

[1] Beechey, *l. c.*, i. pp. 82, 83.

[2] Meinicke, *l. c.*, ii. p. 189.

[3] King and Fitzroy, *l. c.*, ii. p. 513; instr. on Tahiti, Lubbock, *Orig. of Civ.*, p. 478.

[4] Hauser, *l. c.*, i. pp. 174-176.

In the two groups of the *Mendana Archipelago*—the Washington and Marquesas Islands—may be found both the song and dance. In Nukuhiwa, an island of the former group, the dancing place is paved with large, broad, flat stones; it is *Tabu*.[1] The music is a "wild cry"; the instrumental music is entirely played by drums, while the songs are accompanied by a loud, regular tone which is produced by clapping the naked left arm against the body, and by smiting the ribs with the right hand.[2] In the Marquesas Islands, on the other hand, songs and dances are only accompanied by hand-clapping.[3]

In the *Sandwich Islands* there are merely monotonous songs; drum-beating accompanies the dances. The former are very soft and slow, but when the dance movements are more ardent and more lively, the *tempo* of the music becomes quicker and the tone louder. All the dancers execute precisely similar movements, several times repeated, and so exactly as to give the impression of only one dancer.[4] In Hawaii music is now so "civilised" that troups of singers and dancers receive payment for their Art.[5]

The general character of the music of the above-mentioned islands is therefore (in so far as primitive music is concerned) (1) preference for rhythm to melody, if indeed the idea of melody is not entirely subordinate to that of rhythm or of monotone songs; (2) union of the song and dance, and the practice of music here, too, is a source of ever-increasing excitement and of physical exertion.

4. AUSTRALIA.
(TASMANIA AND NEW ZEALAND.)

Australia is the "asylum for the Fauna and Flora of past ages". Here the animal and vegetable world has

[1] Langsdorf, *l. c.*, i. p. 160.
[2] *Ibid.*, p. 164 ; Krusenstern, *l. c.*, i. p. 197.
[3] Meinicke, *l. c.*, p. 255 *seq.*   [4] Kotzebue, *l. c.*, iii. p. 254.
[5] Meinicke, *l. c.*, ii. p. 306.

remained stationary, here even human life has remained
as it was in earlier times and thus affords us an immediate
example of what we once were.[1]   In Australia a similar
history may be recorded of the music which, because of
its original character, gives us a welcome picture of the
simplest Artform.   As everywhere else it is also here
bound up closely with the dance, which, in the form of
mimic representation, affords apparently more variety
than on other continents.   One of the best known and
most important dances is the Corrobberree (whose nature
we will examine more closely later), in which musical
accompaniment plays an essential part.   Beckler states
that the natives show the greatest exactness in both
measure and intonation, the octaves of the women and
children at the performance he attended being "perfectly
in tune, as one rarely hears in a modern opera chorus:
they were in exact accord.   Each note is sung with a
sort of expiration ; every moment the singers can be
heard drawing breath with a sort of convulsive gasp,
which they immediately exhale with visible exertion.
By such almost breathless singing, by such passionate
excitement on the part of the singer, by the almost in-
cessant stamping of feet and by similar movements of the
arms, such a Corrobberree must be made very exhausting
work."[2]   The three melodies quoted by Beckler are not
particularly beautiful; and are too artificial to be entirely
primitive, and for this reason Gerland is probably correct
in considering them too romantic and idealised.[3]   Freycinet's examples, too, are more or less modern in form and
can hardly be quite true to nature.[4]   [Mus. Ex. 5.]

I believe I am confirmed in this opinion by the fact
that the descriptions of Wilkes[5] differ substantially from
those of Freycinet and Beckler.   What Beckler calls a

[1] Comp. Peschel, *Völkerkunde.*   [2] Beckler, *l. c.,* p. 82.
[3] Gerland-Waitz, *l. c.,* vi. p. 753.   [4] Freycinet, *l. c.,* ii. p. 774.
[5] Wilkes, *l. c.,* ii. p. 188.

ballet, Wilkes states to be no dance at all in our meaning
of the word.   It merely consists of violent movements of
the arms and legs, while the instrumental music—if so it
may be called—is nothing more than a few thumps on a
shield which coincide with the rhythm of the songs.   The
natives never sing in harmony, and the only accompaniment is a sort of bass, "a deep-toned grunt, sounded deep
in the throat".   Of harmony, of purity or impurity of
intonation, Wilkes says nothing.   As a rule the Australian
songs begin in high, loud tones and end in deep, soft ones,
while the rhythm is given by boomerangs, drums or sticks,
one of which is held across the breast and beaten with
another.   They have, of course, some instruments of
definite tone ; in Port Essington and Port Jackson they
have a small bamboo flute, the tones of which are considered musical in Australia.[1]   Topinard says: "The
Australians love their song, a thing monotonous and of
indefinite rhythm, constantly repeated in a minor key,
which scarcely strikes the European ear as being beautiful.
In return they are quite insensible to the charm of our
melodies."[2]

In New South Wales the natives are fond of singing
while paddling their canoes, keeping time with their
paddles.   All their new songs come from the North to the
South, "which tends to prove—as Angas says—their
migration from the Asiatic islands".[3]   I think, however,
this only proves their being invented in the North of
Australia.   Howitt divides Australian music into three
classes : dance music, descriptions of comic and pathetic
events which may have interested the composer, and a
fairly large class of songs which "are connected with the
practice of magic".[4]   The simple and somewhat monotonous songs appear to the novice at first to possess little

[1] Gerland, *l. c.*, vi. p. 752.   [2] Topinard, *L'Australie*, p. 72.
[3] Angas, *l. c.*, ii. p. 216.   [4] A. W. Howitt, *l. c.*, p. 327.

melody, but even he gradually sees how powerful an impression they make on the natives.

The character of Australian music depends a good deal on its rhythm, which is strongly marked and very irregular, full of sudden changes and often alternating between duple and triple time; these changes are brought about by a slackening of the *tempo* and a curious gliding of one tone into another, not unlike the slow tuning of a violin string.[1] This all exercises an unmistakable influence upon the feelings of the native; music excites his anger, with it he rushes into the fray, hurries off to the dance or the hunt, or willingly resigns himself to his master's orders.[2] For these different circumstances the native seeks out the definite rhythm which best fits his case, quick for the dance, slow and solemn for love, wild and pathetic for mourning. The music is sometimes not entirely inharmonious, and in the stillness of night when heard from a distance it is both soothing and pleasing.[3] Mr. Lloyd relates of a native whom he met in the neighbourhood of a mission station that he thoroughly aroused the laughter of his audience by his good musical ability and wonderful mimicry.[4] Urged on by promised presents of tobacco and by his own success he played many new pieces. Unfortunately nothing as a rule is done to encourage the peculiar productions of savages, and Howitt regrets that we know so little of the songs of the blacks as they might afford us welcome information about their mental capacity, their intelligence and imagination. To most people they are unmeaning and barbarous chaunts, and to the missionaries, who are in the position to learn more than any others about them, they are merely a sign of heathenism, and must therefore be altogether pushed into oblivion and forgotten. The effect of this must be that sooner or later they will be completely lost.[5]

[1] Howitt, *l. c.*, p. 327.   [2] Salvado, *l. c.*, p. 182.   [3] Eyre, *l. c.*, ii. p. 240.
[4] Lloyd, *l. c.*, p. 455.   [5] Howitt, *l. c.*, p. 327.

But still more than this misunderstood effort at culture is sacrificed to the well-understood action of European Governments. The now extinct Tasmanian is a terrible accusation against this relentless tyranny, from which we can defend ourselves only with very great difficulty. In their wild state the *Tasmanians* were a merry people; it was, in the first place, through their unlucky wars against the whites that they became " morose, sulky, sullenly wretched ". To-day the joyful shouts of the Corrobberree are rarely heard, yet once their songs had melodies which the natives liked no less than the Europeans, and eye-witnesses tell of examples when the deepest emotion was aroused by their national songs : tears were shed until the passionate excitement became almost tumultuous.[1]

Many of their songs and dances were borrowed from other tribes, and many a song was sung without their words being understood. Both sexes joined in the tune. They were fond of making a b-r-r-o by blubbering the lips over closed teeth. Their poetry was chiefly improvised, its subjects being the events in their history of the day.[2]

Labillardiere has declared that the natives sang in thirds, a statement which Bonwick appears to doubt. Dr. Ross also states that the music was nothing more nor less than constant repetitions of the same note,[3] as if syllables were being pronounced in a soft and liquid manner, the character of the music allowing (through its being mere imitation of speech) of this repetition as if dotted notes were used. They begin with the third from the key-note (whether the third above or below is not stated) and cease with the third above; at times they take the octave above suddenly. The music strongly re-sembles the monotonous chaunt of the bagpipes. Possibly with a view to darkening the already indistinct impression of his very superficial description, Bonwick quotes

---

[1] Bonwick, *l. c.*, p. 28.   [2] *Ibid.*, p. 29.
[3] I quote from *Ibid.*, p. 30.

two Australian songs,[1] borrowed from B. Field[2] and
Edward Jones,[3] which are said to be "similar" to the
Tasmanian. It would have been more desirable to quote
the original, so that one might ascertain the exact resemblance; since, however, this has vanished, it is dangerous
to make any attempt to represent it. The women sang
during the absence of their husbands (who are seal-hunters)
a song whose purport was a prayer to their god to protect
the men. It was accompanied by a charmingly graceful
movement, and had a very pleasing melody.[4] " The voice
of the singer, and, in many parts, the sweetness of the
notes, which are delivered in pretty just cadence, and
excellent time, afford a species of harmony to which the
most refined ear might listen with pleasure."

Much more trustworthy accounts come from *New
Zealand*, probably the most ancient land on the earth's
surface. It is—together with a number of smaller islands
—the first or lowest step in geological changes; after it
come, in order, Australia, America, Africa, Asia, Europe.[5]
This circumstance, together with what has already been
remarked about Australia's remaining *in statu quo*, gives
to the examination of New Zealand for our purpose
an especial value. It is said of the *Maoris* that their
music excels that of the other isles of Polynesia.[6] Their
songs are adapted to all phases of life : they row in time
with a melody which is sung by a chorus sitting in canoes;
they dance to music and speak many of their prayers
(*E-Karakia*) in a musical tone : *i.e.*, it is not the cadence
of the voices which characterises these devotions, but the
metrical language ("lengthening and shortening of the
syllables") after the manner of the Talmud reading in
synagogues. In this way it is customary to celebrate all
important events, suitable words being adapted to well-

[1] Bonwick, *l. c.*, pp. 31-33.   [2] B. Field, *l. c.*, p. 433.
[3] Ed. Jones, *l. c.*   [4] Evans, *l. c.*, p. 20.
[5] R. Taylor, *l. c.*, p. 44.   [6] Meinicke, *l. c.*, i. p. 330.

known melodies. Such songs are in the memory of all,
and are transmitted through several generations.

The war-songs of the *Maoris* have a pronounced
rhythm which is marked by certain fitting motions of the
body. On one occasion, when they sang such a song on
board a European ship, the measured steps were so
vehement, and the stamping of feet so powerful, that the
whole ship trembled. The commander sought in vain to
stop them, but they continued singing and dancing until,
quite overcome with their exertions, they were compelled
to cease.[1] Strangely enough Grey declares that the
Maoris observed neither time nor rhythm when singing,
and that the singer retains each note at pleasure. As I
have no reason for deeming either statement incorrect, I
conclude that it is with the Maoris as with the majority
of primitive people—they have both systems of music : the
rhythmic and the free.

How difficult it is to reproduce Maori—and probably
many other kinds of primitive—music in European
notation is seen in a very accurate description furnished
by Mr. James A. Davies.[2] " I beg to state that, though
with great care and the assistance of a graduated monochord, and an instrument divided like the intervals of the
Chinese Kin, I have endeavoured to give an idea of those
airs of New Zealand which I heard, yet so difficult is it to
discover the exact interval, that I will not vouch for the
mathematical exactness. . . . I must also add that I have
studied the subject for more than twenty years . . . but
yet I only offer these airs as an approximation, and if
any one shall be found who may do more justice to them,
I shall be glad to hear of the result." These songs,
however, sung by Mr. Davies himself according to his
annotations, were found by the natives to be correct.[3]
[Mus. Ex. 6.]

[1] Wood, *l. c.*, ii. p. 164.   [2] Davies in Grey's *Polyn. Myth.*—Append.
[3] *Ibid., l. c.*, p. 326.

Among the various songs of the New Zealanders mention may be made of one which is called *Totowaka*. Although as a composition of little value, it meets the case for which it was designed wonderfully well, that is, it makes it practicable for a large number of people to work in perfect accord when drawing huge blocks of wood or pulling up their canoes. Whoever has heard this sailors' song when loading a ship or pulling at a rope will fully understand how it is sung; it varies in *tempo* according to the easiness or difficulty of the labour.[1]

In addition the Maoris have airs which are sung in several parts (*Rurerure*), as a rule " Love-songs "; their performances are usually accompanied by indecent gestures. The *Ngeri* is a war-song, designed to keep the warriors in time in their war-dances. The specimen quoted by Shortland is very ancient, and was imported from Hawaiki. The *Waiata* is designed for singing in one or more parts, but without action;[2] it is thus not dramatic like the Rurerure. The Waiata cited by Shortland was composed by a woman. Of these songs there are two kinds, the *Waiata-aroha*, or love-songs, and the *Waiata-tangi*, or funeral-songs.

In the folklore of the Maoris, fairies play an important part. The Maoris imagine them with fair hair and complexion almost like Europeans. It must be stated, however, that they had an idea of fairies before Europeans came to New Zealand. According to a tale, a chief, Kanawa (who died before the first European arrived), learnt a song of the fairies, which is still preserved among the New Zealand poetry. The chief point of the tale seems to be a dream (or an illusion),[3] the fairies appearing before the terrified chief and his people during the night in a forest on the hills, dancing and singing until early morning, when they disappeared. These Maori fairies

---

[1] Shortland, *l. c.*, p. 139.   [2] *Ibid.*, p. 156.
[3] Grey, *Polyn. Myth.*, p. 292.

were always described as gay, friendly, and singing continually like crickets. So much for the Saga, the motive of which is easily recognised ; modern investigators might have reckoned it among the "phantasms of the living," and have easily explained it by telepathy. Primitive man has his tale and is satisfied.

5. AMERICA.

The original population of North America is doomed to destruction. " Before our very eyes it has to disappear and to perish," says Martius.[1] Whatever may to-day be done in the matter of preservation and education, the difference between the two races—the old and the new— is too great to allow of their being united in one. And America is not the only land in which this is the case. It seems quite impossible to confer the complete benefits resulting from the development of culture, which has been in progress during many centuries, upon a people who have remained at their original level. Such races are never in a position to thoroughly grasp the advantages of culture, while, on the other hand, they learn with extraordinary rapidity all its vices. Oddly enough this is shown in their physical as well as in their mental condition. If they have not innate in them the seed and the strength to aspire to higher things, they cannot obtain them from without. Here, more than elsewhere, do Goethe's words hold good : *Willst du enstehen, entsteh' auf eigene Hand.*

The aborigines of America may, for our purpose, be easily subdivided into several groups ; the Indians of the North and South, the—comparatively speaking—highly

[1] Martius, *l. c.* It would bring us too far out of the way to comment upon the remarkable fact of extinction of savage races by civilised ones, which is also to be noticed on other continents. This social law may, however, hold good in the domain of music as well, and therefore I will refer to Gerland's excellent pamphlet : *Über das Aussterben der Naturvölker.*

civilised people of Central America, the Eskimo in the North, the natives of Tierra del Fuego in the South, and the negro race which is spread over the entire continent.

The *Indians* have no great reputation as musicians, and several travellers have declared that they are ignorant of both harmony and melody. Catlin however denies the truth of this judgment,[1] which he thinks too sweeping, although he agrees that in their "songs" there is an entire absence of melody, and he also says that "their songs are made up chiefly of a sort of violent chaunt of harsh and jarring gutturals, of yelps, and barks, and screams, which are given out in *perfect time*, not only with method, but with harmony in their madness. Among the Indians, in spite of the poverty of their own music, we also find that remarkable imitative talent which we have already seen exists among other primitive people, especially among the Hottentots. Boys frequently indulge in repetitions of extracts from celebrated speeches which they easily remember. It is worthy of note how quickly the natives learn songs and imitate those which they have heard from travellers. They learned the hundredth psalm and also several Scotch hymns very quickly.[2] Indian children, too, learn simple melodies in the Sunday Schools with the greatest ease.[3] Some original Indian compositions have made a deep impression upon European travellers, as did those of the Hottentots. Mr. Powers, who did not consider himself a musician, heard some simple melodies which moved him to tears, and he declared without reserve that in a chorus of Kabinapek voices there occurred a short passage sung by men alone which was one of the most touching he ever heard.[4]

Naturally this is not the same with all tribes. In Port des Français on the west coast of North America La Pérouse frequently heard the Indians singing, and made

---

[1] Catlin, *l. c.*, i. p. 242.
[2] Sproat, *l. c.*, p. 64.
[3] Powers, *l. c.*, p. 407.
[4] *Ibid.*, p. 212.

the following observations thereon : [1] "When a chief
wished to visit him on his ship he rowed out singing, and
crossing his arms over his chest as a sign of friendship,
came on board and performed a pantomime which represented either a fight, an attack, or death.   The song which
preceded this dance sounded very pleasant and tolerably
harmonious."   If the truth of this quotation may be
relied on, it must be confessed that the song could not
easily be sung, the "stronger voices sang a third deeper, the
women a third higher than the natural pitch ".   According
to this they sang in fifths.   La Pérouse only quotes the song
in thirds, and so it is not quite clear whether he has only
expressed himself badly or not given the notes correctly,
for later on he says : "A few sing the octave and make
two-bar rests frequently, when the song lies too high ".
This octave too is not given in notes, from which we may
conclude that he also omitted the fifths in the music.
It is a pity that we cannot place full reliance upon so
important a communication.

At *Nootka Sound* (east of Hope Bay, lat. 49°, long.
233°, west coast, North America) the Indians sing very
well together in spite of the fact that the number of singers
is often very large ; the variations of their songs are both
numerous and expressive, the melodies irresistibly soothing.   In addition to the choruses, solo singers perform
"sonnets" of the same grave character and keep time by
smiting their hands against their thigh.   For accompaniment they use a rattle, which, with the exception of the
fife, is their sole instrument.[2]

Among the *Apaches* (south-west of North America)
old matrons and small children dance until no longer able
to stand, and stop from very exhaustion.[3]

Among the *Hyperboreans* are the *Thlinkeets* (on the isles
and banks between Copper River and River Ness), "who

[1] La Pérouse, *l. c.*, ii. p. 150.   [2] Cook, *Second Voyage*, p. 310.
[3] Schwatka, *l. c.*, p. 51.

cultivate music and art ".[1] At stated hours of the morning
and evening they sing choruses, in which every one takes
part, and if one may judge from the melancholy character
of the songs, one would imagine that they have some deep
interest for them. The males dance, and their wives, who
are "fat and flaccid," accompany them with songs and
tambourines.[2] The *Sitka* (Sitka Sound) tribes, too, dance
and sing continually.[3]

The Indians of *Alaska* near Fort Yukon (once Russian
America, but now belonging to the United States) had a
song which was performed in chorus by boatmen usually
in unison. It seems to have been an obsolete song, for
the present generation did not understand the meaning
of the words.[4] At another time they sang monotonous
choruses accompanied by gongs, the text being " Yung,
iya, iya," etc, while the dance which was given simultaneously was a sort of pantomime.[5]

On the Klamath River in California dwell three
different races, the *Yúrok*, *Károk*, and *Módok* (which names
mean down the river, up the river, head of the river). The
Károk—the handsomest of the three—have a solemn
" Propitiation" dance, which is given by men only,
arranged in a long row and clad in fantastic Indian attire.
Two or three singers then begin an improvised song—a
kind of invocation to the spirits, and occasionally all join
in a well-known " fixed-choral," the words of which signify
nothing and are repeated "over and over *ad libitum* ".
In the recitatives, in which each singer calls independently
on the spirits, as well as in the choral, all keep excellent
time, and that without beating time. The dancers lift
and lower their feet slowly and regularly.[6] A similar report is made of the *Viàrd* or *Wiyot* tribes (Eel River), which
make use of the same monotonous chants and meaningless

[1] Bancroft, *l. c.*, i. p. 242.   [2] *Ibid.*, p. 112 ; Langsdorf, *l. c.*, ii. p. 114.
[3] Lisiansky, *l. c.*, p. 240.   [4] Whymper, *l. c.*, p. 234.
[5] *Ibid.*, p. 134.   [6] Powers, *l. c.*, p. 31.

choruses, and occasionally improvised recitatives, while
the time is remarkably well kept without the use of a
bâton.   More to the south of Humboldt Bay, most of the
tribes *beat* time when singing.[1]

The *Yumas* in California only possess a few monotonous
songs ; their youths steal the affections of their beloved by
means of " flute-playing," the instrument being made of
reed.[2]   Another example may be quoted in favour of the
Darwinian theory on the origin of music (if only others
did not speak against it).   At *Shawanee* (State Tennessee)
the young folk practised flute-playing in the evenings, their
melodies being of a pleasing but plaintive character, and
their object to decoy the women from the villages so that
they could obtain opportunities for declaring their love in
the quiet woods or on the banks of the murmuring streams.
In the day-time gallantry is forbidden, and this has given
rise to the erroneous allegation that the Indians have no
affection for each other.   At night an Indian youth may
frequently be met walking with a lighted calumet in his
hand, with which he enters the cabin of his beloved.
(This is open day and night, for these Indians have no
cause to fear malevolence from one another.)   If she
extinguish it he may embrace her ; if otherwise, then must
he depart " with a disappointed and throbbing heart ".[3]

If we now turn our attention to *Central America* we
light upon the remains of a comparatively high state of
culture in *Mexico*.   Unfortunately Christianity has in
course of time annihilated all that there once was there of
science and art, burned the libraries, destroyed the temples,
and broken the statues, to triumph eventually on the
smoking ruins.   The European Conquest must have the
same meaning for the aborigines of the country that the
migration of nations has for us ; the Europeans had the
same reputation there that the Vandals had with us.

[1] Powers, *l. c.*, p. 105.   [2] Bancroft, *l. c.*, i. p. 516.
[3] Ashe, *l. c.*, ii. p. 69.

What little we know to-day of ancient music in Mexico speaks favourably of ancient culture. Tezcuco was the musical centre; here was a musical Council whose duty it was to encourage art and science, and especially to attend to the education of the youth.[1] The aborigines appear as a fact to have been very fond of music at their public festivals, and at their devotions, and at the sacrifices in honour of their gods.[2] This is true of the Aztecs of Mexico as well as of the Maya or Quiché peoples of Central America, of their drama as well as of their lyric poetry and their dance; and it is thought that their mimic and gymnastic progress must have been so great as to have called forth our admiration had we had an opportunity of witnessing it. This has, however, all fallen a prey to Spanish fanaticism.[3] Even Torquemada still speaks of primitive songs.[4] " Los primeros cantos von en tono baxo, como bemolados y despacio; y el primero es conforme ala fiesta, y siempre le comiencan aquellos dos maestros y luego todo el coro lo prosigue juntamente con el bayle."

High up on the towers of the temples of Teotihuacan (seven leagues from Mexico), whose ruins are still in existence, various musical instruments were placed, the sounds of which, accompanied by the ringing of sonorous metal plates (which Ranking thinks were gongs), summoned the pious to their devotions.[5] At Tlaloe a peculiar custom was observed; the priests of all the temples resigned themselves to a fast which lasted four days, and at night-time they betook themselves to a certain spot accompanied by the sound of horns, conches, and other instruments, where they, stripped of all clothing, submitted to a bloody scourge. Next they plunged into the water, began to beat about with hands and feet, and raised a fearful cry in

---

[1] Bancroft, *l. c.*, ii. p. 492 ; Prescott, *Mexico, l. c.*, p. 81 *seq.*
[2] Nebel, *l. c.*   [3] Brasseur, *l. c.*, p. 8.
[4] Torquemada, *l. c.*, i. p. 593.   [5] Prescott, *l. c.*, p. 92.

imitation of the calls of waterfowl.   After the bath they
returned, still accompanied by music, to the temples, where
they gave themselves up to sleep.   It seems that some of
them spoke in their dreams, others walked about, while
some snored or sighed heavily.[1]   This half-crazy auto-
hypnotism seems to have been materially assisted by
music.   So much for the old reports.

The music which we meet with to-day is too much
influenced by Europeans to be of service for our purpose.
This is, at any rate, the case with the examples given by
Tschudi, and he himself acknowledged this modern influence.[2]   The *Yaquis* in New Mexico are " good musicians "
and imitate everything which they may chance to hear on
their instruments.[3]   The same is reported of the natives
of the province of *Vera Cruz*.[4]   They particularly like
dance-music and song, but they rarely abandon themselves
to them without at the same time drinking to intoxication.[5]
In Guatemala, too, among the uncivilised (and also among
the civilised) inhabitants no musical entertainments are
given unattended by drunkenness, and they only stop when
they have reached the summit of their ambition in this
respect, *i.e.*, by becoming helplessly drunk.[6]   A similar
custom obtains in Honduras,[7] and generally over the
Isthmus.[8]   I presume it is unnecessary to state which
European people this custom reminds me of; it is one of
the very numerous examples of savage life in which
civilised man recognises his own self—not seldom to his
utmost astonishment.

As with the before-mentioned Jesuit who exclaimed on
seeing the Buddhist services that a colleague of his must
already have been there before him, so it is with many

---

[1] Bancroft, *l. c.*, iii. p. 338.
[2] Tschudi, *Reiseskizzen ;* Sartorius, *l. c.*, p. 99.
[3] Bancroft, *l. c.*, i. p. 584.   [4] *Ibid.*, p. 631.
[5] *Ibid.*, p. 635.   [6] *Ibid.*, p. 706.
[7] *Ibid.*, p. 735.   [8] *Ibid.*, p. 774.

others in different parts of the world. In Central America
among the Yukas, Acosta once (lib. v. cap. 27) spoke of an
idol "Tangatanga" which represented the Christian
Trinity, and his only explanation was that the "devil, who
always attempted to imitate the mysteries of the Church,
had invented the idol".[1] At any rate it was more the
creation of his fancy, and its name should be "Acatanca".
It seems to have gone better with the Spaniards on their
first conquest of Yucatan and Mexico. The people looked
so like Jews that they thought they had discovered the
lost ten tribes; others believed that the Spanish Jews
must have already settled there. The same idea, especially
with regard to numerous Israelitish customs and certain
words, occurred among the majority of writers about
Indians up to the present day; and it was at length the
cause of a thorough examination being made, and (as I
believe) a solution of the question[2] being arrived at, with
the result that the ten tribes of Israel, as a race, have long
since vanished. Traces of them, however, may still be
found anywhere.

Among the Yukas there were some solemn funeral
ceremonies for a departed king, at which several men and
women especially engaged for the purpose sang funeral
songs and praised the virtues and deeds of the deceased
king.[3]

The *Iroquois* people seem to possess a highly developed
sense of rhythm in their music, as well as in their dances;
their melodies, however, were indescribably poor. They
were entirely unable to recognise the "natural intervals
of a tone or a semitone". There goes always through
their music a dominant, oft-recurring tone from which the
other tones vary "in every conceivable interval or portion
of an interval". (Does the author mean this to be a
remarkable evidence of the principle of tonality?)

---

[1] Garcilasso, *l. c.*, i. p. 120.   [2] Ausland, 1865, p. 12.
[3] Garcilasso, *l. c.*, ii. bk vi. ch. v. p. 114.

Iroquois melodies, if their rude minstrelsy may be so called, are fairly numerous and varied, and very well adapted for inducing enthusiasm or sadness. In their occasional songs, as in the *Ah-dó-weh*, both music and words were extemporised. The Indian voices, especially of the women, are musical and highly capable of cultivation. Among the Iroquois concerts form an important part of their "*amusements*"; those taking part assemble in a room and seat themselves against the walls in one unbroken line, each holding a rattle. These rattles emit different tones according to the size of the conches placed inside them, and of the holes bored in them. When all is in readiness, one begins a song to which the others beat time with their rattles, occasionally, too, joining in the chorus.[1]

As in Central America so also in *South America*, music appears to be a mixture of primitiveness and of culture, and it is only in a few instances that it is retained in its original purity. In *Peru* and *Bolivia* music seems to have reached a fairly high standard, but it is all under European influence.[2] Weddell quotes two melodies—the *Waiños* of the *Quichua* Indians, and the *Callahuayas* of the tribe which bears this name, in two towns of the province of *Muñecas*.[3] This writer says "it may be supposed those airs which are most usually heard in Bolivia are imported from the mother-country: at the same time it cannot be said that no purely national melodies exist". Of these, however, none are given. Among the *Incas* of *Peru*, the Amantas and the Haravees or poets had to keep the national annals; they selected the chief events of their history for their ballads, and so many names have been

---

[1] Morgan, *l. c.*, p. 289.

[2] Two Peruvian songs (modern), harmonised by Ambroise Thomas, quoted by Comettant. *l. c.*, p. 584; Peruvian instr., *ibid.*, pp. 577-585.

[3] Weddell, *l. c.*, pp. 199, 202.

preserved for future generations by their connection with rural melodies.[1]

According to Inca Roca it is the upper classes who must be taught sciences, and not the lower, because they will otherwise become overbearing and so do injury to the State. To the duties of teachers in ancient Peru belonged those of thorough acquaintance with the calendar and music. The Peruvians "understood a few chords, possessed a sort of shepherd's pipe made of four reeds, each of a higher pitch than the other. The four notes were descant, tenor, bass, and contra-bass." [2]

In *Chile* the national dance " *Samacueca* " is very important. The music, however, is a mixture of Spanish and Indian, and is performed in a Chingano (amphitheatre) exclusively by women. An old-fashioned, long, narrow harp is their musical instrument, one end of which is placed on the player's lap, while the other, which is ten feet distant, rests on the stage. Another female musician beats time lustily on the sound board while a third plays the guitar—playing full chords by plucking all the strings together.[3] The songs of the *Araucanians* in Chile are less of a mixture but positively atrocious, while their sole instrument is a fife.[4] Equally bad are the songs of the *Caribs*, who use their instruments merely for signalling.

In *Paraguay* the *Abipones* on their first acquaintance with Europeans seem to have been more or less susceptible to music. The *viola d'amour* made a great impression upon them, when played by the Jesuit Dobrizhoffer when on one of his successful proselytising missions.[6] On the birth of a boy the natives perform certain plays which last eight days, during which time the men drink freely and beat drums and sing alternately.[7] At their funeral

---

[1] Prescott, *l. c.*, i. p. 117.   [2] Bastian, *Altes Amer.*, ii. p. 884.
[3] Wilkes, *l. c.*, i. p. 170.   [4] Waitz, *l. c.*, iii. p. 515.
[5] *Ibid.*, p. 387.   [6] Dobrizhoffer, *l. c.*, i. p. 70.
[7] *Ibid.*, ii. p. 218 ; instr. from Paraguay, Comettant, *l. c.*, pp. 541-543.

ceremonies a woman beats two big drums and sings at the same time a funeral hymn, " the rest observing the same measure of voice"; this also lasts eight days. Dobrizhoffer declares that women are more easily moved to tears than made to keep silent, and this accounts for the fact that at night in this district there is so rarely peace.[1]

The *Patagonian* Indians, too, have their funeral rites at which they sing songs of mourning, the women beating the ground meanwhile, to keep off the evil one.[2] Even here the Tehuelches learned with ease to play the ordinary signal-horn which they were accustomed to hear at Rio Negro and Punta Arenas. Moreover, the majority have a good musical ear, but their peculiar songs are unmelodious and are a mere empty repetition of words which have no signification. In past times the old men used to sing the traditions of their race and also a number of hymns, but this custom is now fallen into disuse.[3]

The Indians of the Roráima Mountains in British Guiana had very obstreperous music which was performed at their dances and orgies. Men and women led by a conductor sang their monotonous songs to the accompaniment of drums and fifes. The conductor used a bamboo stick to beat the ground, so that the tone produced from it marked the rhythm. The text of the songs was an endless repetition of " Heia, heia ".[4]

The *Charruas* of Uruguay know neither play nor dance, neither song nor instrument, nor even social amusements; their deep earnestness seems to overpower all their passions. Their laugh is nothing more than a pursing of the mouth, and they never laugh nor speak aloud, and even when dying their moaning is low. This characteristic is carried so far that they never call to each other even when at a distance of only ten paces, but they prefer to approach closely in order to speak. They

[1] Dobrizhoffer, ii. p. 278.   [2] Falkner, *l. c.*, p. 118.
[3] Musters, *l. c.*, p. 181.   [4] Appun, *l. c.*, ii. p. 297 *seq.*

worship no God, have no religion, no laws, no government.
They are covered with vermin, which the women like to
catch ; they put them on the tip of their tongue, bite them,
and eat them up. (This habit is said to be common to
all Indians.[1]) The same lack of musical feeling is found
among the Guanas too (who are variously reckoned to
number from 8300 to 20,000).[2]

The *Guarani*, who also never laugh loudly, had at one
time no inclination for either dancing or music.[3] De
Azara, when among the Guanas, saw some youths dancing
to a noise, and so in all three related tribes a regular
dance accompanied by a suitable noise is found, though
it is not so general and public as with other tribes. This
fact induced me to state my opinion that every tribe in
the world has its music (given at the beginning of the
book) as merely probable. At the same time, however, I
must call attention to what Mr. Wied has said of all
Indians : " Quite apathetic indifference to all joyful or sad
events is to be found among all American tribes ; they are
seldom seen to laugh, and rarely heard to speak aloud ".
(Wied-Neuwied, *l. c.*, p. 311.)

In *Brazil* primitive music of the Indians is rarely met
with, but the result of the influence of culture is in many
ways interesting. The performances held by Indians in
the upper reaches of the Amazon on holidays are simply
processions, masquerades, animal pantomimes, a melody of
drums and fifes, and, to a great extent, slow but deep
drinking.[4] These Indians keep the Roman Catholic
saints' days with the greatest regularity, and on Sundays
they may be seen going in long processions to church.
Three old women carry the " Sairé " dressed in cotton and
bedecked with jewellery and mirrors. By means of these
mirrors the Jesuits induce the " savages " to go to church,
for they like to see themselves, and therefore run after the

---

[1] De Azara, *l. c.*, pp. 77-78.
[2] *Ibid.*, *l. c.*, p. 122.
[3] *Ibid.*, *l. c.*, p. 111.
[4] Bates, *l. c.*, ii. p. 201.

mirrors until they eventually and unconsciously get into the church.[1]

At *Alagôas-Douradu*, in the Brazilian Highlands, Mr. Burton found more European than Indian music, although this was primitive enough in another sense. The natives sang during their meals, a fact which moved Burton to write a short essay on the subject of "table-music," which closed with a classical receipt from *Crambambuli*.[2]

Among the Coroados in Brazil, song, dance, and drink were all united in one art-work; a jug was passed round among the singers, and the oftener it came round the more general and noisy became the music and the dance. To this they sang the text, "Hy, ha, ha".[3] On the island of Mexiana at the mouth of the Amazon it is customary to celebrate in verse (many times repeated) every important event. For instance one singer will begin with "*The padre was ill and could not come*". Chorus, "The padre was ill," etc. Then the music begins without the chorus, which hunts up some other event to turn into verse. Next another sings, "He told us we should come next day to see if he were better," which is immediately repeated by the chorus. And so it goes on to the end of the story.[4]

When during a drinking bout of the *Yuruna* (Shingú River) the excitement was at its height, a few lads got up and walked singing up and down the tent, each one performing a sort of monologue by himself.[5] On another similar occasion the herald walked up and down between the graves in the hut (the Yuruna bury their dead within their huts) holding a trumpet in his hand and singing a monotonous song. Each verse of this almost endless song lasted for quite a minute and was immediately re-

[1] Bates, *l. c.*, i. p. 310. [2] Burton, *l. c.*, i. p. 155.
[3] Martius, Spix, *l. c.*, ii. p. 235.
[4] Wallace, *Amaz. and Rio Negro*, 2nd edit., p. 65.
[5] Von der Steinen, *l. c.*, p. 260.

peated again in the same words; meanwhile the singer
offered the others a drink—not forgetting himself. "Läva
náim, Läva náim," it sounded without ceasing.[1] In South
America if we wish to find genuinely primitive music we
must go to *Tierra del Fuego*. The famous American
Expedition under Wilkes found that the natives of Nassau
Bay were excellent mimics both in voice and gesture, and
they imitated every English word with great correctness
of pronunciation. Their imitation of other sounds was
really astounding. One of them ascended and descended
the octave perfectly, following the sounds of a violin.
Later they found that he could sing the common chord
and the chromatic scale with scarcely an error. They all
have musical voices, speak in the note G sharp, ending
with the semitone A when asking for presents, and
were continually singing.[2] Their mimicry prevented the
expedition from getting at any of their words or ideas.
The usual manner of interrogation for names was quite
unsuccessful. On pointing to the nose for instance, they
did the same. This kind of imitation seems to be almost
a disease, and resembles certain cases of aphasia where
the weakness of the nervous system and of the activity of
the brain causes the patient to imitate all he hears spoken
or sees done in his presence. Among savage races it is
in some instances endemic (morbid mania of imitation),
e.g., in the Philippines, in Java, among the Maniagry,
the Cossacks, and Jakuts in Siberia.[3]

Wilkes says that the natives of Tierra del Fuego had
no regular songs of their own composition, only, when they
wished it to be understood that they were friendly, they
would take a visitor by the arm, stand in front of him, and
jumping a few inches into the air, would compel the guest

[1] Von der Steinen, p. 266 ; instr. by Comettant, *l. c.*, pp. 534-540.

[2] Wilkes, *l. c.*, i. p. 125.

[3] Jagor, *Philip*, p. 159. On the importance of imitation for primitive
art compare my essay : " Das musikalische Gedächtnis.," *l. c.*, p. 219.

to keep time to a simple monotonous song.[1] This, however, seems to hold good only of one particular tribe, for
Mr. Bridges, who dwelt for many years in Tierra del Fuego,
mentions a long list of their songs of different kinds.
Lóinra is the name of a song of a man about to wreak a
bloody vengeance. *Telaníu* is a song of mourning for the
dead, *Aona* is the doctor's song. *Tacóus* is sung for the
amusement of the people. This last is the best. In
addition to these there is a number of songs with which a
sort of superstition as to their origin is connected, and
which were handed down from father to son; they are
songs with no definite import but with original names:
Upóush, the west wind; *Hahni saf*, the north sky; *Shúcoosh*,
the Kelp goose; *Aloocoosh*, the loggerhead duck; and
indeed the name of almost every bird is used to designate
the different kinds of songs.[2]

That they derive pleasure from European music is
confirmed by other travellers as well, and this seems to be
general among these tribes. The music of a concertina
delighted all and apparently had some special attraction
for them.[3]

In the extreme parts of North America music plays an
important part, although we must carefully discriminate
between the music produced by the *Eskimo* themselves
and that they have learnt from Europeans. Wood states
that they knew little of music and of musical instruments,
while Mr. Hall, in his report, says practically nothing
about music,[4] and the very little he does say shows that
his expedition did not hear much. Their favourite song
is Amnnaya, which has no particular melody, sounds very
poor,[5] and is accompanied by "ridiculous gestures".[6]
Other short songs serve to greet guests.[7] The ability

[1] Wilkes, *l. c.*, i. p. 127.   [2] Bridges, *l. c.*, pp. 207, 208.
[3] Snow, *l. c.*, ii. p. 15.   [4] Hall, *l. c.*, pp. 66-76.
[5] Wood, *l. c.*, ii. p. 717.   [6] Sabine, *l. c.*, p. 201.
[7] Ambros, *l. c.*, i. p. 6.

shown in their original productions differs greatly from
their reproductive talent, which is manifestly greater. As
both these are always described by the term "musical"
(about which different authors have the most extraordinary
notions), it follows that the most contradictory opinions
are heard. Waitz, for instance, says[1] that the Eskimo
possess "real musical talent," and Nansen calls them
"astonishingly musical people";[2] they invented some
satirical songs directed against their friends or against the
members of the European Expedition. The melodies
often had their origin in some well-known European song,
but not infrequently they were really original. Even
these latter, however, are undoubtedly influenced by
European music, sacred and secular.[3] From this it is
clear that Wood's opinions, which at first seem contradictory, and those of other travellers lead to the result
that the unmistakable musical gifts of the Eskimo first
found expression under European influence. This is
particularly the case in Greenland. Mr. Parry states that
the Eskimo spoke in very loud tones, and screamed as
they rowed out to his ship, but among all their utterances
there was no real song, not even an articulate note.
Having reached the deck of the ship, their exclamations
increased with their astonishment, and they expressed
their delight by loud and repeated cries which continued
until they were quite hoarse and breathless. During
extremely cold weather conversations held in an ordinary
tone of voice could be heard at a distance of an English
mile, and songs even farther than that.[4] A curious custom
is, that when a bargain has been concluded the vendor
beats time on a drum, the purchaser on his own back, to a
song which has for its subject a description of the articles
which have been purchased.[5] Eskimo songs and declama-

[1] Waitz, *l. c.*, iii. p. 309.   [2] F. Nansen, *l. c.*, ii. p. 344.
[3] *Ibid.*, p. 347.   [4] Parry, *l. c.*, p. 143.
[5] Ratzel, *l. c.*, ii. p. 731.

tions were sometimes performed in the open air, and generally at feasts immediately after the meal by men only. The singer beat time on a drum with a stick, gesticulating and dancing at the same time.[1] In Greenland there exists a sort of musical duel at which an insult may be wiped out by the public performance of ironical songs, the public acting as umpire.[2] At the dancing festivals which the Greenlanders hold at the time of the reappearance of the sun, the pieces produced consist of several divisions in which each of the musicians sings four songs; the two first were entirely made up of the theme "*Amna-ajah*," the others being recitatives whose short rhymeless verses alternated with the chorus "Amna-ajah".[3] The Greenlanders are excellent pupils for organ-playing; their manual dexterity is as highly spoken of as their musical ear and their beautiful voices, both of which are more or less universal.[4]

There still remains to be mentioned one race which is spread over all America and whose musical powers have attracted the attention of many Europeans—the negro race. It may seem inappropriate to treat of the negroes in this place, but it is of their capabilities under the influence of culture that I wish to make a few remarks. I think I may say that, speaking generally, these negro-songs are very much overrated, and that as a rule they are mere imitations of European compositions which the negroes have picked up and served up again with slight variations. Moreover, it is a remarkable fact that one author has frequently copied his praise of negro-songs from another, and determined from it the great capabilities of the blacks, when a closer examination would have revealed the fact that they were not musical songs at all, but merely simple poems. This is undoubtedly the case with the oft-quoted

---

[1] Rink, *l. c.*, p. 34.   [2] *Ibid.*; Crantz, *l. c.*, i. p. 164.
[3] Crantz, *l. c.*, p. 164.   [4] Etzel, *l. c.*, p. 551.

negro-songs of Day[1] and Busch.[2] The latter declares that the lucrative business which negroes made by singing their songs in the streets of American towns determined the whites to imitate them, and with blackened faces to perform their own " compositions " as negro-songs. We must be on our guard against the selections of so-called negro-songs which are often offered to us as negro compositions.

Miss M'Kim and Mr. Spaulding were the first to try to make negro-songs known,[3] the former of whom, in conjunction with Allen & Ware, published a large collection which for the most part had been got together by the negroes of Coffin's point and in the neighbouring plantations at St. Helena. I cannot think that these and the rest of the songs deserve the praise given by the editors, for they are unmistakably " arranged "—not to say ignorantly borrowed—from the national songs of all nations, from military signals, well-known marches, German student-songs, etc.; unless it is pure accident which has caused me to light upon traces of so many of them. Miss M'Kim herself says[4] it is difficult to reproduce in notes their peculiar guttural sounds and rhythmical effects, almost as difficult, in fact, as with the songs of birds or the tones of an æolian harp. "Still the greater part of negro-music is *civilised* in its character," sometimes influenced by the whites, sometimes directly imitated. After this we may forego the necessity for a thorough examination, although it must be mentioned here, because the songs are so often given without more ado as examples of primitive music. It is, as matter of fact, no longer primitive, even in its wealth of borrowed melody. Feeling for har-

---

[1] Day, *l. c.*, ii. p. 121.   [2] Busch, *l. c.*, i. p. 254.

[3] M'Kim in Dwight's *Journ. of Music, l. c.;* H. G. Spaulding, *Under the Palmetto, l. c.*

[4] Allen, Ware, M'Kim, *Slave Songs, l. c.,* p. vi. : another interesting collection of Æthiopian negro melodies by Christy, *Plantation Melodies.*

mony seems fairly developed. Soyaux heard melodies sung
by negro girls in Sierra Leone—their African home—which
were accompanied with perfectly correct harmonies.[1]
Barbadoes negro melodies must be excepted from the half-
civilised negro music of North America—as Mrs. Marknengo Cesaresco observes [2]—although she agrees that they
lose their original character very quickly under the influence of the whites. To these belong to a certain extent
some songs of the Bahama negroes (east from Cuba) which
were sung before the hut of a dying friend and which had
reference to his death : —

> If every day was Judgment day, somebody's dying here to-day.[3]

This verse must have made a strange impression on the
sick person. Mention, too, must be made of the " song
of the porters " at Rio de Janeiro,[4] which is nothing but
a " call " to render the work easier and more regular.

6. EUROPE.

The attempt in Europe to find traces of primitive music
may be glanced at. As a rule the Jews and gipsies, who
have retained much of their primitiveness, are considered
in archæological studies. But the Jewish, even the
synagogue, music has been modernised, notwithstanding
the fact that many of their old songs have been preserved.
Their sickly sweet *" lamentabile "* is still unmistakable in
Mendelssohn's compositions.[5]

The music of gipsies is very debatable ground, and
Liszt declared [6] that all so-called Hungarian national
music was pure gipsy music ; still numerous writers have
stated that gipsy music and poetry, " ragged and motley
in colour as are they themselves," is begged, borrowed, or

---

[1] Soyaux, *l. c.*, ii. p. 174.   [2] Marknengo Cesaresco, *l. c.*, p. 5.
[3] Edwards, *l. c.*, p. 525.   [4] Wilkes, *l. c.*, i. p. 53.
[5] Exampl. by C. Engel (*Mus. Anc. Nat.*, p. 349).
[6] *Des Bohémiens et d. leur Mus. au Hongrie.*

stolen from everywhere and anywhere,[1] and that, on the other hand, music must be "almost drubbed into the gipsies on the large Hungarian estates".[2]

Liszt's theory, which caused great excitement all over Hungary, was contradicted by Brassai, Bartalus, Simonffy, Kálmán, Adelburg, Czeke Sándor, Scudo, and Thewrewk. The latter, especially, said that the law of accent of the Hungarian music is the same as that of the Hungarian language, and is opposed to the accent of the ancient gipsy language.[3] Again, Liszt is said to have recognised the "decisive value" of the argument of rhythm, but insisted upon the fact that the "gipsies brought something with them," and maintained that the harmony was introduced into the Hungarian music by the gipsies.[4] I confess I cannot see the "decisive value" of the argument of rhythm, for we can never say that, *e.g.*, Italian music has a rhythm peculiar to the Italian language. On the contrary, musical rhythm shows such great variations that it can be adapted to any language. On the other hand, I cannot understand how the gipsies could have brought *harmony* from *India*, where there was no harmony in music. Decisive, however, seems to me the fact that the melody of an English gipsy song has nothing in common with Hungarian gipsy music.[5] Still I think that gipsy music will, like the gipsies themselves, remain a puzzle for many an anthropologist and musician,[6] while the romantic and poetic glamour of gipsy music will soon

---

[1] St. Bartalus, *l. c.*, p. 60.

[2] A. v. Adelburg, *l. c.*, p. viii., literature on gipsies by Liebich, *l. c.*; instrum. by Comettant, *l. c.*, pp. 282-284.

[3] Thewrewk, *l. c.*, p. 316.   [4] *Ibid.*, *l. c.*, i. p. 317.

[5] Sampson, *l. c.*, pp. 81-84.

[6] A most complete list of the literature on gipsies is given in the book of the Austrian Archduke Josef (*l. c.*, pp. 327-343), himself an authority on this subject. As the book is unfortunately written in Hungarian only, I was obliged to use the English abstract of it in *Journ. Gyps. Lore Soc.*, ii. pp. 148-160. Ten original melodies of Transylvanian tent-gipsies in *Journ. Gyps. Lore Soc.*, i. p. 100.

disappear if we bear in mind what all the writers on this subject say : " The Bohémiennes sing only when they are paid for ".

> Sorciers, bateleurs ou filous
> Reste immonde
> D'un ancien monde ;
> Sorciers, bateleurs ou filous
> Gais bohemiens, d'ou venez-vous ?

Despite all that has been said as to the influencing and modernising of primitive music in all parts of the world, *it is not yet entirely lost,* and we still have too many writings of travellers who were the first Europeans to enter strange countries, to ignore or pass over the entire music of primitive people, as is so often done as to be almost the rule. Of the music of savages we possess not only more direct knowledge than of the Greek and Roman music, we have in many instances also, not only the musical but the primitive condition before us, in which mankind existed in the most ancient geological period.

In any attempt to turn the musico-ethnological material to account by systematising and classifying it perfectly, I do not think myself bound to search out laws and all that bears upon the matter of music, race, climate, etc., because I do not think any such necessity has arisen out of the nature of the subject itself. Nevertheless I cannot refrain from stating that some such attempts have been made.

Fétis in his day had the idea of calling ethnological studies in music to his aid in determining the race of a people.[1] For this purpose he specially used the musical system, or rather the musical scale, but I am afraid this method can lead to no exact results. Far from it in fact, for if two races have the same scale there follows nothing to show its common derivation. Correctly enough at the time when Fétis declared his idea, Gaussin[2] had promulgated the notion that the music of a nation developed as civilisation increased, and might very soon assume a totally different form from that of a branch of the same

---

[1] Fétis, *Classificat. des races humaines, l. c.,* p. 134.   [2] *Ibid., l. c.,* p. 143.

race which has stagnated. Among quite primitive people the idea of a systematic "scale" is useless. At any moment they may be able to systematically arrange and retain a succession of notes, and to this extent differ from others of the same race; or they can even adopt the system of civilised people. It is true that Broca [1] and Topinard [2] seem to have declared for Fétis, and there are certain cases in which the community of musical systems along with many other characteristics coincides with the community of origin; but none are productive of more satisfactory results than are skull measurements or divisions according to the colour of the skin or hair. It is quite as difficult a matter to scientifically establish a pure musical type as the purity of a race. My own attempt to find out a conformity between certain races and musical talent has been, so far as I am concerned, completely unsuccessful, although I recognise the fact that in the matter of systematisation there will always remain something for speculative minds to do. As already three distinct musical stages have been found which are said to correspond with the use of certain instruments, I would not be surprised if some one were to discover (say) seven different races with sevenfold musical gifts. However this may be, it would be better to omit all gratuitous and subjective ideas of "musical talent" in expressing "ethnological judgments," and at the same time to state clearly if composition or reproduction is meant, beautiful voices, songs, or the playing upon instruments, love of music in general, or individual efficiency, teachableness, or diligence or merely possessing imitative talent, good ear, feeling of rhythm, feeling or judgment, memory for absolute pitch or melody, feeling for harmony or melody, etc. All this is usually called "musical," and one can only think how various opinions must be.

[1] Fétis, *Classificat. des races humaines*, *l. c.*, p. 145.
[2] Topinard, *L'Anthropologie*, p. 6.

CHAPTER II.

SINGERS AND COMPOSERS IN PRIMITIVE TIMES.

OVER almost the entire African Continent we find a sort
of wandering minstrel, a person whose vocation is the
glorification of the mighty chief in whose service he may
be, and to demonstrate for the spreading of his fame the
inexhaustible power and beauty of art. This is remarkable,
as art, or at any rate music, is a popular festival in which
every one takes part, not merely as one of the audience but
as a performer. So it cannot be said that art is indebted
to these professional artists for its origin, and they, for
their posts, to the graciousness and munificence of the
chief. On the contrary, what is achieved in this way is
throughout a lower kind of art, and, it appears to me, a
product of later—although still a very primitive—state of
culture.

These singers are, in Africa, a sort of sycophants.
Each chief keeps two or three of them who have to
accompany strangers by way of state, and to sing songs in
praise of the white man and of the king. It is, too, their
duty to praise the "wit and genius" of any great man
into whose service they may for a short time be taken. If
the expected presents are not given they go to the villages
round about and retract all that they have previously said
in praise of their "protectors". They are renowned for
their great wealth, and their wives possess more "blue-stones
and crystals than does the chief's wife". Despite this,
they are considered disreputable ; they are even denied the
common rite of burial, and their corpses are placed upright
in a hollow tree-trunk and there left to rot.[1]

[1] *Astley Collect.*, ii. pp. 277-279.

It is remarkable at what an early date art was employed for economic purposes, how from the very beginning this manner of practising art was despised, and yet how these "artists'" power was bowed down to in fear, while at the same time the contemned economic effect was assisted and propagated by voluntary contributions.

Mr. Jobson found on the Gambia each chief surrounded by a number of such musicians who were called "*Jelle*" or "*Jellemen*". The most important occasions upon which they had to perform were the festivals of circumcision and at funerals. At the former the entire country-side assembled, while music, yelling, and dancing were indulged in all through the night.[1] In addition, male and female singers celebrate every event of interest in suitable songs. "Flattery is naturally the standing reproach against this class of bards,"[2] and in this respect culture has not induced the slightest improvement.

Mr. Lenz says of these Griôts (as they are called in some places) that they are invariably attached to the suites of *Sheiks*, they laud them in their melodious songs, and, indeed, any one else who will pay them for it. They are not greatly respected, and are compelled to go out with war expeditions and on predatory excursions in order to encourage the others ; they also act as spies.[3]

In Bechuanaland Mr. Mohr came across a troop of these wandering minstrels (who are there called Amatongas), natives with six wives, who were *en route* to the Bechuana chief Matcheen, to give performances and to dance.[4]

Among the Niam-Niam there are musicians who generally perform in the most fantastic costumes, decorated with feathers, roots, etc. Several travellers have called them Minnesingers ; the Arabs of the Sudan call them "Lashash" ; the Niam-Niam "Nzangah" ; in

[1] H. Murray, *l. c.*, p. 74; *Jelles of the Soulima*, Laing, *l. c.*, p. 368.
[2] *Ibid.*, *l. c.*, p. 443.   [3] Lenz, *Timbuctu*, ii. pp. 217-218.
[4] Mohr, *l. c.*, i. p. 165.

Senegambia they are known as "Griôts,"[1] among the negroes of West Africa as "Guéhués".[2]

As often as one of this brotherhood appears, he begins at once to set forth every detail of his journey and experiences in an emphatic recitative, at the end of which he never forgets to appeal to the generosity of his audience.

Among the numerous unedifying examples there may be found here and there noteworthy exceptions. Thus we hear of a blind man who at certain times visited Ukuin in East Africa, where, without being led even by a dog, he could find his way through every street. Hundreds of the inhabitants welcomed him and listened to him, among them being the Sultan, and all united in a chorus "of almost devotional music". Holding his hand before his mouth he produced a quite pleasing tone which could be heard at a great distance, and every one was delighted, especially with the peculiar shrill falsetto notes. Another blind man taught the village youth the songs of their country—they have really charming national songs—to which he beat time with his foot.[3]

In Australia too, there are to be found such professional singers, and some tribes have whole families of bards. Many of these compose under natural, others under "supernatural" influences. To the latter belongs the case in which the bard receives in a dream his songs (poetry too) from the spirit of some departed person—usually a relation.[4]

Among the Australian poets one or two are mentioned as being greatly renowned. Grey was, however, not in a position to determine if they still lived and worked or if they only existed in folklore.[5]

It is surprising to find in the lower strata of society—at any rate as regards artistic invention—the idea of

[1] Schweinfurth, *l. c.*, i. p. 295.　　　[2] Caillie, *l. c.*, i. p. 93.
[3] Grant, *l. c.*, pp. 83, 84.　　　[4] Howitt, *l. c.*, p. 330.
[5] Grey, *Austr.*, p. 304.

intellectual copyright, as it were. It is the case that not only is the poet who writes a song—music or only text— recognised as its owner, but he also receives handsome gifts as payment for his master-work. We have already mentioned an example of this kind in Fiji; the whole institution of professional singers in Africa affords us further evidence, although in this case it is tinged with something other than the artistic. This custom is most decisive in the Andamans, where, at the great music festivals, the composer only may sing his own songs, however popular they may be. His rights are fully recognised, and it is just on solemn occasions that the honour of performance should be his.[1] This recognition on the part of the public is as remarkable as the wish of the artist. Two M'Quichis once performed their dances before Herr Schütt, during which the native members of his expedition sang to a drum-accompaniment and made handsome presents to the dancers of pearls, powder, and some tools. Again and again did they stretch out their hands asking for more, and the people invariably gave what they could possibly spare.[2]

The vocal art, as such, consists almost everywhere of the same very simple principle: the louder the better. This, in Africa at least, is with very few exceptions everywhere the case, and primitive people generally have the means of carrying out the principle. In Madagascar the strength of the "musical voices" was especially satisfactory, and although male voices there sound very nasal and rough, yet they are uncommonly powerful, and it is very easy for a speaker at a public meeting in the open air to hold the careful attention of an audience of several thousands of people.[3] The Sinhalese voices, too, are loud, harsh, ill-toned, and disagreeable. Some of the hill Veddas seem to have lost their capacity for modulating

[1] Man, l. c., p. 389.   [2] Schütt, l. c., p. 116.
[3] Ellis, Madag., i. p. 273.

their voices, "probably from disuse".[1] In Tahiti the
natives have both good voices and ears, and in addition
make very apt pupils in the European music-classes, but
their own manner of singing was not satisfactory to the
Europeans ; it was monotonous, the voices nasal, and full
of sudden transitions from the highest to the lowest notes.[2]
In Australia it was deemed a sign of specially great vocal
art to be able to sustain the last note for a long time.[3]
This too has not been much altered by culture, the chief
change being the trill which is sometimes sung on the last
note. Among the Papuans at Finchhaven there exists a
sort of " Meistersinger-school " of the Middle Ages, according to whose rules certain songs might only be sung by
persons of certain rank.[4] Although it is extremely difficult
to reproduce these songs in our notation, Mr. Schelling
believes that he has done so, and he quotes eighteen
different melodies. [Mus. Ex. 11.]

It is worthy of note to what extent each of the sexes
participates in the art of singing, and what ideas half-
civilised and quite uncivilised races have of it. The
practice of music as a profession stands high among the
Siamese, the loftiest ambition of whose females is to be
able to perform the graceful movements and sing the
enchanting melodies of the Lakhon-pu-ying or "dancing-
girl," who from her youth up is taught these arts. The
close of each day is the signal for the commencement of
music and dancing. If one consider for a moment how
much time is given to it daily by the women whose almost
sole occupation it is, it may well surprise us that the Siamese
have not attained greater proficiency in the art.[5] In their
concerts they perform part-songs in which the women
sing the bass part.[6] Again, in Persia singing and dancing

---

[1] Le Mesurier, *l. c.*, p. 340. [2] Wood, *l. c.*, ii. p. 404.
[3] Lumholtz, *l. c.*, p. 156. [4] Schelling, *l. c.*
[5] Bowring, *l. c.*, i. p. 150. [6] Turpin, *l. c.*, p. 596.

are considered *infra dig.*, and are left as in almost all the Orient to prostitutes.[1]

In ancient Jewish synagogue music it was held that female voices offered too much physical attraction, and for this reason the seats for men and women were separated during divine service. In many Catholic dioceses this *maxim* has remained unto this day. On Nukahiwa (Washington Islands) that part of the dancing place on which the music was arranged was tabooed to the women.[2] Otherwise in primitive culture the women always take a prominent part in music festivals. The young women of the Yaribs, who have loud clear voices, are selected as wives or concubines of the monarch. They lull the king to sleep, play instruments, and whistle together. Moreover, they are accustomed to pay court to the men (as is often the case in Africa), the most extravagant encomiums being lavished on the beauty and blandishments of mankind by this gentler part of creation.[3] The women of the Sudan are famous for their singing; they accompany themselves on the "Erbab".[4] Gardiner remarks of the Zulu women that they perform their parts with such a degree of sustained effort that a European girl would be compelled to go on crutches for the remainder of her life were she to work so assiduously.[5] In Tanga (East Africa) women are the chief propagators of songs, of which some know an incredibly great number.[6] In Madagascar the female voice is usually much more suitable for training than the male, and the women sing much more frequently.[7] On Hervey Island (Friendly Isles) the women often amused Cook with their songs. Their voices were very extensive in compass, and their music as well as their voices sounded

---

[1] Della Valle, *l. c.*, pp. 19, 203, 225.   [2] Langsdorf, *l. c.*, p. 164.
[3] Lander, *Rec. of Clapp.*, i. p. 291 ; ii. p. 197.
[4] Lyon, *l. c.*, p. 161.   [5] A. F. Gardiner, *l. c.*, p. 58.
[6] Baumann, *Usumbara*, p. 51.   [7] Ellis, *Madag.*, p. 274.

very harmonious.[1] They accompanied themselves while
singing by snapping their fingers. The Kanaka women
in Honolulu have wild, shrill voices like those of the
peasants in South Germany,[2] but they often sing and are
always willing to do so.

By far the greater number of Japanese songs are sung by
girls; men would make themselves ridiculous by singing, just
as they would never dance with their ladies in an evening
party.[3] That in New Zealand the women write poetry,
and probably also compose (as music and poetry are there
so bound up together), we have already stated. The
greater part of those Chinook songs (North America) that
Mr. Boas collected was composed by women. The composer either invented a new tune to each song or used old
well-known tunes.[4] The Nishinam women (Indians)
have a sort of musical contest which is won by the woman
who sings loudest and longest.[5] Barbarian as it may
appear to be, such performances are still in use in America,
the modern counterpart being the " musical " contest which
took place at Huber's Museum, New York, on the 23rd
October, 1892. We are told the condition was that there
should be no stop of any sort in the performance, so that
from time to time each competitor had to be fed with a
spoon, and both, it seems, drank beer. They started at
9 A.M. on the 23rd, and at 1·52 A.M. on the 24th the lady
was " knocked out," her hands falling to her lap after
sixteen hours fifty-two minutes of pianoforte pounding.
The gentleman went on for eight minutes more, when he
too stopped, his thumbs then being twice their usual size,
while the lady's right wrist was swollen, the finger tips

[1] Cook, Second Voyage, p. 220.　　　　[2] Buchner, Ocean, p. 399.

[3] v. Holtz, l. c., p. 13, mus. examples; other Jap. songs, as taught
in schools, quoted by Fr. Eckert, l. c., pp. 422-428.

[4] Boas, Chinook Song, l. c., p. 224; with mus. examples: Ponka and
Omaha songs, quoted by Fletscher, l. c., p. 225 ; Dorsey, l. c., p. 271.

[5] Powers, l. c., p. 326.

were blistered, and she was very sleepy. Both performers talked freely to the people while they played, and Miss Melville received no fewer than three proposals of marriage within the first seven hours, besides two more before she stopped playing.[1]

Among the Apache Indians the women dance and sing;[2] the *Samacneca* in Chili, too, is performed only by women, as is the music which accompanies it.[3] On Buru Island (between Celebes and Papua), on the other hand, the woman's part is very small. Mr. Forbes tells us of a musical performance where the men sang an improvised song to the accompaniments of the native Tifa (drum), and they amused themselves royally, laughing heartily at their own improvised conceits. But the women sat around on stones, taking no part in the proceedings, resting their heads on their arms, elbows on their knees, and looked like veritable automata.[4] On the Marianna island Radack, Chamisso heard a song by women only.[5] The song of the Botocudo (Amazon) men resembles an inarticulate war-cry; the women, however, sing less unpleasantly, but only a few notes, which they constantly repeat.[6]

In the playing of instruments too women sometimes hold a peculiar position. Among the Mississippi negroes the girls play upon a brass tube several feet long, from which many of them produce excellent tones, and sometimes even complete melodies.[7] The Papuans have two kinds of flutes of which only one may be played by women.[8] The Karagwe tribes in Africa make the women beat their

---

[1] *Daily News*, 19th Nov., 1892.   [2] Schwatka, *l. c.*, p. 51.
[3] Wilkes, *l. c.*, i. p. 171.   [4] H. O. Forbes, *l. c.*, p. 399.
[5] The words run as follows (Chamisso, *l. c.*, p. 67): " Untertauchen in die See sechs Mal. Auftauchen aus der See sechs Mal. Sieben Mal." Simmel says of this song (*l. c.*, p. 284): " In Radack the women sing even songs that deal with war and navigation " (?).
[6] Wied-Neuwied, abstract, vol. lxi. p. 155.   [7] Busch, *l. c.*, p. 260.
[8] Schelling, *l. c.*

war-drums,[1] and the Radack women go in the rear of battle beating their drums at the command of the leader ;[2] in times of peace too the drum, which always arouses their joy, is to be found in the women's hands.[3]   In New Guinea and New Britain several instruments are played by women only, as the pangolo, a bow with a string,[4] and the wuwu (= wind, air), a globular fruit with four holes, one of which is blown into while the others are fingered. (Since 1884 it is out of use.[5])   The Tongala-up, a stick with a string whirled in the air, is played by women and children.[6]   The large heavy wooden drums, however, called angramut, are tabooed for the women.   While manufacturing it, the men are not allowed to call on women.[7]   The Australians allow themselves to be drawn into all sorts of passionate actions by the music of the women.[8]   Four or five old women can stir up thirty or forty men to commit any bloody deed ;[9] they also have mourning-songs which they alone sing, while men only perform the war-songs.

Wallace when voyaging up the Amazon found a tribe, the women of which were not allowed even to look upon a certain instrument on pain of death.[10]   In Ceylon the women of a family sit the whole day long round a timbrel (Rabani), and from it produce a monotonous but most agreeable sound, by drumming with their fingers.[11]

With the Finnish Laplanders marriageable girls are not allowed to touch a certain drum.[12]   The chief instrument of Japanese young ladies of " quality " is the guitar (Samsic), and this they take to every entertainment, where they play upon it one after the other, and sing.   So it seems that in Japan, too, the poor guests have their musical troubles.

[1] Wood, *l. c.*, i. p. 447.   [2] Chamisso, *l. c.*, p. 118.
[3] *Ibid.*, p. 119.   [4] Finsch, *Erfahrg. Südsee*, iii. 2, p. 112.
[5] *Ibid.*, p. 110.   [6] *Ibid.*, p. 117.
[7] *Ibid.*, p. 111.   [8] Gerland, *l. c.*, vi. pp. 747, 775.
[9] Grey, *Austr.*, p. 303.   [10] Wallace, *Amaz.*, pp. 348-49.
[11] Tennent, *l. c.*, i. p. 88, note 1.   [12] Schefferus, *l. c.*, p. 53.

The part taken by women in music and song among primitive people is therefore a fairly large and exceptional one, more especially because of the intimate relationship between music and dancing, to which the women are everywhere passionately devoted.   For this reason I purpose speaking in a later chapter (" Music and Dancing ") of the part which woman plays in primitive music.

In some places the children, separated from the adults, sing choruses among themselves, and under certain circumstances they are the chief support of the practice of singing.   On Hawaii Ellis found boys and girls singing in chorus, with an accompaniment of seven drums, a song in honour of a quondam celebrated chief.   Even during supper with the Governor table-music was performed by a juvenile bard of some twelve or fourteen summers, who sang a monotonous song to the accompaniment of a small drum.[1]

The men do not everywhere take part in the musical performances.   In Fiji a man of position deems it beneath him to sing, and he leaves it to his wives and children, so that women sing with women only, and children with children.[2]   On the other hand, on the Andaman Islands as a rule only the men sing, the women contenting themselves with beating time,[3] and among the Thlinkcets (Indians) the men dance while the women sing.[4]   Among the Greenlanders men drum and sing all day long, women only at dancing parties.[5]

It has frequently been observed that the male singers sing so unusually high, as do the women at times, but in the former case it is much more surprising when compared with civilised races.   In Abyssinia,[6] in Madagascar,[7] among

[1] Ellis, *Hawaii*, pp. 74, 75.   [2] Gerland, *l. c.*, vi. p. 604.
[3] Jagor, *Andam.*, p. 45 ; Portman, *l. c.*, p. 196.
[4] Bancroft, i. p. 112 ; Langsdorf, *l. c.*, ii. p. 114.
[5] Graah, *l. c.*, p. 85.   [6] Lobo, p. 27.
[7] Pfeiffer, *Madag.*, pp. 185-186.

the Maoris,[1] the song is pitched as high as possible and
performed amid the greatest excitement. In a troop of
Sudanese soldiers who once visited Europe the frequency
of high tenor and bass voices was striking.[2] All up the
Niger and its tributaries the prevailing voice among men
seems to be high baritone, and among women contralto.[3]
Among the male voices in a Hottentot chorus not a single
baritone was heard; every one sang tenor, somewhat
hoarsely it is true, but not unpleasantly.[4] The men in
Samoa, who have exceptionally good voices, sing a
second tenor part.[5] The Tasmanians, too, used to sing
tenor.[6] With the Andamanese "falsetto" is common
among both sexes, though their general "timbre" is not
as nasal as that of more civilised Oriental races. The
usual compass of the voice in both sexes of the "Öngé"
tribes is about an octave, the prevailing male voice being
baritone, the prevailing female voice being contralto. All
the notes of the women are distinctly head, not chest
notes.[7] Among the Nahua nation (North America) bass
singers were rare, and were prized in proportion to their
rarity.[8] As a rule, however, the compass of Indian male
voices is almost identical with that of the whites, and
there was not one who was unable to sing tenor F easily,
while the average compass was two octaves, F-f or A-a.
Their voices are pleasant, but when the Spaniards first
went to America they said the Indian voices sounded
somewhat rough, but that they improved immensely under
careful tuition.[9]

With these facts some interesting conclusions have
been connected. Mr. Berg [10] imagines that the male
voice was formerly higher than now, and that this is only

[1] Wood, *l. c.*, p. 162.　　　　[2] Zöllner, p. 447.
[3] Day, *Niger*, p. 272.　　　　[4] Michaelis, *l. c.*, p. 527.
[5] Wilkes, *l. c.*, ii. p. 77.　　　[6] Bonwick, *l. c.*, p. 32.
[7] Portman, *l. c.*, p. 183.　　　[8] Bancroft, *l. c.*, ii. p. 294.
[9] Th. Baker, *l. c.*, p. 16.　　　[10] Berg, *l. c.*, pp. 18, 19.

the phylogenetic analogy to the ontogenetic fact that our boys also have at first high voices which acquire the deeper tones of a man after the mutation. But with this the tenor voice of a few primitive people obviously has nothing to do, for if the higher voices of savages should be analogous to boys' voices they ought to have female voices, for in this consist the characteristics of the mutation in falling directly from the female "timbre" into the male one, from the soprano or alto to bass or tenor, instead of gradually sinking from soprano to alto and then to tenor or bass. This hypothesis, however, that savage races had female voices, would be entirely unfounded, although some singular exceptions speak in favour of it at first sight. Thus the Australians frequently sing in falsetto and use a sort of tremolo;[1] the Chinese sing and speak in descant[2] during theatrical performances; those who play women's parts must therefore pitch their voices considerably higher. The women of the Kamchadales have an astonishingly hollow and thin voice "in speaking". According to Mr. Erman this is due to their small stunted snub noses.[3] The Kafirs sing in falsetto,[4] as do the natives of Tierra del Fuego, and, moreover, as Wilkes says the latter "sing continually when speaking," I imagine they must also speak in falsetto. But Mr. Bridge, who lived many years among them, makes no mention of this; although it is well known that when conversing with each other they do so in whispers (possibly this points to a falsetto voice), Mr. Foster simply mentions their "soft melodious voice".[5] This example is therefore not certain enough to warrant an acceptance of the idea that the male of primitive people have female voices; in all other mentioned cases this particular tone-colour, so to speak, is only used when singing, or, as in China, at

[1] Curr, l. c., iii. p. 170.   [2] Görtz, l. c., iii. p. 59.
[3] Erman, l. c., vol. i. 3, p. 209.   [4] Shooter, l. c., p. 237.
[5] Foster, l. c., i. p. 180.

the play ; they *have*, then, male voices and screw them
up to a high pitch only on special occasions. As they
become much more excited over singing than we, so they
are able to pitch their voices with more ease in the higher
registers, in which also they can continue singing freely
in spite of the great exertion, because they have neither
to preserve nor train their voices. Even the ordinary
conversations of primitive people are carried on with the
greatest excitement, a fact which led so many travellers
falsely to believe they were discussing very important
intelligence, the natural consequence of this too being
high-pitched voices.[1] Taking this into consideration I
would neither share Mr. Stumpf's more reasonable presumption that the male voice in general was higher
originally than now, in its entirety.[2] When he alleged
that the old-time tenor parts, *e.g.*, those in the St.
Matthew-Passion, were written so high, that therefore the
tenors of Bach's day were better than those we have now
as far as compass of voice is concerned, it must not be
forgotten that Bach wrote for a lower pitch than that now
in use, as Ellis has shown.[3] Moreover, the space of time
which has elapsed since Bach's death is much too short
to have effected so important a difference in the human
voice. It can rather be said that we have a natural
tendency to constantly raise the pitch. In favour of this
is the fact that theatre and concert pitch is always being
lowered artificially and forcibly at many of the congresses ;

[1] Thomson, *Heart of Africa*, p. 43.
[2] Stumpf, *Tonpsych.*, i. p. 340.
[3] Ellis, *Hist. of Mus.-pitch*, p. 305. This low pitch of Bach's explains
to me why he always wrote the trumpet part so high that our players are
scarcely able to play it. Consequently it has unnecessarily been supposed
that the art of trumpet-playing has decreased in quality in course of time.
High tones, however, can more easily be played on trumpets of lower than
of higher pitch, and as the pitch called B flat was actually lower at Bach's
time than to-day, our players are naturally at a disadvantage compared with
their colleagues in the seventeenth century.

also, that in tuning several strings each higher than the preceding, and not each according to the first, we invariably err towards raising the pitch.[1]   Nevertheless Ellis's historically arranged tables of comparison of different pitches show a certain fluctuation both upwards and downwards. For my part I venture to say that in consequence of the constant training and selecting of good voices, in course of time high tenors and sopranos as well as deep basses and altos are more frequently found ; at any rate the demands of modern composers have become much greater, and the number of both male and female singers incomparably so. The number of choral societies and theatres will corroborate this ; what is not required of these to-day, and what has not been overcome in course of the past fifty years ! So it appears to me that progress and development in this particular line are in every way remarkable.   It is with the vocal organs as with those of hearing ; there has been practically no change in historic times at any rate, although to-day we may perhaps be better able to realise their capabilities than heretofore.

[1] Stumpf, *Tonpsych.*, i. p. 303.

CHAPTER III.

INSTRUMENTS.

(a) GENERAL REMARKS.

THE use of instruments in the first development of music (phylogenetically and ontogenetically) furnished the necessary hold and the equally necessary definiteness for the melodic frame-work. Further than this, however, the use of instruments does not seem to go, all subsequent development proceeding from vocal music. But in earliest times it required whole centuries before all the capabilities of even the most simple and primitive instruments were completely understood and made use of. Possibly this may in some degree account for the surprising antiquity of many comparatively complicated instruments, the full appropriate use of which would otherwise be quite incomprehensible.[1] Concerning this antiquity the following archæological discoveries furnish the desired explanation: At a meeting of the Archæological Institute (3rd June, 1864) the Earl of Dunraven exhibited the bone of an animal of which the original use was at that time unknown. The report of the *Archæological Journal* states [2] that it was thought to have formed part of a musical instrument or a

[1] In the following chapter I wish to call attention to the names of instruments (primitive and modern), the sound of which sometimes imitates the sound of the instruments ; compare flute, pipe (the German Pfiff), tube, tam-tam, gong, rattle, drum. Only later such names were given to other objects of similar form but different use, *e.g.*, chibouk, originally a herdman's pipe or flute in Central Asia. Compare the rich collection of examples in Tylor's *Primit. Cult.*, i. p. 188 *seq.*

[2] *Archæolog. Journ.*, 1864, p. 190.

crossbow. It was found in Ireland in a moat at Desmond
Castle. Professor Owen pronounced the material to be a
bone of the Irish elk (*cervus alces*) ; from this others drew
further conclusions and declared the bone to be the remains
of an "Irish lyra". This last hypothesis is somewhat
hazardous, but not at all because of the improbability that
at the time of the Irish elk there were instruments which
could be used for musical purposes. On the contrary,
this latter presumption has been made more probable
through further discoveries of a less hypothetical nature.
Among the relics of the Troglodytes of the Dordogne
valley was a reindeer bone pierced at one end by an
oblique hole, reaching to the medullary canal. It was
possible to produce a shrill sound from it by blowing as
one would a hollow key.[1] Paul Broca called this instrument a "rallying whistle," but it is questionable if this is
a correct definition ; [2] still other and more complicated
instruments have been found which give more definite
evidence of their being used for a musical purpose. M.
E. Pietto in 1871 found in the cavern at Gourdan (Haute-
Garonne), in a layer of charcoal and cinders mixed with
flint implements, an instrument which he called a neolithic
flute made of a bone and pierced with holes (it is not
stated how many) at the side. Wilson considers this
discovery to be an undoubted example of the very earliest
musical practice.[3] Mr. Fétis,[4] too, mentions and gives a
diagram of a flute of stag-horn (found near Poitiers), which,

---

[1] The first of these reindeer whistles was found, according to Christy
and Lartet (*l. c.*, p. 48), in 1860 in a grave in Aurignac. Since then so
many similar whistles have been found that they are by no means rare
specimens in our ethnological collections.

[2] Lartet is of opinion that this is a hunting whistle. Besides there are
other similar pieces of bone which also emit a shrill tone, but which, according to Ch. Lyell (*l. c.*, p. 128), were pierced with holes for the mere purpose
of being strung over the arm and so used as ornaments. Comp. C. Engel,
Descript. Catal., *South Kens. Mus.*, *l. c.*, p. 10.

[3] D. Wilson, *l. c.*, i. p. 41.   [4] Fétis, *Hist. Gen.*, i. p. 26.

judging from the surroundings in which it was found, has been supposed to date from the stone period. It had three holes bored at equal distances, thus producing four diatonic tones. Another instrument is a sort of rule or paper-knife made from a light greyish green nephrite spread over with brown colour, wonderfully polished, 18·4 cm. long, 1·8 cm. broad in the middle, 3·4 mm. thick, tapering towards the ends and somewhat thinner at the sides. The broader sides are quite smooth and shining, while the ends and edges are rounded off. In the middle of one of the narrower sides is a small round "relief" with flat rounded inlets, which is pierced with two holes, the one slightly larger than the other, but both bored conically from each side so that the middle is the narrowest part. (It came from Tocuyo, west of Valencia, in Venezuela.) It was obviously hung up on a string drawn through the two holes, and it is quite possible that it was struck upon great functions, i.e., that it was a sort of musical instrument, for it emitted a powerful, high-pitched tone when struck. It was similar to an East Asiatic gong.[1]

Of later date is a bronze tube found in a ravine in Schleswig; it lay beneath a pile of gold and silver ornaments and emitted a deep note. The specimen is now in the museum at Copenhagan.[2]

Though the fact is sufficiently remarkable that musical instruments were first made at a time when the artistic capabilities of mankind were confined to working in stone or in animals' bones, yet the boldest hypotheses of musicians have been surpassed by the existence of ancient Egyptian flutes which were brought to London in 1890, and which, to the astonishment of all, produced the diatonic scale. From the surroundings in which they were found it was thought they dated from 3000 years B.C. (i.e., the Egyptian bronze period). Thus the flute

---

[1] D. Wilson, l. c., i. p. 41.   [2] Fétis, Hist. Gen., i. p. 26.

and fife are, with the gong, the most ancient instruments so far as can be definitely ascertained. Sounding plates (like gongs), however, are proved by their very polish to belong to a somewhat later period. (Lubbock's *Period of Polished Stones*.)

It is also remarkable that even to-day there exist people who use the same materials and principles in making their instruments. Flutes and fifes made from the bones of animals or wings of a bird are not uncommon. The Caribs in Guiana use the bones of the jaguar for this purpose. Wood says[1] they formerly used human bones. This remark of Wood is, I am sorry to say, incorrect; the truth is, as a matter of fact, just the opposite. *Formerly* jaguar bones were used, but as these became scarce, human bones were brought into requisition, and they still are used.[2] The jaguar flute has three holes like that mentioned by Fétis, but Mr. Im Thurn unfortunately does not give the notes. Flutes made from human bones are also found in New Zealand,[3] among the Surinam in Guiana [4] who use the bones of slain enemies for this purpose, and among the Indians of Columbia River[5] who use animals' bones.

Even the human skull is used as a musical instrument —as a rattle (on the Fly River in New Guinea). Its construction is as follows: The cleansed skull is covered with a wax mask stained with the red juice of the *Arbus precatorius* and rattan stripes. The eyes are replaced by cowry-shells, and to the temples are fastened ear pendants as the natives wear them. The lower jaw is bound to the upper, and the whole skull tied up with a thong and filled with stones, hard kernels of fruit, and pumice-stone,

---

[1] Wood, *l. c.*, ii. p. 630.   [2] Im Thurn, *l. c.*, p. 309.

[3] Angas, *Savage Life*, p. 529 ; *Polyn*., p. 158.

[4] Stedmann, *l. c.*, i. p. 409.

[5] Bancroft, *l. c.*, i. p. 201 ; Jewitt, *l. c.*, p. 88, mentions the flute from animal bones as a general Indian instrument.

occasionally serves for a sort of rattle during a dance. On Eremitanos Island near New Guinea, the lower jaw, hair, and teeth are fastened to a frame of bast in the shape of a horse-shoe and hung up on the houses.[1]

Ethnological inquiries, and more especially archæological discoveries, have destroyed a hitherto generally accepted theory that the drum is the oldest, and the stringed instrument (of whatever name) the most recent of musical instruments.[2] The most ancient is the flute. The division into instruments of percussion, wind, and strings helps nothing in deciding their origin, although it may be the most useful in connection with the modern orchestra. The reasons which speak against it are manifold and are all specially opposed to Rowbotham's theory, which assumes not only three different types of instruments, but also a corresponding development of music itself.

1. The most ancient discoveries (from the youth of mankind) of flutes and pipes, but not of drums, are definite facts which no speculation can put aside. The early appearance of the bow (as a stringed instrument) among the Damaras and Hottentots also declares against the theory that we are indebted to a much later period for stringed instruments. Rowbotham, however, makes light of this fact, and designates the Hottentot bow a "mere idle experiment," and behold his theory is saved. I am rather inclined to believe that Mr. Wagener was correct in saying that a wind instrument was undoubtedly the first.[3] He mentions especially the bamboo tube, while the abovementioned discoveries decide in favour of the bone whistle and flute. Folklore in Java, too, states that the origin of music is due to accident, that the wind blew through a suspended tube and produced a musical *tone*.[4]

[1] Andree, *Ethn. Par.*, p. 139 ; similar description by Albertis, ii. p. 379.
[2] I need scarcely quote any authors as the supposition is a general one.
[3] Wagener, *l. c.*, p. 48.
[4] Raffles, *l. c.*, p. 472.

Carl Engel (*Anc. Nat.*, p. 10) considers the drum the most ancient instrument. But when he says we find drums earlier than any other instrument his statement is opposed to all discoveries of prehistoric remains. I can find nothing but speculative reasons and common consent for the drum being the most ancient instrument.

2. The existence of combination instruments in primitive periods and their importance makes the above-mentioned division utterly impossible, unless we simply pass over these facts. I mention the goura as a combination of wind and stringed instrument, the marimba as a combination of wind and percussion instrument, and the jew's harp as a wind instrument combined with the principles of the vibrating string, *i.e.*, principle of stringed instruments.[1]

3. As a rule the simplicity of construction of a drum as opposed to the complexity of stringed instruments is held out as a reason for its being the most primitive instrument. If this be sound reasoning, it is manifest that the drum cannot be the most ancient instrument. Compare existing illustrations of primitive instruments and you will see that the primitive bow (or guitar or zither, lyre or harp, or whatever you may call it) is the simplest, the flute and tube coming next, while the drum—in ancient days not rarely a richly ornamented work of art—is the most complicated. A simple bow or a primitive harp or zither (just as used in primitive times) any one of us could construct; every shepherd boy cuts his flute in a few moments—but a drum, especially such a one as is in use among savages, made of a hollowed-out tree trunk, would take days to make with the aid of several practised hands and appropriate implements. Nevertheless, on this basis Mr. Rowbotham builds up his theory of the three periods, drum, pipe, and lyre stages which should correspond with

---

[1] The mere name is characteristic enough: the Germans say "Maul-trommel," the English jew's *harp*.

the stone, bronze, and iron ages, and as the stone and bronze were replaced by the iron, so must the drum and flute be by stringed instruments. This seems to me a most unfortunate and unnecessary theory, as such distinct periods of musical instruments never existed, and the drum has held its own up to the date of the modern orchestra quite contrary to the part played by stone and bronze.

4. The above classification, further, is impossible, on the ground that it must not be made according to the mere appearance of the instruments and the use to which *we* think they would have been put, but rather to that to which the savages have put them. The character of instruments can decide nothing as to the condition of music. Again and again may examples be adduced to prove that savages tuned their drums together by applying pressure with the fingers, or by holding the drum near a fire ; drums, too, which produce a different tone from each end, and therefore are not used merely as rhythmical instruments, were used in Guiana.[1] On the Tonga Islands there is a bamboo tube in use, which is not blown but beaten on the ground ;[2] the same thing occurs in Samoa, too.[3] Mr. Crawfurd mentions an instrument made of different tubes (like the pipes of an organ) which is not blown but shaken about in a frame.[4] The Kafirs have a " fiddle " or harp from which they can produce no melody, but merely one note.[5] In Fiji the natives had flutes with five openings of which only one was used,[6] and the Bechuanas played their reed pipes more for the sake of time than of melody.[7] The Mandingoes are said to play but one note on their flutes, " nor would they play better if they had European flutes ".[8] The ancient Armenians

---

[1] Im Thurn, *l. c.*, p. 309.   [2] Mariner, *Quar. Rev.*, *l. c.*, p. 35.
[3] Turner, *Samoa*, p. 125 ; *Polyn.*, p. 215.
[4] Crawfurd, *l. c.*, p. 334.   [5] Wood, *l. c.*, i. p. 232.
[6] Wilkes, *l. c.*, iii. p. 189.   [7] Fritsch, *Eingeb.*, pp. 190-91.
[8] *Astley Collect.*, ii. p. 278.

had a stringed instrument which they *beat with a stick*.[1]

Under the circumstances, then, nothing of the character of music can be argued from what is known of the instruments as such. But though melody and harmony are the most recent developments of primitive music, yet they in no way decide the period at which stringed instruments came into use. *Drumming*, it is true, was the first attempt at the practice of music, or rather of time-keeping, but the *drum* was by no means the first instrument.

There are a good many savage tribes which perform their music without any instruments: thus the natives of the Philippine Islands have no instruments;[2] the same is said of the aborigines on the Caroline Islands in the West, and of Lugunor and Kusai.[3] Only in Ponapé there is a drum, flute, and shell-trumpet used in war and during religious feasts,[4] in Bornabi a nose-flute and a wooden drum covered with shark's skin.[5] The Melanesiens, too, have no instruments, at least not in the smallest islands,[6] nor have the Veddas in Ceylon,[7] and the natives in Tierra del Fuego. The Andamanese know only the sounding board (Pakuda), on which they beat time.[8] The Ainu on the Island of Yezo do not themselves make any instruments; those which they use are all introduced from Japan.[9] The women beat time to the dancers on empty coops and accompany their songs with clapping their hands.[10] The Hassanyeh tribes on the White Nile had no musical instruments. Girls clapping their hands and singing a song, and young men clapping too, although not joining in the song, was sufficient to excite the dancers. All kept good time.[11]

---

[1] Peterman, *l. c.*, p. 366.' [2] Fr. Müller, *l. c.*, p. 137.
[3] Gerland-Waitz, *l. c.*, v. 2, p. 90. [4] Meinicke, *l. c.*, ii. p. 383.
[5] Angas, *Polyn.*, p. 384. [6] Ratzel, *l. c.*, ii. p. 228.
[7] Brown, *l. c.*, p. 241. [8] Jagor, *Andam.*, p. 63; Portman, *l. c.*, p. 183.
[9] Siebold, *Aino*, p. 48. [10] Scheube, *l. c.*, p. 237.
[11] Petherick, *l. c.*, p. 137.

The natives of Australia, too, had no instruments (except at Ports Jackson and Essington), and they accompany their songs by beating one arm against the other.[1]   At Moorunde (Australia) the natives carried branches of green boughs, which they waved and shook to the time of the song.[2]   Speaking of the Finmark Laplanders, Mr. Leems says they have no musical instrument.[3]   Linée, however, found in the hills of Lapland a sort of trumpet (" lur ") and pipes made of the bark of the quicken tree or mountain ash (sorbus aucuparia).[4]

In spite of their having no instruments the above-mentioned tribes know songs and dances; anything making a noise may be used to accompany the performers.

Thus the negroes are said to use everything for their musical performance that claps: wooden sticks, tin boxes of preserved meat, keys, etc.[5]   Some tribes even use their pans, such as they have for meals, pierce holes round them with copper plates fastened with copper pins.[6]   The Indians use for the same purpose mussel or cockle shells tied together[7] (original of the castanets?).   When commencing an attack the lords of " Tezcuco " (Mexico) struck two bones together as a " musical " signal.[8]

No wonder the appreciation of European instruments in savage countries is so different from ours.   Burchell's flute did not impress the Bushmen, nor did the sound of a flute strike the Fuegians in any degree.[9]   On the Tonga Islands the sounds of European drums excelled—according to the natives—all other music;[10] the high opinion the savages had of the musical boxes has been

[1] Salvado, *l. c.*, p. 183.   [2] Eyre, *l. c.*, ii. p. 236.
[3] Leems, *l. c.*, ii. p. 452.   [4] Linnæus, *l. c.*, ii. p. 51.
[5] Buchner, *Kam.*, p. 13 ; Ratzel, *l. c.*, i. p. 617.
[6] *Astley Collect.*, iii. p. 227.   [7] Jewitt, *l. c.*, p. 88.
[8] Bancroft, *l. c.*, ii. p. 426.   [9] Foster, i. p. 180.
[10] Erskine, *l. c.*, p. 152.

mentioned before.[1] The music of a Scotch bagpipe once considerably frightened the poor Australians; later on, when they saw that no harm would come out of it, they got used to the music, and the performance met with general approval.[2] In Hapai (Tonga) none of the European musical instruments which Cook brought with him was held in the least esteem except the drum, and even that they did not think equal to their own. The French horns, in particular, seemed to be held in great contempt.[3] At Loango (Africa) the natives often gather under a tree to hold concerts; they use all sorts of stringed instruments, trumpets, fifes, and drums, and mix their verses to the sound of instruments. The more noise is made the better the piece is performed. "Our military musicians would soon become new Orphei, but the best opera musician would just as soon be laughed at."[4] The Fûlis (West Africa) love music, and though the kings and princes of the neighbouring Jalofs think it a disgrace to touch an instrument, yet some of that rank among the Fûlis pride themselves in understanding several. At the same time they are extremely fond of dancing.[5]

Mr. Lander tells us that in every class of society from the monarch down to the lowest slave instrumental music is in favour, and a European fiddler might travel with ease and comfort from Badagry to Bornu. He would be received everywhere with open arms, lodged in palaces, and sumptuously fed, although he might, perhaps, feel some trifling inconvenience from excess of kindness.[6]

At Griqua-Stad, near the conflux of the Vaal and Grote

---

[1] It may be well to mention that our "civilised" population as well takes great delight in a monster musical box—the street organ.

[2] Globus, xiii. p. 123.

[3] Cook, *First Voyage*, i. p. 248; *Pink. Collect.*, xi. p. 667.

[4] Proyart, *l. c.*, p. 575.

[5] Brüe, *l. c.*, p. 63d.

[6] Lander, *Rec. of Clapp.*, i. p. 293.

Rivers (tributaries of the Orange River), the European mouth-harmonica was in particular favour, to the playing of which the swollen up lips of the natives seemed especially fitted.[1] Their extraordinary feeling for time is even on such occasions unmistakable. The natives on Solomon Islands were much pleased with an imitation of the boatswain's call, and seemed to like a German student song which the sailors sang.[2] The real boatswain's call so much impressed the Papuans that they at once offered a high price in gold for it.[3]

(b) FLUTES, FIFES, FLAGEOLETS.

The ancient Greeks had a sensible saying about the importance of a reed : it contributed to subjugate nations by furnishing arrows, to soften men's manners by the charm of music, and to unfold their understanding by affording the first instruments for tracing letters. To this Humboldt remarked that these three uses of reeds mark in some sort three different periods in the life of nations.[4] However, the bone-flute existed long before the reed-flute and also before the reed-arrow, and to soften men's manners primitive music with all its flutes has contributed next to nothing ; on the contrary, it inspired the savages with a desire for fighting, it aroused their anger, excited their fanaticism, and by accompanying their war-dances, also in time of peace, it aroused their lust for war. Among warlike nations music is most developed, and directly arises from an excess of vigour which is to be trained and strengthened for the struggle for life. This saying of the ancient Greeks, and still more Humboldt's attempt to divide the life of nations into three periods, is

[1] Fritsch, *Die Eing.*, p. 190 ; 3 *Jahre in Süd. Afr.*, 252.
[2] Zimmermann, *l. c.*, i. p. 239.
[3] *Ibid.*, ii. p. 186.
[4] Humboldt, *l. c.*, iv. p. 465.

certainly unsuccessful from a scientific point of view, although no one will deny its poetic beauty.

Bearing in mind all that prehistoric discoveries have made manifest, apart from all romantic combinations, we may say: the original of the flute was an ornament, the bone of a captured animal or of a slain enemy was pierced with a hole and hung up as a war trophy. By this one approached to the possibility of producing tones from it. It is not possible to determine from the earliest of these fifes if the openings were used merely for hanging the instruments up, or if they were meant to be blown into, but we may consider the latter to be the correct idea, as pipes of the same shape and construction which are used for producing tones have been found to-day among primitive people. These tones were at first used as signals, next, with some modifications, as signs of recognition, thus showing a practical purpose side by side with the artistic use made of it in accompanying the dancing songs.

For its extreme antiquity and for its wide dissemination, this instrument is indebted in no small degree to the great simplicity of its construction, which was only surpassed by that of the bow. Humboldt says he was surprised to see with what promptitude the young Indians constructed and tuned these pipes when they found reeds on the bank of the river.[1] Schweinfurth also says of the Bongos in Africa that they constructed small flutes with little trouble and with the poorest of materials.[2] It is remarkable in what a simple manner savages sometimes tune their flutes together. Cook noticed in Tahiti that the natives used for this purpose the shortest flute, which they lengthened by means of a rolled-up leaf that could be pushed in or drawn out until the requisite pitch was arrived at. This they determine by the ear alone " with

---

[1] Humboldt, *l. c.*, iv. p. 465. [2] Schweinfurth, *l. c.*, i. p. 130.

great nicety ".[1]   Here we have as good an example of the
harmonic use of the flute as former examples have given
of its rhythmic use.

A somewhat more complicated construction of the
flageolet was reported by Baker among the Iroquois (he
strongly marks the distinction between the flute and the
flageolet).   The intonation is rarely quite pure, and the
notes are generally the first four to six of the minor scale
with (although not in all instruments) their octaves.[2]

Very frequent among primitive people is the custom
of blowing the flute by means of the nostrils, when one
nostril is closed by the finger and the entire force of the
breath blown into the flute through the other.

Mr. Tylor agrees with C. Engel in explaining this
curious custom as a prejudice of the Hindus ; no man of
higher rank would ever touch with his lips a flute which
a low caste man has made and put to his mouth before.[3]
From India this custom spread all over the islands of the
Indian Ocean.

Flutes, fifes and flageolets are to be found in all
continents and in all stages of culture.   We mention the
reed-pipe of the Makalaka,[4] the flute of the Ashantis,
which is larger than any kind used in Europe and through
which the natives profess to be able to hold conversation
with each other,[5] the flute of the Mandingoes [6] and the
Malagasy.[7]   The Kafirs use their pipes not for an artistic
purpose but for calling their cattle from a distance.   They
are made of bone or ivory, and are used by being held to
the lower lip and sounded as we blow a key.   Without an
instrument, too, the Kafir whistles with his lips alone or
by the aid of his fingers so loudly " as to half deafen any
one who may be near ".   Cook found flutes in the islands

[1] Cook, *First Voyage*, vol. ii. p. 205.   [2] Th. Baker, *l. c.*, p. 55.
[3] Tylor, *Study of Customs*, pp. 81, 82.   [4] Mauch, *l. c.*, p. 43.
[5] Beecham, *l. c.*, p. 168 ; Bowdich *Mission*, p. 361.
[6] Mungo Park, *l. c.*, p. 878.   [7] Gerland, *l. c.*, v. p. 169.

of Amsterdam and Middleburgh,[1] and Hamilton mentions
the pipe in Pegu (East India).[2] We find flutes among the
Dayaks in Borneo,[3] and a pipe of deer-bones among the
Indians of Columbia.[4] A peculiar species seems to be the
flute of the Papuans of New Guinea. They have two
sorts, the "male" and the "female" flute: the latter
constructed like a German "Schalmei," the former rather
a small trombone, so far as the construction is concerned,
as the natives prolong and shorten the hollow tube by
means of a slide to produce different tones. Women are
forbidden even to see these flutes, as their superstitious
belief says they would die at once in face of them.[5]
Catlin found with the Indians of North America a war-
whistle, a "deer-skin flute," and an instrument which he
calls a "mystery-whistle" because it was very difficult
to understand the mode in which the sound was produced.[6]
In travelling along the Amazon River Mr. Wallace saw the
natives with flutes and pipes of reed, pipes of bones and
skulls.[7] The Botocudos (Amazon Valley) have a reed-
flute commonly played by women.[8] The Yuruna (Xingu
River), especially, have a great number and variety of
flutes; a long one called Panetatadu, with a tone like a
trumpet, and small bassoons played by women, and pan-
pipes.[9] The aborigines of Surinam,[10] the Caribs in Guiana,
and the natives in New Zealand have flutes of the bones
of slain enemies,[11] and the latter a nose-flute as well.[12]

[1] Cook, *Second Voyage; Pink. Collect.*, xi. p. 594.

[2] Hamilton, *l. c.*, p. 427.   [3] Hein, *l. c.*, pp. 113-116.

[4] Bancroft, *l. c.*, i. p. 201 (Columbian River); a bone-whistle only used
by the king, the chief, or some important person. Jewitt, *l. c.*, p. 88.

[5] Schelling, *l. c.*   [6] Catlin, *l. c.*, i. p. 242.

[7] Wallace, *Amazon, l. c.*, p. 504.

[8] Wied-Neuweid, *l. c.*, abst., xli. p. 155.

[9] Von d. Steinen, *l. c.*, p. 259.   [10] Stedmann, *l. c.*, i. p. 409 (illust.).

[11] D'Urville, *l. c.*, ii. p. 446; Lubbock, *l. c.*, p. 467; Angas, *Sav. Life*, p.
392; *Polyn.*, p. 158.

[12] D'Urville, *ibid.*

The flute "Bendu" of the Kimbunda people (Africa) is said to be a "hell for the ear ";[1] something akin is said of the flutes of the Fulah and Susu (West Coast of Africa).[2]

In some instances it is particularly mentioned in the accounts of travellers that it is possible to produce several tones on the flutes. The reed-pipe of the Bechuana (called lichâka) is played by the natives in one tone only, but they tune it to any required note by pushing or withdrawing a movable plug. They take great pains in getting the precise note which they want.[3] The Karagwe tribes have a pipe with six finger holes.[4] Prominent among the Niger people is the "lera," constructed of a hollow pipe of cane, with four to six finger-holes. At the end of the pipe, upon the upper side, a notch is cut, forming the embouchure. Such flutes appear common throughout Africa.[5] Another wind instrument of that country, the "furi," is played with three finger-holes only, covered respectively by the thumb and finger of the right hand, and the first finger of the left. Instruments sounded by single or double reeds, which are in use in the Niger territories, are, in Capt. Day's opinion, "distinctly of Mohammedan introduction".

Brown speaks of an Indian flute with six holes;[6] in ancient Mexico there was a pipe with four holes (c d e $\bar{c}$);[7] in Guiana a flute (Quamu) with three tones,[8] "very much resembling the howling of a dog in distress". The New Zealanders have a pipe (He Koauan) with two holes, made of a whale's tooth;[9] in Amsterdam and Middleburgh (or Tongatubu and Eua) there is a flute with four holes, on Tahiti with two holes,[10] on Tonga a nose-flute (played with the right nostril) with five holes (fango-fango),

[1] Magyar, l. c., p. 311.   [2] Corry, l. c., p. 153.
[3] Burchell, l. c., ii. p. 598.   [4] Grant, l. c., pp. 184, 185.
[5] Day, Niger, p. 268.   [6] Brown, l. c., p. 291, Nos. 10, 14.
[7] Sartorius, l. c., p. 203.   [8] Bernau, l. c., p. 45.
[9] R. Taylor, l. c., p. 316 (illust.).   [10] Cook, Second Voyage, i. p. 220.

on Fiji Islands one with five holes, but the natives scarcely vary the tone by the closing and opening of the holes.[1] A Polynesian flute (played through the left nostril) is mentioned by Ellis; it had three holes at the top and one at the bottom.[2] The Chukmas (one of the wild races in South Eastern India) are famous for their flute-playing. Their instrument is simple enough, being merely a joint of bamboo pierced with holes; but from this rough medium they evoke "wondrous soft music".[3] In New Britain and the York Islands there is a pipe with three tones,[4] and in North Luzon (Philippine Islands) a flute with three holes.[5]

From the above it may be seen that the number of holes is a very limited one (as a rule two to six), a fact most important for the construction of the scale, as we shall see later on.

Contrary to the limited use savages make of their instruments, we hear of some instances where the natives themselves are able to play regular airs on them. As the Carib approaches home he generally plays his quamuh (flute), and preparations for his reception are immediately made.[6] [Mus. Ex. 13.] An Iroquois youth always plays a certain melody when he wishes to entice his love from the hut.[7] The Warrau Indians in Guiana have flutes of reed bamboo or of thigh bones of animals. In large settlements they have a band master or hohohit, whose duty it is to train his pupils to blow upon the flutes, in which a small reed, on the principle of the clarionet, is introduced. Their playing produces an effect similar to the Russian horn-bands;[8] in the same manner as these

---

[1] Wilkes, *l. c.*, iii. p. 189; Williams, *l. c.*, p. 141.
[2] Ellis, *Pol. Res.*, i. p. 285.   [3] Lewin, *l. c.*, p. 188.
[4] Powell, *l. c.*, p. 73 (illust.).
[5] A. B. Meyer, *l. c.*, viii., table 17, Nos. 13, 16.
[6] Schomburgk, *l. c.*, p. 274.   [7] Baker, *l. c.*, p. 56.
[8] Schomburgk, *l. c.*, p. 274.

Russian bands play the Tipperahs, who use reeds on which each performer plays his one tone as his turn comes round.[1] The natives on the Máhádeo Hills (Central India) sang and danced to the music of half-a-dozen bamboo flutes.[2]

A peculiar instrument of the pipe class is the pan-pipe or syrinx. It was commonly supposed that the pan-pipe represents the first attempt to produce different tones from one instrument,[3] and that later on men were induced to obtain the same end by perforating a pipe with holes. The above-mentioned examples of prehistoric archæology seem to point to the contrary. The oldest specimen of pan-pipe appears to be a syrinx found in Peru. It is cut out of a solid mass of a compact, softish stone (Lapis ollaris). There are eight pipes or cylindrical tubes, but the second octave of them, and even a third octave, may be obtained by an expert performer. The condition of the stone material seems to indicate that "the Peruvian artist knew also how to amend the tone by stopping the bottom of the pipe when necessary". Although it is calculated to be of considerably anterior date to the Spanish conquest, the first-mentioned prehistoric flutes are still the most ancient we possess.[4]

Double flutes and pipes are to be found on almost all the continents, although not so frequently as the ordinary flute and pipe. Among the Iroquois Mr. Baker saw a double flute in the shape of a V;[5] the Surinam Indians in Guiana had a syrinx called quarta,[6] "a set of pipes of different length". In Guiana Mr. Im Thurn found a double flute of wood and a pan-pipe of reed;[7] double flutes also

---

[1] Lewin, *l. c.*, p. 217. The Russian horn-band (invented by Maresch, 1751) originally consisted of sixteen horns of different pitch. Each player played one tone only, but by a clever combination they succeeded in executing the most complicated compositions ; compare Hinrichs, *l. c.*

[2] Forsyth, *l. c.*, p. 119.   [3] Daniel, *Fantaisie, etc.*, p. 388.

[4] Traill, *l. c.*, p. 124.   [5] Th. Baker, *l. c.*, p. 55.

[6] Stedmann, *l. c.*, i. 409 (illust., p. 423).

[7] Im Thurn, *l. c.*, p. 309.

occur on Savage Islands (Polynesia),[1] a pan-flute of reed on the islands Amsterdam and Middleburgh with ten to eleven tubes of different length,[2] a pan-flute with seven tones in Sumatra,[3] North Luzon,[4] New Britain, and the York Islands [5] (seven to fifteen notes), the Fiji Islands,[6] Admiralty Islands,[7] with the Papuans (with thirteen tones),[8] the New Hebrides (eight tubes),[9] and in Samoa ; [10] here the flute is beaten with a stick.

The Tipperahs have a most curious musical instrument, in sound something between an organ and a bagpipe. It is made from a gourd, into which long reed pipes of different lengths are inserted, which have each one hole-stop.[11]

Mr. Ives found with the Keres in New Mexico an instrument with an end like a clarionet [12] (Bancroft nevertheless calls it reed-*flute*) ; [13] one end is put into a water basin, by blowing into which the warbling of birds was imitated. The Keres often use the bagpipe, not for an artistic purpose but while at work, to keep time to its music.[14] This is one of the numerous examples where music has to serve a practical purpose. I particularly wish to call the attention of the reader to such examples, as we shall have to make use of them in our conclusions in the tenth chapter. At Tascala and Natividad an Okarina was in use (Teponastle) three feet long with a human face in front.[15]

[1] Turner, *Polyn.*, p. 470.

[2] Cook, *Second Voyage*, i. p. 220 (illust. No. 5).

[3] Bastian, *Indon.*, Liefg. 3, table 2.   [4] Meyer, *l. c.*, viii., table 17, No. 16.

[5] Powell, *l. c.*, p. 73.   [6] Williams, *l. c.*, p. 141.

[7] *Challenger Exped.*, i. 2, p. 723.

[8] Miklukho Maklay, *l. c.*, p. 845 ; Schelling, *l. c.*

[9] Turner, *Polyn.*, p. 337 (illust.).   [10] Turner, *Samoa*, p. 125.

[11] Lewin, *l. c.*, p. 217.   [12] Ives, *Colorado River*, p. 121.

[13] Bancroft, *l. c.*, i. p. 552.

[14] Davis, *El Gringo*, p. 119.

[15] Bancroft, *l. c.*, iv. p. 478 (illust.); a clarionet (Chirimiya) of the Lacandones mentioned by Bancroft, i. p. 705.

What we know as the modern bagpipe seems to be derived from common reed pipes (single and double) by a process recently described in a very interesting and elaborate paper by Mr. H. Balfour, and in his collection of horn-pipes (historically arranged) in the Oxford Museum. At first the reeds were protected from injury by a large mouthpiece of gourd or of horn.[1] By perforating the cover a secondary use was found for it as a mouthpiece, through which the reeds could be sounded.[2] Later on a skin was substituted for the sake of a continuous blast, the necessity of which seems to have been felt long before. Thus the Bhotanese were able to sustain prolonged blasts upon the hautboy, and so, too, did the Brahmins of India.[3] Mr. Balfour concludes that horn-pipe instruments were very probably " brought to the British Islands with the Celtic immigration, and that they have survived particularly in those regions in which the Celtic blood has held its own ".[4] From such instruments the Picborn (identical with the horn-pipe) is derived.

Another theory is that the bagpipe might probably have been brought to England by the gipsies. Pennell leaves this question open.[5] In other countries she thinks the gipsies' influence is more clearly noticeable. Thus the Spanish name for bagpipe, " gaita," belongs to the Greek dialect of Romani,[6] and is the same as " gaïda," applied to the same instrument by the Turkish gipsies, " from which the inference is that Spain owes this name, if not the instrument itself, to the gipsies ". The editor of the *Gyps. Lore Soc. Journ.* further calls attention to Walker's statement (*Irish Bards*, p. 165) : " The Wal-Pipe of the Finns seems to be the Cala-Mala of the *Zingari* of Swinburne, and Mala-Pioba (or piob-mhāla) of the Irish ". For the British Islands, however, the immigration of

---

[1] H. Balfour, *l. c.*, p. 147.   [2] *Ibid.*, p. 152.
[3] *Ibid.*, p. 147.   [4] *Ibid.*, p. 152.
[5] Pennell, *l. c.*, ii. p. 276.   [6] *Journ. Gyps. Lore Soc.*, i. p. 302.

gipsies seems to be too late a date for the introduction of bagpipes, and therefore Mr. Balfour's theory has in itself a far greater historical probability. Even the Spaniards may have got bagpipes from the ancient Romans (Nero was a bagpipe player). Very likely the gipsies brought the bagpipe and reed-pipe from India with them, and may have brought it in fashion again in *some* countries, but were certainly not the first who imported it to Europe.

(c) TRUMPETS, TUBES, HORNS.

If the peculiar custom of playing the flute with the nose has struck us as being remarkable, so, in the case of the tube, equally noteworthy is the habit of playing it like a European flute, and this, too, in spite of its huge size and weight.[1] Consequently its tone is not unlike that of a fife or flute, but is both louder and fuller. The signal horns of the Bongos (Central Africa), which are made from the horns of antelopes, are said by Schweinfurth to be very similar in tone to the fife.[2] They have three holes like a small flute and are called " Mangoal " by the natives; the Mittu signal horns are constructed on exactly similar lines.[3] The Congo people frequently make them of very costly materials, and for this reason, I think, they are the property of persons of royal blood. This certainly is the case with the ivory trumpet, " Embuchi," of the Angola tribes.[4] Very early, it seems, arose the need for making the inconvenient form of the tube more handy, and while Europeans succeeded in artistically bending the tube, the Karagwes were content to construct their instruments like a telescope to draw out and in.[5] Ivory horns are found among Niam-Niams,[6] the Mandingoes,[7] the Jebus,[8] and in the Niger coun-

---

[1] Wood, *l. c.*, i. p. 627 ; Day, *Niger*, p. 268.
[2] Schweinfurth, *l. c.*, i. p. 130. [3] *Ibid.*, p. 197.
[4] Carli, *l. c.*, i. p. 622; Tuckey, *l. c.*, p. 373 ; Merolla, *l. c.*, p. 244.
[5] Grant, *l. c.*, pp. 184-185. [6] Ch. Long, *l. c.*, p. 279.
[7] M. Park, *l. c.*, p. 878. [8] Avezac, *l. c.*, p. 90.

tries[1]; horns of the Harrisbuck among the Makalaka[2] and the M'balunda negroes.[3] In East Africa they use wooden horns,[4] which Burton calls " noise instruments ". Even this is something, however, for the valuable ivory horns of the Ashantis are so badly treated that now and then they crack and at last give no tone at all. But their tone at the best of times cannot be particularly beautiful, for the instruments are always covered with snake skin.[5] Still this remark of Wood's is not invariably accurate, for several reports mention not only the " powerful sounds " of these horns, but also the fact that each Cabucir plays upon it his own peculiar song which is known to all. This working up of different tones of the horn into a melody does not occur in sentimental serenades or the like as has been said, but is used to communicate the position of the chief to his warriors in a battle.[6] In times of peace this " *leit-motiv* " may also be used for other purposes ; its original idea however is connected with war, as may also be seen in the trophy fastened to the instrument, and which is a man's upper jaw.

On the upper Amur wooden horns are wrapped in the leaves of a lime tree ;[7] on the Malay Peninsula bamboo tubes pierced with holes are hung upon trees in the forest (and are called " Buluperindu "). The effect of the wind passing through suggests the " soft and tender tones of the flute as well as the deep, full notes of an organ ". Some of the bamboos give fourteen to twenty notes.[8] The Maoris use their seven foot wooden tubes (*putura-putura*)

[1] Day, *Niger*, p. 268.

[2] Mauch, *l. c.*, p. 43 ; the Jewish Schoffat is evidently a buck's horn from primeval times.

[3] Soyaux, *l. c.*, pp. 175-176.   [4] Burton, *Centr. Lakes*, ii. p. 98.

[5] Wood, *l. c.*, i. p. 627.

[6] Beecham, *l. c.*, p. 168 ; ivory trumpets in Guinea by Bosman, *l. c.*, p. 394.

[7] Andree, *Amurgeb.*, p. 173.

[8] Tennent, *l. c.*, i. p. 88, note 1 ; Bickmore, *l. c.*, p. 191.

for purposes of war; during an uproar they blow them with such vigour as to be heard at a distance of several English miles.[1]

The Indians of the Uaupés (tributary of the Rio Negro) make and use huge tubes "which resemble bassoons," and of which eight different sizes are used in the Juripari or devil's music. The tone is not unpleasant, and the Indians play them tolerably well together. Wallace says the instruments are made of bark spirally twisted and with a mouthpiece of leaves.[2] The natives waved their instruments vertically and sideways attended by corresponding movements of the body, and played a regular melody accompanying each other very correctly. The women are not allowed even to look upon these instruments under pain of death, which is caused by poison. It is said that fathers have been the executioners of their own daughters, husbands of their wives.[3] It might be wished that a symbolical remnant of some such prohibition might be found in the course of the general development of instruments from the Indian tube to the modern pianoforte of our periods of culture.

A bamboo tube (Caracasha) on the Lower Amazon[4] and a wooden trumpet in Guiana[5] are mentioned among the wind instruments of Northern South America; the children of the Batéké (Congo) make trumpets from rolled-up banana leaves.[6]

A much simpler tube is found on the isles of the Pacific Ocean, where a mussel-shell is used for this purpose; this is also used on the Congo,[7] in Fiji,[8] and on the Cornwallis Islands.[9] The tone of a mussel trumpet

---

[1] Angas, *Savage Life*, p. 152.   [2] Wallace, *Amaz.*, pp. 348-349.
[3] *Ibid.*   [4] Bates, *l. c.*, i. p. 311.
[5] Im Thurn, *l. c.*, p. 309.   [6] Johnston, *Congo*, p. 432.
[7] Tuckey, *l. c.*, p. 373.
[8] Wilkes, *l. c.*, iii. p. 189; Williams, *l. c.*, p. 141.
[9] Chamisso, *l. c.*, p. 113.

as used in Fiji by the priests in their temples was more
terrific than that of the drum.   The instrument was a foot
long and seven inches in diameter at the mouth.   In order
to facilitate the blowing a three foot long bamboo reed
was introduced and blown into.[1]   These sea mussel-shells
were always used when processions went into the temples.
On other occasions bamboo tubes (Thura) are used.   The
Papuans have a trumpet made from the shells of *tritonium
variegatum*,[2] which is probably used for alarm signals.[3]
A shell trumpet, found in Madagascar, sounds like a
post-horn; with it the husband, father, or son calls the
women together, who then approach their masters
crawling on hands and knees.[4]

The Haussa (Guinea) have the kakaki, a long brass
instrument which sounds like a trombone; it is an attribute of a chief.[5]   In Sumatra a tube made of an ox horn
is in use.[6]

(*d*) CASTANETS.

Cook in his *Voyages* mentions a peculiar dance and
song of women on the islands of Amsterdam and Middleburgh.   As they sang, they marked time in a very simple
manner by snapping their fingers.[7]   It appears then that
in a very primitive state of culture there is a general
tendency to give rhythmic movement during songs by the
use of the fingers.   Compared with hand-clapping, foot-
stamping and beating the hips, this is undoubtedly the
most elegant substitute for instrumental accompaniment.
Naturally later it was replaced by a definite instrument,
which has remained with us to the present day.   In
Africa the natives were acquainted with it.   The home
of the castanets, or at any rate the land in which they

[1] Ellis, *Polyn.*, ii. p. 283.   [2] Schelling, *l. c.*
[3] Rosenberg, *l. c.*, p. 93.   [4] Drury, *l. c.*, p. 67.
[5] Flegel, *l. c.*, p. 25.   [6] Bastian, *Indon.*, table 2, Lfg. 3 (illust.).
[7] Cook, *Second Voyage*, in *Pink. Collect.*, vol. xi. p. 594.

were most commonly used, appears to be America, where
Indians used a couple of mussel-shells tied together for
this purpose.[1]   This custom is particularly mentioned
among the Hyperboreans.[2]   Among the Indians of
Yucatan both kinds of finger movements were in use,
with and without instruments.   When at their amusements the Indians changed their native dance to a
Spanish one, they from time to time snapped their fingers
instead of using castanets.[3]   Possibly these instruments
were introduced by the Spaniards from their American
colonies to Europe, where even now they are popular in
national dances.   Another, and a very much beloved,
instrument with Indians is the

(e) RATTLE.

This is made from a gourd or mussel-shell, or from raw
hide filled with small pebbles or dried fruit stones, and is
shaken about "to mark the time and rhythm[4] of dances
and songs".   On Columbia River the Indians use the
skin of a seal arranged like a fish and filled with stones.[5]
The Abipons[6] in South America and the Mississugua
Indians[7] use a gourd filled with fruit stones; to this the
Abipons make by way of accompaniment a peculiar noise
by drawing their fingers rapidly over their lips.   The
Uaupé Indians of the Amazon use a tortoise-shell as a
rattle.[8]   Some tribes seem to have a highly trained ear
for the "tone" of a rattle, and to be particularly fond of
it.   It is not always a mere "instrument of noise"; in
Virginia (North America), for instance, several rattles are
tuned together and the natives have "bass, tenor, counter-
tenor, alto and soprano rattles".[9]

[1] Jewitt, *l. c.*, p. 88.   [2] Bancroft, *l. c.*, i. p. 112.
[3] Stephens, *l. c.*, i. p. 145.   [4] Catlin, *l. c.*, i. p. 242.
[5] Bancroft, *l. c.*, i. p. 201.   [6] Dobrizhoffer, *l. c.*, i. p. 66.
[7] Chamberlain, *l. c.*, p. 158; Neuwied, *l. c.*, ii. p. 190; the rattle is called
Chichikoue.
[8] Wallace, *Amaz.*, *l. c.*, p. 504.   [9] John Smith, *l. c.*, p. 38.

In Africa, too, the rattle is well known. Hottentot dancers fasten a number of small ones to their ankles and so very distinctly mark time.[1] The Congo people[2] also know the rattle; they have it in war and are so clever in its use as to be able to shake them in a variety of tones; by this they indicate to the rest of the warriors behind in what danger they are.[3]

A sort of rattle seems to be the "fly-fan with bells" with which the Bashilange chief, Chingege, received the European travellers: he stood in the midst of a semi-circle, his feet on the legs of his wives, and allowed his majestic movements to be accompanied by a big drum.[4]

In the West Torres Straits rattles also occur; they are called Pădătrong.[5]

It has already been stated that the human skull is used as a rattle ready made. So it appears that it is with the rattle as with the flute: a part of the slain enemy's body is carried triumphantly as an article of ornament, and is later on used as an instrument to produce tones. It has here, too, a military not an artistic purpose which leads men to use and to appreciate a variety of tones, a signal, a melody. So it is with the flute, the rattle, the trumpet, the drum, the gong and the tamtam. This shows once more how intimately primitive musical instruments, and with them primitive music, are connected with a practical purpose.

(f) TAMTAM AND GONG.

The sounding stone plate (gong), together with the flute, are the most ancient prehistoric instruments. Even at the present day the Chinese have an instrument which merely consists of a number of resounding stone plates of different sizes, which are hung up in a sort of frame in

---

[1] Burchell, i. p. 66. [2] Tuckey, l. c., p. 373.
[3] *Astley Collect.*, iii. p. 281. [4] Wissmann, *First Voyage*, p. 72.
[5] Haddon, *West Torr.*, p. 374 (musical exampl.).

two rows. The Javese gong differs from this, but even in Java the union of several gongs into one instrument is well known (Bonang or Kroms), and, in addition, there is the Gambang, which is made of wooden or brass bars of various lengths laid crosswise over a trough.[1] Moreover, in Java the natives have huge Gomgoms shaped like hollow iron bowls of different sizes, and each giving a different tone from the others when struck with an iron or wooden stick.[2] The Malay gong, which is also common among the Dyaks in Borneo, produces by no means so clear a note as that of the Chinese; its tone is muffled, and the instrument is used at night for signalling. Krusenstern, however, mentions some Malay gongs made of copper which produced a charming tone.[3] Despite the obvious simplicity of the instrument, the natives modulate its tone excellently, and keep time so accurately that the effect is "anything but inharmonious".[4] In Borneo there are gongs made of brass pans which vary in tone between tenor and bass; to the music of these is added that of resounding chains, which are thrown in the air, or of small, crooked pieces of iron, which are hammered. Mr. Beeckmann compares this music to the sounds heard in "a butcher's establishment or in a copper smithy".[5] It forms a sort of musical prelude performed on the evening before a wedding.

In Dahomey a tamtam purloined from an enemy is a very much sought after trophy by the victor, and is decorated with human skulls![6] In Guiana the tamtam is made of rolled bark covered in tiger skin;[7] in Aduma (Ogowe, West Africa) a hollow piece of wood is used with goat skin drawn tightly over it,[8] in East Africa a thin

[1] Bickmore, *l. c.*, p. 191 (illust.).   [2] Stavorinus, *l. c.*, p. 172.
[3] Krusenstern, *l. c.*, i. p. 197.   [4] Marryat, *l. c.*, p. 84.
[5] Beeckmann, *l. c.*, p. 122.   [6] Bouche, *l. c.*, p. 95.
[7] Bernau, *l. c.*, p. 45.   [8] Lenz, *l. c.*, pp. 286-288.

iron plate.[1] In many parts of West Africa it is played
by slaves, for it is a wearisome and exhausting work.[2]

The sound of a tamtam excites the natives visibly.
During a dance of medicine-men in Ashuka (West
Africa) several young people were made positively ill
by the sound and the general exciting scene. They broke
suddenly from the line, ran about on all fours like animals
on the grass and commenced to rave, and were only with
difficulty overcome and taken aside. In the villages, during
the terrible dances of the Oganga (priests), such fits had
no end; wherever one looked, one saw these unhappy
creatures rolling about, and it was all that the old men
and women could do to get them to their huts.[3] The
Bakalai, too, become frenzied at the sound of the tamtam,
but are calmed by the tone of an Ombi[4] (guitar, with
strings of tree roots).

(g) BELLS.

The bell was originally a kind of rattle.[5] In its most
primitive form it was made from a nut-shell or of some
other hard fruit. Further progress in its construction was
marked by the use of hollowed-out pieces of hard wood,
and lastly iron. The original form of the bell, as figured
by Wood (Lane Fox Collection), is precisely similar to a
species of the number of rattles in use among the Maganja
tribes. In Dahomey iron bells[6] are found *employée par les
féticheurs;* others are worn by the leader of female water-
carriers. At the sounds of them the men rush to the
bushes, for they are afraid of being compelled to be

[1] Burton, *C. L. of Afr.*, ii. p. 98.   [2] Lenz, *l. c.*, p. 301.

[3] *Ibid.*, p. 199.   [4] Du Chaillu, *Equ. Afr.*, p. 391.

[5] Sir J. Stainer calls the bell a double gong or tamtam. This derivation
is no doubt correct as far as the more modern iron form is concerned. As
the most primitive form, however, is made of hard fruit, I think I may
suggest the bells being derived from the rattle.

[6] Bouche, *l. c.*, p. 96.

answerable in case of a jug falling or being broken. Doubtless the blame would be put upon the men.[1] Among the people of the Congo an iron double bell, Longa, is carried before princes.[2] "The Ogangas (Ogowe Lake) carry clumsy iron 'magic bells, everywhere a sign of a priest'; with them they go in procession from the villages, and firmly believe they will always find treasure on their return—which, indeed, they do. For the priests arrange these processions only when they know that a transport is going up country from the coast." Mr. Lenz closes this report with the words: "It is here, among these raw children of nature, as everywhere else in the world; he only speculates well who speculates in the stupidity of others".[3]

The Maoris in New Zealand have a bell, "Pahu," which is used for purposes of war.[4] The Pegu in East India unite twenty bells into one instrument, which is beaten with sticks, "and they make no bad music".[5]

In view of the already mentioned ethnological examples and especially of the Fox Collection, Gardiner's opinion "that the bell is of Chinese origin and like the ancient gong was generally made of copper" cannot be maintained.[6] It is one of the most common errors to commence history with one of the civilised races of Asia, if not with the Romans and the Greeks.

The *Glockenspiel* of Tima, which consisted of five brass plates on bamboo cylinders mentioned by Bastian,[7] is rather a form of the marimba (*q. v.*). The Javese bells on Banda Island, to the number of twelve, sounded from a distance like a string orchestra.[8]

[1] Wood, *l. c.*, i. p. 635.
[2] Angelo and Carli, *l. c.*, p. 160; Merolla, *l. c.*, p. 244.
[3] Lenz, *l. c.*, p. 317: bells of the Mandingoes, M. Park, *l. c.*, 878.
[4] Angas, *Sav. Life*, p. 152.   [5] A. Hamilton, *l. c.*, p. 427.
[6] W. Gardiner, *l. c.*, p. 269.   [7] Bastian, *Indon.*, table 2, Lfg. 2 (illust.).
[8] *Challeng. Exped.*, i. 2, p. 567.

(h) MUSICAL-BOXES.

The *principle* of our musical-box is not unknown among primitive people. The Batoka and Manganja tribes on the Zambesi, which possess a large number of musical instruments, have one of the earliest forms of this instrument which they call *sansa*. It consists of a board upon which a number of wooden pegs are fastened on end, so that when one end is pressed down and released a sort of musical note is produced.[1] This, with certain modifications, is frequently found in Central Africa and "differs from the modern musical-box only in that the teeth of ours are made of steel and not of wood, and the tone of ours is produced by cylinders and pins, theirs by the fingers". An advance on this type is the *mbira* of the Makalaka; a square piece of wood upon which metal tongues, made fast to one end between thick iron wire and pieces of wood, bring forth tones. "This has a compass of some two to three octaves" (unfortunately the exact notes are not given). It is fixed inside a calabash on the rim of the opening of which are mussel and spiral shells.[2]

We have already spoken of the popularity of the European musical-box. Specimens with a *glockenspiel* and drum are preferred to any other kind by the negroes,[3] and sometimes they are even feared. "The people of Máyolo's clan took to their heels at once when they heard the musical-box, presuming that a devil must be in it."[4]

(i) DRUM, KETTLE-DRUM, TAMBOURINE.

The drum is the most important and most widely spread instrument of savage races. It has already been mentioned that it is not at all the most ancient instrument we know, and that there is a small number of tribes who do not know even the drum. It is curious that the New

---

[1] Wood, *l. c.*, i. p. 392. [2] Mauch, *l. c.*, p. 43.
[3] Elson, *l. c.*, p. 269. [4] Du Chaillu, *Ashongo Land*, p. 192.

Zealanders, who themselves do not possess a drum, should find so much pleasure in a noisy European drum, while delightful music—as Thomson remarks—does not excite their emotions.[1] The Australians, too, do not know the drum, and yet they have a better ear for rhythm than for melody, and did not appreciate Mr. Lumholtz's songs in any way.[2] A thick piece of hard wood in form of a club, to beat time with, is rare; sometimes the natives beat sticks together,[3] or beat on rolled deer hides,[4] or beat a stick against a flat board.[5] The natives of the Fiji Islands use sticks to drum with (but the drum as well); they beat the long ones with the small ones, and get quite "clear notes" out of them.[6] The Molua, in Africa, beat a wooden box (ginguva), open at the upper end, like a kettle-drum.[7] The Niam-Niam beat a sinon-like wooden horse on its sides with drum-sticks; several performers beat successively upon different-sized pieces of dried wood fixed across parallel banana trees.[8] Among the Columbians, on the Columbia River, the instruments are boxes and benches struck with sticks, a plank hollowed out on the under side and beaten with drum-sticks about a foot long.[9]

With the Greenlanders the drum is the only musical instrument; it is played with the right hand and held with the left. This is accompanied by many wonderful motions of the head and whole body, and performed in common musical time, so that two strokes fall in every crotchet.[10] The Finnish Laplanders have a drum called kannus or œnobdus, made out of a hollow piece of wood. It must either be of pine, fir, or birch tree, which they

---

[1] Wood, *l. c.*, ii. p. 137.   [2] Lumholtz, *l. c.*, p. 156.
[3] Eyre, *l. c.*, ii. p. 228.   [4] *Ibid.*, p. 237.
[5] Grey, *Two Exped.*, ii. p. 305.   [6] Williams, *l. c.*, p. 141.
[7] Pogge, *l. c.*, p. 241. (Kalunda tribes near Mussumba, 23° long., 9° lat.)
[8] Ch. Long, *l. c.*, p. 279.   [9] Bancroft, *l. c.*, i. p. 201.
[10] Crantz, *l. c.*, p. 162.

believe very acceptable to the sun, which they worship. They draw near the middle of the drum several lines quite across it, and upon these they place the image of Christ and the apostles, above this the stars, the sun, and the moon. Below the sun there are terrestrial things and living creatures.[1]

This heathen fetish has become obsolete among the Laplanders in the Christian era. Worshipping the drum is still a most frequent custom, especially in Africa.

Peculiar shapes of drums are to be found with the Hottentots. They are called water drums; the instrument is a wooden bowl or bamboo, on which a piece of skin has been tightly stretched. A little water is previously poured into the bowl, which keeps the skin continually wet. It is beaten with the forefinger of the right hand, and is kept at the proper pitch of the songs.[2] The Chukchi have a hand kettle-drum, which they keep wet with water. When drumming they sit down, while two others stretch a strap over the drummer's head. Then the drummer slightly jumps up and the strap is quickly thrown over and drawn away under him by the others.[3] At Kerian the Erubians (south of New Guinea) had a drum in shape like a very elongated hour-glass, made of a hollow piece of wood, emitting a low, resonant sound.[4] The same shape is to be met with in the Niger territories.[5] In New Guinea the drum is only known in some districts;[6] the Papuans have several varieties of them, large and small, the sound of which is to be heard for as many as four and a half miles;[7] the Dyaks have some of an iron-wood block covered with the skin of different animals (Ntawan);[8] others are decorated with

[1] Schefferus, *l. c.*, p. 47 (illus.).

[2] Burchell, *l. c.*, i. p. 66 ; Fritsch, *Eingeb.*, p. 327 ; Thunberg, *l. c.*, p. 33.

[3] Merck, *l. c.*, xvii. p. 65.   [4] Jukes, *l. c.*, vol. i. pp. 177, 274 (illus.).

[5] Day, *Niger*, p. 270.   [6] Albertis, *l. c.*, ii. p. 97.

[7] Miklukha Maklay, *l. c.*, p. 845.   [8] Hein, *l. c.*, p. 114.

beautiful ornaments.[1] Some splendid specimens are to be found in Mexico; the "tunkul" (drum with sheep skin) in South Mexico,[2] the "huehuetl" and "teponaztli" of the Nahua nations are curiosities of the first rank, although of course not quite primitive ones.[3]

It is not always an artistic purpose that the drum has to serve. Just as pipes, whistles or flutes are used to call the cattle, or the fellow-hunters, as horns are used to give a signal to the warriors, so the drum in many instances merely serves a practical end. The M'balunda negroes are expert in distinguishing the drum for dancing (n'dungo) and for war purposes (n'koko).[4] With the Wogago and Wanyamwezi (between Lakes Victoria and Tanganyika) the drum often calls to war. They celebrate the arrival, the departure, or the passing through of a traveller by beating the drum.[5]

Native carriers would never take a burden upon their backs unless they hear the drum being beaten, which is to them like a signal of permission to travel with the white man. With the Ashantis music is the horrible accompaniment of the human sacrifices permitted in their country. They have drums of an enormous size, "the entire trunk of a tree being hollowed out for the purpose," sounding frightfully in the night, when giving the signal for new sacrifices. Their fetish drums and fetish trumpets have a very grotesque appearance, and are sometimes made with remarkable ingenuity.[6] On Tahiti the largest of their drums was placed in front of the temple; its terrific sound, when beaten at midnight, made every one tremble with fear of being seized as the victim for the religious sacrifice.[7] Drumming is also taken up as a profession

[1] Hein, *l. c.*, pp. 113-116.
[2] Bancroft, *l. c.*, i. p. 664.
[3] *Ibid.*, ii. p. 293.
[4] Soyaux, ii. pp. 175, 176.
[5] Wood, i. p. 432.
[6] Wood, i. p. 627 (illus.).
[7] Ellis, *Polyn. Res.*, i. p. 283.

(*e.g.*, all along the Kworra, Africa), and affords a livelihood to numbers of men at each village.[1]

Peculiar to Africa is the custom of using drums as a means of communication from great distances. There are two distinctly different kinds of this drum language, based upon different principles. The first kind imitates the sound of the language, as is shown in an example of Mr. Schauenburg. He saw at Kujar a negro beating the drum with the right hand, and varying the tone by pressing his left on the skin, so as to imitate the sound of the Mandingo words. During the wrestling match it sounded : " Amuta, amuta " (attack) ; during the dance : " Ali bae si," and all the participants understood it.[2] I can fancy that a drum can fairly well reproduce a sound like " a " or " u " (pronounced in the German way), but it is very hard to imagine the drum reproducing the " m " and " t ". At any rate, the natives understood it, perhaps by the aid of the peculiar rhythm of certain words or sentences, so important in primitive languages. Sir A. C. Moloney observed this system of language among the Yorubas (southern neighbours of the Nupes, right bank of the Niger, 4° to 6° longitude), and says it is an imitation of the human voice by the drum. To understand it one has to know " the accents or pronunciation in the vernacular, and to be capable of recognising the different and corresponding note of the drum ".[3]

The second kind of drum language (among the Dwalla tribes) is based entirely upon a rhythmical principle, but not upon the *natural* rhythm of the words, but a conventional one, by means of which the natives keep conversation between each other for miles. Not only signals are given, but real speeches delivered.[4] The natives understand this language as a modern telegraphist understands his working apparatus without

---

[1] Day, *Niger*, p. 2 ff.   [2] Schauenburg, *l. c.*, i. pp. 93, 94.
[3] Moloney, *l. c.*, p. 609.   [4] Buchner, *Kamerun*, p. 37.

seeing what it is writing. The same rhythm can also be produced by the mouth, and this is a sort of secret language used especially in presence of a white man who understands the ordinary Dwalla.[1]

Another mode of making oneself intelligible by means of a drum is the fixed drum signal, as in use in the Unyan-yembe country.[2] It is doubtful whether in Bondei and East Usumbara (German East Africa) the natives have a real drum language or only a highly developed drum signalling. They give the signals on the " Vilangwe ". This consists of two parallel banana trunks over which pieces of wood are laid crosswise and played with sticks.[3]

Every large country in Africa has its own style of drumming ; Grant observed that the drumming of Unyan-yembe was more musical than the jumble of drums in Ukumi. The conductor had always the largest drum ; the rest watched him for the time, while at his feet a little black youth rattled as hard as he could : if ceasing the music would have lost its stirring effect.[4] Mr. Buchner tells us that the drummer in Kamerun does not beat the time, but a perpetual roll, the time being marked by the songs of the lookers-on.[5] The Madi tribes beat the drum with one stick.[6] The Camma tribes, which have perhaps the most noisy music of all the African peoples, beat the drum with immense energy and disproportionate noise ; at the same time they hang a row of brass kettles on poles and bang them with sticks.[7] During the happy

[1] This secret language has been invented because the savages were afraid of the white man in consequence of bad experiences they had had. Mr. Buchner often observed (*Still. Ozean.*, p. 274) how the most stupid and wretched European sailor considered it his duty to threaten the black man like a beast. The most striking case occurred in Madagascar, where the white men behaved in such a manner as to be taken for cannibals (!) by the " savages " (Rochon, *l. c.*, Germ. edit., p. 78).

[2] Grant, *l. c.*, p. 103.
[3] Baumann, *Usumbara*, pp. 136-137.
[4] Grant, *l. c.*, p. 103.
[5] Buchner, *Kam.*, p. 29.
[6] Wood, i. p. 480.
[7] Wood, i. p. 567. (Rembo River.)

palm-wine season all the natives, including the king himself, are in various stages of intoxication, just as certain
civilised nations on like occasions, the king, of course,
excepted.[1] The Apono (Ogowe R.) gently tap the drum with
their fingers; so do the Hottentots and the natives of the
Society Islands,[2] the islands along the West Torres Straits,[3]
and the Ashantis with their small drums.[4] The Malagasy,[5] Balonda,[6] and Angola tribes south of the Congo
mouth,[7] and the natives in Tahiti [8] play it with the palm
of their hand. The Cammas sit down or kneel when
playing the drum,[9] the Ashantis carry the war drum
on their heads and have it beaten by another man
behind; again, the Bafiote hold their drum "ndunga"
between the legs,[10] the Tibbu and Fezzan (North Africa)
play it with the hand on one side and with a stick on the
other.[11]

The Balonda drum has a small square hole in the side
covered with a piece of yellow spider's web of wonderful
toughness and elasticity. This allows the escape of air
and has a resonant effect at the same time. This custom
of using the spider's web prevails through a very large
portion of Africa.[12]

It is not always the rhythm alone which has to be
marked by the drum. In some cases the drummer is very
careful in getting a peculiar note which he varies during
the performance. The "nkonko" drum of the Bafiote
(looking like a small canoe closed at the upper end leaving
only a small slit free) has on each side of this slit different
tones.[13] The Balonda tune the drums by holding them

[1] Wood, i. p. 542 (illust.).   [2] Ibid., ii. p. 404.
[3] Haddon, l. c., West Torr. St., p. 375.
[4] Beecham, l. c., p. 168.   [5] Ellis, Madag., i. p. 273.
[6] Livingstone, l. c., p. 293. (Bantu group.)
[7] Angelo-Carli, l. c., p. 160.   [8] Cook, First Voyage, ii. p. 205.
[9] Wood, i. p. 567.   [10] Guessfeldt, l. c., p. 76.
[11] Lyon, l. c., p. 234.   [12] Wood, l. c., i. p. 414.
[13] Guessfeldt, l. c., p. 129.

to the fire,[1] the Hottentots by pressing the fingers on the skin. On Tahiti the natives know how to tune two drums of different notes into concord.[2]

Drums are often played *en ensemble*. When the chief of the Bashilange received the European travellers he was accompanied in his movements by a great drum with a splendid bass tone. When he declared friendship four well-tuned drums began to play, while the assembly sang a melody of seven tones, repeating it several times.[3] In the house of the Prince of Zebu (Philippines) four girls, entirely naked, played drums, kettle-drums and cymbals (of metal or bronze) in a harmonious manner.[4] During the ceremonies after new moon the Karagwes played on thirty-three drums, all arranged in one row.[5] On the Marquesas Islands the natives produced a terrific noise with an "army of drums," formed of the hollow trunk of large trees, at least fifteen feet in height. Behind these instruments were built slight platforms, upon which stood a number of young men, beating violently with the palms of their hands upon the drum heads. Every few minutes the performers hopped down, and were replaced by fresh recruits.[6] In speaking of the army of Dutugaimunu (Ceylon), the Rajavali says that in the march the rattling of the sixty-four kinds of drums made a noise resembling thunder breaking on the rock from which the sun rises. The band of Devenipiatissa, B.C. 307, was called the talawachara, from the great number of drums ; "the triumph of effect consisted in the united crash of every description of sound, vocal as well as instrumental". Although a full band is explained in the Mahawanso to imply a combination of "all descriptions of musicians," no flutes or wind instruments are particularised, and the

---

[1] Livingstone, *l. c.*, p. 293. [2] Cook, *First Voyage*, ii. p. 205.
[3] Wissmann, *First Voyage*, p. 72. [4] Pigafetta, *l. c.*, p. 337.
[5] Grant, *l. c.*, pp. 184-185. [6] Melville, *l. c.*, pp. 184-186.

incidental mention of a harp only occurs in the reign of Dutugaimunu, B.C. 161.[1]

Some of those drums with different tones might equally well be called kettle-drums, for it is hardly possible to distinguish both instruments according to modern ideas. Kettle-drums especially are mentioned with the Kimbunda (West Africa), whose instrument, longoma, is to be heard for miles.[2] Kettle-drums and tambourines occur among the Makalaka,[3] and in Morocco, where the kettle-drum (ganga) is beaten with a knot tied in a rope;[4] the Karagwe have kettle-drums of copper,[5] the natives on the Island of Saleyer kettle-drums of bronze with beautiful ornaments;[6] again, in Cuba kettle-drums were in use covered with human skin.[7] The "Keeloun" of the Eskimos is something like a tambourine, "being formed of a very thin deer skin, or the envelope of the whale's liver, stretched over one side of a wooden hoop. A handle is attached to the hoop, and the instrument is struck with a stick, not upon the membrane, but upon the hoop."[8]

(k) THE MARIMBA.

One of the most characteristic instruments of savage races is the marimba. It is taken by some writers as the original of our piano, although the resemblance is very slight as far as the construction is concerned, while its tone is pretty similar to that of our piano.[9] It consists of a number of gourds (as many as sixteen) covered with a flat piece of wood, beaten with a stick, and produces different tones according to the size of the gourd. According to Wood it has been brought to England under the name of xylophon.[10] For a time it was commonly

---

[1] Tennent, *l. c.*, i. p. 471 (illus.).
[2] Magyar, *l. c.*, p. 311.
[3] Mauch, *l. c.*, p. 43.
[4] Nachtigal, *l. c.*, i. p. 745.
[5] Grant, *l. c.*, pp. 184-185.
[6] A. B. Meyer, *l. c.*, iv. table 16.
[7] Waitz, *l. c.*, iv. p. 325.
[8] Wood, ii. p. 719.
[9] Bancroft, *l. c.*, i. p. 664.
[10] Wood, *l. c.*, i. p. 392.

supposed to be of American origin, until recent expeditions
brought the same instrument back from Africa. It seems to
have been overlooked that the marimba is mentioned as an
African instrument as early as in the seventeenth century.[1]

We find the marimba in use among the Manganja and
Batoka,[2] all the Congo people,[3] the Mandingoes,[4] Kimbunda[5] (with fifteen calabashes), the Fans (with seven
tones, "hunju"),[6] in Mussumba,[7] all over East Africa,[8]
among the M'balunda negroes,[9] and the Bashislange (or
Mushislange, or Tushislange, or Kashislange),[10] in South
Mexico,[11] and with the North American Indians. Mr.
Froebel saw at Telica an improved marimba, the construction of which had evidently been influenced by
Europeans. Instead of gourds or calabash shells they
made use of wooden tubes, and had steel instead of
wooden flats. To produce the music the musician had a
stick of elastic wood in each hand, and while playing on it
he became more and more excited, till at last he fell into
a kind of musical frenzy, his hands flying so quickly above
each other that the eyes could scarcely follow them. One
might almost fancy that Froebel was describing a modern
pianist.[12]

There are several varieties of the marimba, *e.g.*, the
mandida, *i.e.*, a marimba without sounding-boards,[13] the
" kas " of the Angola (Africa), *i.e.*, a basket of the stock
of the palmetto tree, carved in flowers and covered with a
board.[14] Mr. Heuglin saw at Chief Mofio's court some
blind musicians playing a very complicated instrument
made from the leaves of bananas, and a sort of " har-

[1] Carli, *l. c.*, p. 160 ; Merolla, *l. c.*, p. 245.

[2] Wood, *l. c.*, i. p. 392.   [3] Johnston, *Congo*, p. 433.

[4] M. Park, *l. c.*, p. 878.   [5] Magyar, *l. c.*, i. p. 311 (illust.).

[6] Du Chaillu, *Equ. Afr.*, pp. 87, 88 (illust.).

[7] Pogge, *l. c.*, p. 241.   [8] Cameron, *l. c.*, p. 267 (illust.).

[9] Soyaux, *l. c.*, ii. pp. 175-176.   [10] Wissmann, *Second Voyage*, p. 306.

[11] Bancroft, *l. c.*, i. p. 664.   [12] Froebel, *l. c.*, i. p. 323.

[13] Ratzel, *l. c.*, i. p. 865.   [14] *Astley Collect.*, iii. p. 274.

monica," similar to the marimba. It was a long stick to which cross booms were attached, decreasing in length, and with clay vessels at the end, which were beaten with small wooden hammers.[1] A sort of marimba is evidently the balafoa (or balafen, or ballard) of the Mandingoes, consisting of seventeen wooden keys with two gourds on each of them hanging down like bottles. The keys are beaten with sticks.[2] A balafoa without gourds and played with a notch stick is to be found in West Africa.[3] Similar to the marimba is the "toztze" or "igedegbo" in the Niger territories, formed of a wooden box instead of gourds.[4]

The marimba is often played *en ensemble*, and, strange enough, we find not unfrequently a regular quartette of marimbas, or marimbas and other instruments. Among the Angola four marimbas form a concert.[5] Livingstone saw a marimba quartette combined with three drums ; [6] in other cases it is combined with two "cassuto". The latter is a hollow piece of wood about a yard long, covered with a board cut like a ladder. Running a stick along it gives a sound within which passes for a tenor. The bass to this concert is the quilando, made of a very large calabash, two spans and a half to three in length, very large at one end, and ending sharp off at the other. Mr. Merolla says of this concert : "The harmony is grateful at a distance but harsh near at hand".[7] I am afraid that all the African music is intended for great distance only. In Guatemala several marimbas play together in perfect accord with some song.[8]

(*l*) THE GOURA
(or *gourah, goriah, gorah*).

Savage tribes of South Africa have an instrument which has neither been introduced into other countries nor

---

[1] Heuglin, *Weisser Nil*, p. 216.   [2] *Astley Collect.*, ii. p. 278 (illust.).

[3] Corry, *l. c.*, p. 154.   [4] Day, *Niger*, p. 271.

[5] Merolla, *l. c.*, p. 244.   [6] Livingstone, *l. c.*, p. 293.

[7] Merolla, *l. c.*, p. 245.   [8] Bancroft, *l. c.*, i. p. 705.

modified in any way by the influence of culture. It is the goura. The goura is an instrument in shape like the bow of a double bass, with a cat-gut to which a small piece of quill is attached. The player takes the quill in his mouth and by strong inspirations and respirations makes the cat-gut vibrate, thus producing a few soft notes. The natives sit down if they play, grasp the bow in the middle with the right hand, and strike the string in several places with a small stick five or six inches in length, which they hold in the other hand; one forefinger is put into the player's ear and the other into his wide nostril very likely in order to increase the sound for the player, for this sound is so soft that it cannot be heard at all beyond a certain distance.[1] The natives seldom succeed in playing a regular melody on the goura; it is only a change of the same tones long protracted, the principal tone being struck before every tune. These tunes, however, are only the effect of chance.[2] The instrument produces but five tones, the principal tone, its octave, and three tones between, evidently the open notes of every wind instrument, although not properly in tune. When several gouras play together they are never in unison, and the instrument only emits certain twangs, like those drawn in a particular manner from a violin.[3] Burchell compares the tone of the goura with a "grunting sound which would have highly pleased the pigs; and if any had been in the country, it would indubitably have drawn them all round the player, if only out of curiosity to know what was the matter". Mr. Fritsch, too, calls the goura a terrible instrument which is "maltreated in a nerve-shaking manner".[4]

[1] Moffat, *l. c.*, p. 58; Burchell, *l. c.*, i. p. 458; Lichtenstein, *l. c.*, ii. p. 379; Michaelis, p. 528.
[2] Elson, *l. c.*, p. 257.
[3] Moodie, *l. c.*, ii. p. 226.
[4] Fritsch, *Eingeb.*, p. 427.

(*m*) THE JEW'S HARP.[1]

We need hardly give a detailed description of the instrument which in its most primitive form is still in use among civilised nations. Among savage races we can follow it in the Niger territories (called " to "),[2] on the Society Islands,[3] New Britain and the York Islands,[4] the Fiji Islands;[5] among the Tingianes (North Luzon, Philippine Islands)[6] and the Manegres on the Upper Amur[7] (by these made of latten-plate and called " kamuti "). The jew's harp has become national with the Mapuchés (Araucanians), as much so as the guitar with the Spaniards, and no young gallant is considered fully equipped and provisioned to lay siege to a lady's heart if unprovided with a jew's harp. They play it almost entirely by inhaling instead of exhaling, and have ways of expressing various emotions by different modes of playing, which the Araucanian damsels appreciate.[8]

Mr. Brown does not take the jew's harp for a primitive instrument, because the traveller Mr. Finsch, who once asked for the instrument " pagolo," got the answer : " No more pagolo; pagolo die, the jew's harp make him kill ".[9] This example, however, only proves what it strictly says, *i.e.*, that in this particular instance the pagolo was replaced by the jew's harp. Moreover, Finsch himself describes the pagolo as a bow with a string, whose one end is put into the mouth, while the string is pressed by the thumb of the left and struck with a stick in the right.[10]

---

[1] I mention Mr. Pennant's suggestion that it ought to be spelt jaw's harp (*Pinkerton Collect.*, iii. p. 95).

[2] Day, *Niger*, p. 269.   [3] Wood, *l. c.*, ii. p. 404.
[4] Powell, *l. c.*, p. 73.   [5] Williams, *l. c.*, p. 141.
[6] A. B. Meyer, *l. c.*, viii. table 17 (illust.).
[7] Andree, *Amur*, p. 173.   [8] E. R. Smith, *l. c.*, p. 247.
[9] Brown, *l. c.*, p. 237.
[10] Finsch, *Erfahrg. Südsee*, ii. p. 2, 122 (illust.).

(*n*) THE GUITAR, ZITHER, HARP, MANDOLINE, LUTE, BANJO, LYRA.

In this class some confusion is hardly avoidable in applying the correct names to the instruments, as the majority of travellers were not careful enough in distinguishing a guitar from a harp or mandoline, the specimens used by savage races being so different in shape from the corresponding modern instruments.[1] Of course, where a detailed description of the instrument is given we may easily correct inappropriate terms. Where, however, the instruments are not accurately enough described, we will simply follow the original terminology.

The name guitar is most frequently mentioned. The *Dôr* have three different kinds of this instrument ; one can be tuned by means of a ring passed over the neck which can be slipped up or down ; besides this, however, the notes cannot be altered by pressure of the fingers upon the string. This reminds us of the principle of the harp, while the large body of it resembles the modern guitar. In fact, the instruments are something between a harp and guitar.[2] The Bunda people have a guitar "nsambi," with strings made of the thread of palm trees, and played with the thumbs,[3] the Karagwe a guitar "nanga" with seven to eight strings ; six of the seven notes are a perfect scale (diatonic ?), the seventh being the only faulty string ; in another three strings were a full harmonious chord.[4] Similar to it is the "para," very likely of ancient Egyptian origin.[5] The Hottentots have the "rabekin," a guitar with three to four strings, tuned by screws,[6] another "gabowie" with three strings over a hollow piece of wood with a long handle ;[7] the Mandingoes a guitar "kunting" with three strings,[8] and in West Africa there is a guitar

---

[1] On the difference between these instruments compare Hipkin's masterly Lecture "Mus. Instr.," *l. c.*

[2] Tuckey, *l. c.*, p. 373.   [3] Merolla, *l. c.*, p. 245.
[4] Grant, *l. c.*, p. 183.   [5] Day, *Niger*, p. 266.
[6] Thunberg, *l. c.*, p. 90.   [7] Barrow, *l. c.*, i. p. 149.
[8] M. Park, *l. c.*, p. 878.

"kilara" made of huge calabashes (details not given).[1] The Ashantis have the most perfect guitar (lanku). The instrument is a hollow wooden box perforated with holes and covered with a skin, to which a long stick or neck is attached; it has eight strings, in two rows, supported perpendicularly by a bridge; it produces a soft soothing tone.[2] The Malagasy have a guitar with two strings.[3] The common guitar, or rather "zither," of the negroes, called "sansa," is to be found among all the negro tribes. Mr. Pogge saw it with the Kalunda at Mussumba. Only professional musicians play it, and they have certain compositions which they always repeat.[4]

The Kayans of Baram have a guitar with two strings of the fine threads of rattan twisted and drawn up tightly by means of tuning keys.[5] On the Upper Amazon there is a wire guitar;[6] on the Molucca Island a guitar is made of bamboo, the fibres of which are cut out and a bridge put under in the middle, while the ends are left in the bamboo.[7] On the same principle is made the guitar "valitra," in Madagascar, on which short monotonous melodies are played; the guitar "lokango" is louder in tone.[8]

The Mrung tribes (India) have a guitar, "pankho," with one string over a hollow gourd attached to a bamboo tube; the Magh tribes a bamboo "zither," the strings of which are of reed fibres stretched over a wooden bridge.[9] The Kamchadales have a three-cornered guitar, "cellalika," with two strings, and rude violins, products of their domestic industry.[10] A guitar of the Ginnaanes (North

[1] Corry, l. c., p. 154. [2] Beecham, l. c., p. 169.
[3] A. Schulz, l. c., p. 192.
[4] Pogge, Muata Jamwo, p. 241 ; Ratzel, l. c., p. 54.
[5] St. John, l. c., i. p. 118. [6] Bates, l. c., ii. p. 203.
[7] Bastian, Indon., table 1, Liefg. 1. [8] Ellis, Madagascar, i. p. 273.
[9] Riebeck, Hügelstämme, table 15 ; "Indian Instrum.," see Riebeck, Sammlung, table 4.
[10] Kennan, l. c., p. 162.

Luzon, Philippine Islands) is mentioned and illustrated by Meyer.[1]

The Ostyaks have two stringed instruments (inventions of their own), one with strings, called "dombra" (the name is said to be akin to the tombora of the Magyars), another with eight strings, called "naruista juch chotuing" (chotuing = swan). In Russian folk-songs the comparison of instruments with aquatic birds frequently occurs, particularly in the bride-songs.[2] The swan especially is considered to have the most silvery voice of all animals; even the Chinese goose, "ritais roi gus," is called "swonroi," *i.e.*, possessing a beautiful voice. Mr. Erman supposes that the Russian harp, "gusli," has its name from "gus" (goose), like the chotuing of the Ostyaks from swan.[3] I may mention that in Slavonian, too, "husa" means goose, and "husle" a violin.

A peculiar instrument is the harp of the Kafirs. It is sometimes called guitar or fiddle; in fact, it is a bow with a hair string which can be tightened by means of a ring. Near one end of the bow a round hollow gourd is firmly lashed by means of leathern thongs. The cord is struck with a stick, and the instrument produces tones scarcely audible at some distance. "It is intended for time rather than tune."[4] This simple bow seems to be the original of all the stringed instruments, from which the goura and perhaps also the jew's harp is developed; Mr. Andersson at least called the bow a sort of rude jew's harp,[5] and the mode of playing the latter is very similar to that of the goura. The n-kungu in Angola is a bow like the Kafir's harp, tightened by means of a thread instead of a ring. The bow is a curved whip, and the string is a plant fibre.[6] Another similar instrument

---

[1] A. B. Meyer, *l. c.*, viii. table 7. [2] Erman, *l. c.*, p. 520.
[3] *Ibid.*, i. 1, p. 671. [4] Wood, *l. c.*, i. p. 231.
[5] C. J. Andersson, *Ngami*, p. 230.
[6] Shooter, *l. c.*, p. 236 *seq.*; Soyaux, *l. c.*, ii. p. 177.

is the bow of the Damaras. They tie a piece of reim round the bow-string and the handle and bind them tight together, then they hold the bow horizontally against their teeth, and strike the tense bow-string with a small stick. They attend more to the rhythm than the notes, and imitate with its music the gallop or trotting of different animals to perfection.[1]

The *harps* of savage races have in their most primitive form an almost funny appearance. The harps of the Bakalai,[2] with eight strings, of the Niam-Niam,[3] and of the Kroo negroes[4] are examples. The former consists of a triangle of sticks (the strings between) unequal in length, the longest being put into a gourd. The Akelle (Ogowe R.) are said to be famous for their beautiful harps, which Mr. Lenz mentions, without, however, describing them;[5] the Mandingoes have a harp, "korro," with eighteen strings, and another, "simbing," with seven strings;[6] in Guinea there is a harp with six to seven reeds, on which the natives play "very finely";[7] among the Moors there is one with fourteen strings of sheep gut.[8] The natives of Guiana had a sort of Æolian harp, formed from the leaf-stalk of the æta palm, the parallel fibres of which are separated, and a bridge placed under; then the whole instrument is fastened upright in some exposed place, and the wind passing through the strings causes a soft musical sound.[9] The Zuñians (South Mexico) have a whizzer, which they twirl during the dance. It is a flat stick with a string which, when whirled about in a circle, gives a peculiar sound. It is found among American tribes as well as among the Australians (called "turndun" or bribbun), in New Zealand, Zululand, and West Africa.

---

[1] Galton, *Travels*, p. 117; Andersson, *l. c.*, p. 230.
[2] Ratzel, i. p. 618.
[3] *Ibid.*, p. 534.
[4] *Ibid.*, p. 618.
[5] Lenz, *Skizzen*, p. 286.
[6] M. Park, *l. c.*, p. 878.
[7] Bosman, *l. c.*, p. 530.
[8] Caillie, *l. c.*, i. p. 95.
[9] Im Thurn, *l. c.*, p. 309.

In Australia it is used to warn the people from the dance; the Zuñians, however, use it simply to imitate the wind. The instrument is carried by the Koy-e-a-mashi, a very old organisation among the Zuñians, and borne by the Zuñi mythological personage, Pan-ti-va.[1]

The *mandoline*, "dourou," is a favourite instrument in Dahomey. A proverb says of it: "Vous n'avez pas encore entendu résonner le dourou, et déjà vous danser gaiement ".[2] The mandoline of the Niam-Niam has five strings, which can be tuned by means of screws.[3]

On the Lower Congo there are *lutes* with strings of an elephant tail or threads of palm trees. By playing upon them the natives are said "to express their mind almost as intelligibly as with their tongues ".[4] At Fort St. Louis the natives sing to the accompaniment of a lute.[5]

In New Britain and the York Islands the natives have a primitive *banjo* with two strings on a flat piece of bamboo, fastened across a sort of drum. This banjo, as well as their fifes, pan-pipes, jew's harps, are to be seen in any village, only the larger drums are carefully hidden, belonging especially to the chiefs.[6]

The Maoris in New Zealand have a lyre with three to four strings.[7] On the Congo there is one with five strings.[8] Old Egyptian lyres had four to eighteen strings,[9] and are to be met with as early as at the time of Amenophis I. (about 3000 years ago).[10]

Mr. Rowbotham objects to the bow being considered the first string instrument, and the lyre being developed from

[1] Fewkes, *Sum. Cerem.*, p. 23, note 1; *cf*. A. Lang, *Cust. and Myth*, pp. 28-44; *Myth. Rit. Rel.*, i. p. 284.

[2] Bouche, *l. c.*, p. 96.   [3] Heuglin, *l. c.*, p. 216.

[4] *Astley Collect.*, iii. p. 249.   [5] Brüe, *l. c.*, p. 48.

[6] Powell, *l. c.*, p. 73.   [7] Dumont d'Urville, *l. c.*, ii. p. 446.

[8] Johnston, *l. c.*, p. 434 (illus.).   [9] Wilkinson, *l. c.*, i. p. 475.

[10] *Ibid.*, p. 477.

it, for, he says, the New Zealanders do not use bows as
weapons and yet possess the lyre.   Rowbotham takes the
jew's harp for the original of the lyre.   Unfortunately the
New Zealanders have no jew's harp either.   Meanwhile
Mr. Tylor has pronounced the hunting-bow as the origin
of stringed instruments (*l. c.*, p. 184).   The Damaras at
least use the bow for the double purpose of hunting and
twanging.

(o) THE VIOLIN.

Were the origin of bowed instruments to be called in
question, the first thing to be explained would be the
peculiar custom of producing tone by "stroking" as
opposed to percussion or wind.   The Bawili in Loango
have a very primitive instrument—simply a notched stick
planted firmly against some fixed object and stroked along
in strict time.   It is played in the hut in which the
maiden, N-Kumbi, is made familiar with the secrets of
matrimony.[1]   In Louisiana the jaw-bone of a mule is
rubbed with sticks,[2] and in Zuñi Pueblo two sticks are
rubbed together.[3]   In New Zealand pieces of wood which
produce tones when rubbed with the hands are common.[4]
In New Britain there is an instrument, called kulepa-
ganeg, consisting of a round thick piece of wood with
three notches (wider at the bottom).   It is stroked with
the wet palms of the hand and gives three different tones.[5]
Mr. Finsch, who describes the instrument, seems, however, to be mistaken, if he calls it "unique in the world".
The above jaw-bone instrument is similar, and still more
similar is the instrument charra or kwatscha in Usumbara (East Africa).   It is a solid piece of wood over which
a notched stick is slightly bent.   Along this stick another
is stroked.   The sound is of so wonderful effect that in

---

[1] Soyaux, *l. c.*, ii. pp. 175-176.   [2] Fortier, *l. c.*, p. 137.
[3] Fewkes, *Sum. Cerem.*, p. 37.   [4] Ratzel, *l. c.*, ii. p. 228.
[5] Finsch, *Erfahrg. Südsee*, iii. 2, p. 140.

comparison with it—as Mr. Baumann said—wood-sawing must be called harmony.[1] Thus the idea of producing tone by rubbing or stroking—*i.e.*, a sort of primitive fiddling—is not unknown among savage races, and we may easily imagine how a stick or bow furnished with a plant fibre may have been subjected to similar treatment, without taking into further consideration the connection with the above-mentioned ceremony. As a matter of fact this stroking or rubbing of a stick by means of a bow often occurs; the Damaras hold the leather string of their bows in their teeth and play on it with a stick,[2] while the Patagonians play their flutes with a bow. Among them the flute is used as a kind of sound-post,[3] which obviously sounds better than the stick, and is stroked with a bow instead of with the hand. This flute-playing with a bow will only be understood through its connection with the above examples of the " stroked " stick; [4] we have already mentioned that the Ashantis *beat* a sort of flute with a stick.

The Bongo have a " monochord " which externally resembles the gubo of the Zulus, and is common in South Africa; [5] one end is held to the lips, while the string is struck by a piece of bamboo.

The M'balunda negroes have a violin with three strings and a bow all made of plant fibre.[6] The Malagasy also play a violin with a bow which is no less rudely shaped than the violin itself. Its tones do not sound " particularly harmonious," but nevertheless are said to be just as pleasant as those of the stringed instruments of China, Japan, or Turkey.[7]

The Malays have a sort of two-stringed violin,[8] but as

---

[1] Baumann, *Usumbara*, p. 137. [2] Ratzel, i. p. 331.

[3] Musters, *l. c.*, p. 77 (illust., p. 176).

[4] Mr. Rowbotham openly declares that he cannot make anything out of it.

[5] Schweinfurth, *l. c.*, i. p. 130. [6] Soyaux, *l. c.*, ii. p. 177.

[7] Wood, *l. c.*, ii. p. 772. [8] Waitz-Gerland, *l. c.*, v. p. 169.

no description of it is given, and no bow mentioned, I am unable to determine if it has anything more in common with the violin proper than its name. In Banjowangi (East Java) a bowed instrument is known. It is a flat two-stringed violoncello, the neck of which is about one and a half feet long; its body consists of a very thin cocoa-nut of a special nature, which is both extremely rare and costly, and only found on the Islands of Baly and Madura. Malay princes pay fabulous prices for it. Its strings are horsehair, and the bow is made of a crooked rotang. The instrument stands at right angles to the ground like our double bass, which is also very similar in tone. From time to time the musicians cease playing in order to sing, which they do in a miserable manner almost continually in the same tone.[1]

Bastian mentions a monochord—as he calls it—in the Molucca Islands. Its body was one half of a cocoa-nut shell, its neck of bamboo, its foot of carved wood : so it is rather a sort of bass or violoncello. It is played with a bow made of wood and a horsehair stretched on it.[2] Possibly it is related to the East Javese instrument already described, but it is difficult to say which is the original. The Dyaks have a violin with two strings, and tones like those of an organ ;[3] stringed instruments made from cocoa-nut shells, iron-wood hemispheres, Labu fruits, over which one or two rattan strings are stretched, and bows of bamboo and rattan strings.[4] In Zubu (Philippine Islands) the natives have a "sort of violin" (bow not mentioned) with copper strings.[5] The Apache Indians (south-west of North America) have a violin with a horsehair string and bow.[6] In British Guiana fibres are stretched over a hollow branch under which a bridge is

---

[1] Tombe, *l. c.*, ii. pp. 6 and 7.   [2] Bastian, *Indon.*, table 1, Lfg. 1.

[3] Bock, *l. c.*, p. 77.   [4] Hein, *l. c.*, p. 115.

[5] Pigafetta, *l. c.*, p. 337.   [6] Schwatka, *l. c.*, p. 45 (illust.).

placed : "thus the natives make a rude violin," says Mr.
Bernau, without, however, mentioning the bow.[1]

As the origin of the violin the rebab (rebeb or rebába)
is frequently mentioned ; but this belongs rather to semi-
civilisation and is described at one time as a guitar, at
another as a bowed instrument.

The Beduin rebába is a sort of guitar.[2] At Nejd
and among the Sinai Arabs it is considered indecent to
play it before an audience. A "rebebb" with two
strings (bow not mentioned) is given as a Moorish instrument.[3] Negroes alone sing here, for public singing is
regarded as a slavish occupation.[4] A rebab in Java
with two strings and played with a bow is said to be of
Mohammedan or Persian origin.[5] The Sudanese "erbab"
consists of a gourd over which a skin is stretched, like
that on a drum ; over this a string is fastened and played
with a horsehair bow.[6]

Never has neglect of ethnological research led to such
hypothetical results as in the history of the violin, a fact
which is all the more surprising and grievous because the
" Queen of the orchestra " has so often given rise to very
complete and obviously painstaking historical investigations.

As a curiosity I mention Jean Rousseau's (not Jean
Jaques) theory, who begins his history of the violin with
the creation and arrives at the conclusion, " si Adam avoit
voulu faire un Instrument, il auroit fait une Viole, et s'il n'en
a pas fait, il est facile d'en donner les raisons".[7] Fétis was of
opinion that India was the home of our bow instruments.[8]

---

[1] Bernau, *l. c.*, p. 45.   [2] Burckhardt, *l. c.*, p. 43.

[3] Shaw, *l. c.*, p. 643 ; Lempriere, *l. c.*, p. 773.

[4] Addison, *l. c.*, p. 439.   [5] Crawfurd, *l. c.*, pp. 335-339.

[6] Lyon, *l. c.*, p. 161.

[7] Rousseau, *l. c.*, p. 3. I quoted the original French words, as Rousseau
has often been supposed (for instance by C. Engel) to have said that Adam
actually was the first violinist.

[8] Fétis, *Stradivari*, p. 4.

He seems to have overlooked that there was a time when
India represented the climax of human civilisation, and
that therefore the very primitive bow instruments ought
to be sought in the savage world rather. As it is, we
have no better proof of the Indian origin of our violin
than for a probable African one. Mr. C. Engel begins
his history of the violin with the "rebab". This,
however, was not a bow instrument until the time of
Mohammedan culture, while its original shape was a
guitar, and not the most ancient we know of.[1] It seems
to me that a simple bow played with a stick approaches
much more the modern violin than all the guitars played
with the fingers. Again Mr. Hart says that the peoples
of antiquity seem to have had no knowledge of bow
instruments, and "it is satisfactory to know that upon
this point writers on the subject of the early history of
the violin seem agreed".[2] Mr. Rühlmann goes still
further and concludes that the home of such a magnificent instrument as the violin must be the fatherland.
There is to be found the most ancient and simple form
of the "Trummscheidt," which Mr. Rühlmann takes for
the original of the violin. He thinks, however, that the
invention of bow instruments was made by *civilised* peoples
quite independently, at different times and different places,[3]
everywhere starting afresh from the rudest form.

(*p*) ORCHESTRA.

We have already had occasion to remark that several
instruments of the same class are played together among
primitive people. There were, for instance, flute, drum,
and marimba orchestras, while the union of several different
kinds of instruments into an *ensemble* also occurred. I must

---

[1] C. Engel, *Viol.*, p. 24. The oldest European bow instrument is said
to be the "Welsh crwth".

[2] Hart, *l. c.*, p. 2 (edit. 1874).

[3] Rühlmann, *l. c.*, pp. 6, 23.

confess my surprise that the quartette form is so frequently found, for at first I thought it an accidental arrangement, especially in the case of the drum quartette; but the arrangement of a marimba quartette and the union of a marimba with other instruments, intentionally chosen according to their pitch, must have innate musical grounds. On the other hand savages trouble themselves little about a melody, which—when they have it—is seldom really definite. Could, under these circumstances, a harmonious accompaniment and *ensemble* be possible? Probably in such cases the melody moves within a restricted radius and is kept within a fairly definite traditional modulation. I believe that active tradition, direct imitation, little originality, and a lack of sudden and unexpected innovations in the leading of a melody take the place here of a systematic study. Even the productions of European gipsy bands, whose performances by ear often greatly astonish us,[1] are more or less stereotyped; everything really artistic is previously studied.

A distinguished Molua in Mussumba always has at his court an orchestra, which consists of two marimbas and a gingwoa.[2] In Moody Schweinfurth met with four young men of the Bongo tribe who came together every evening for quartette playing: there were two drummers and two tube players.[3] Why in this and in numerous other cases the number four should be chosen could only be ascertained if the travellers had reported correctly what and how the natives played, but unfortunately nothing is said on this subject.

Larger orchestras, generally a sort of military band, are found at the courts of many African chiefs. Mr. Avezac states that a music corps is considered almost an attribute of a chief.[4] Rumanika, the Karagwe chief, had

---

[1] Liebich, *l. c.*, p. 58 (with bibliography on the gipsies).
[2] Pogge, *l. c.*, p. 241.   [3] Schweinfurth, *l. c.*, ii. p. 249 (illust.).
[4] Avezac, *l. c.*, p. 91.

a band of sixteen men—fourteen tubes and two drums—
which were arranged in three set, the drums placed at the
back; they played when marching and swayed their bodies
in time with the music, the conductor touching the ground
with his knee at each beat.[1] The pieces were played in
waltz and march time. Grant declares that their playing
was much better than he had ever expected to witness,
but at the same time he states the remarkable fact that
at Karagwe hardly a single dance was known.[2] I must
mention that Grant visited districts where no European
had previously been.

Mr. Speke was received by the Waganda with a band
of twelve flutes and five drums.[3] Sepopo, King of the
Marotse Kingdom (Upper Zambesi), had a band of twenty
men, of which, as a rule, only eight played at one time,
while the others were kept in reserve.[4] Several drummers
played with the palms of their hands, or with their fingers,
on long conical or cylindrical kettle-drums or double
drums in the shape of an hour-glass, which were suspended from their necks by a strap. The principal
instrument was the marimba; besides there were the zither-
like sylimba, iron bells, rattles, and various pipes. All
these instruments are to be found everywhere among the
population, but the more elaborate ones belong exclusively
to the royal band. The common method of playing them
is purely mechanical and the melodies are somewhat
monotonous. Mr. Holub says that a little cultivation
of music among the Marotse-Mabundas would soon be
crowned with success. In Lunda, too, there are regularly
organised bands which play fairly well but always the
same melody.[5] Further mention is made of the Dembo

[1] Wood, *l. c.*, i. p. 448 (illus.); another illus. by Clement, *l. c.*, pp.
152-155.

[2] Grant, *l. c.*, pp. 184-185; *Lake Vict.*, p. 192.

[3] Ratzel, *l. c.*, i. p. 463.

[4] Holub, *l. c.*, p. 168; Zambesi orchestra, illus. by Clement, p. 153.

[5] Ratzel, *l. c.*, i. p. 561.

bands, which consist of five reed-pipes, two gourds which are filled with stones and shaken like rattles by little boys in time to the fife music.[1] The chief Kasongo had a band of wooden drums, marimbas, and globular gourds which were played like wind instruments by men and women, and emitted a sound similar to that of a bugle.[2] At human sacrifices in Dahomey chorus and orchestra were united. The old To-no-num and his fifty men went round the half-circle singing and dancing and clapping hands. Then came the Pani-gan-ho-to or gong-gong men, four in number, and carrying single and double cymbals, whilst a correspondingly numerous chorus of women and twenty more male singers promenaded up and down preceded by a drummer playing upon the Ganikbaja, a drum borrowed in idea from the Ashantis.[3]

At Timé among the Mandingoes there was a band of four large drums, four cymbals, six oboes, small children rattling baskets in time, and the whole was led by two conductors. The musicians were Bambaras.[4]

How much musical talent some African races possess is shown by the band of the Ashantis at Cape Coast Castle, which plays English melodies by ear in " a most astonishing fashion ".[5] In Cape Colony, too, many families make use of the natural inclination of the slaves, especially of the Malays, for music, to develop it by teaching, and so to arrange small orchestras. They play then upon European clarionets, horns and bassoons, violins, basses and flutes, and always by ear.[6] In Brazil, negroes are amazingly quickly trained for the music corps.[7]

The influence of culture is also distinctly traceable in the band of the Fulbe, which consists of eight musicians on horseback who played the drum ganga, a wind instru-

---

[1] Ratzel, *l. c.*, i. p. 561.   [2] Cameron, *l. c.*, p. 355 (illus.).
[3] Burton, *Mission to Gelele*, i. p. 377.   [4] Caillie, *l. c.*, ii. p. 34.
[5] Beecham, *l. c.*, p. 169.   [6] Lichtenstein, *l. c.*, i. p. 45.
[7] Kerst, *l. c.*, pp. 303-304.

ment pampámine, a flute elgaita, a sort of double tympanum, kalángo, another koso, an Egyptian double darabuka or jojo, and a small horn, kafo. The wind instruments together are called by the Haussa "bushé-bushé," which the Féllam (as the Fulbe are called by the Haussa) have turned into "fufe-fufedji". These well-equipped musicians can make any amount of noise on their instruments, but it is neither harmonious nor peculiar to them. Mr. Barth thinks they learnt this from the Arabs, and he vastly preferred the music of a single native Maimolo.[1]

A very primitive *ensemble* is common on the Society Islands. For the purpose they—strangely enough—tune such instruments as the drum, jew's harp, and a flageolet (hoe) together. The musicians then seat themselves in a circle, bend their bodies over their knees and play wonderfully well in time, "although the same praise cannot be awarded to their melodies".[2] On Solomon Islands there was a band of twenty men with pan-pipes (twenty-three tubes), long bamboo flutes with two to three openings. It is said they play in thirds and fifths.[3] From this example I am afraid I cannot draw a safe conclusion as to the use of consecutive fifths, for even European village musicians play sometimes in fifths without (unfortunately) knowing or caring about it.

European influence is already noticeable in the Malay orchestras in Sumatra. They have drums, flutes, and European fiddles.[4] St. John describes a Malay band which played waltzes, but nothing else, by ear.[5] Javese orchestras are renowned, although they are to-day under European influence, yet from time immemorial the natives have been accustomed to play in an orchestra. The instruments are so expensive that a collection of some

[1] Barth, *Afrika*, ii. p. 53.
[2] Wood, *l. c.*, ii. p. 405.
[3] Ratzel, *l. c.*, ii. p. 228.
[4] Bock, *l. c.*, p. 281.
[5] St. John, *l. c.*, ii. p. 184.

twenty of them costs 600 to 1000 dollars.[1] The tone of
such an orchestra coming from a distance has been likened
to that of a glass harmonica.[2] The melodies, although
simple and monotonous, are never wearying if played by
the "gambany Káyn"; this is a peculiar arrangement of
instruments in an orchestra. Another is called "Gamelan";
its concerts sometimes last for several days and nights
together without intermission. At Lamajang there was
an orchestra which consisted of one two-stringed fiddle
and several instruments of percussion made of wood and
brass; the former were mere wooden pans hung by
strings to a wooden box. The melodies with their irregular
rhythms reminded Jukes a little of Scottish songs.[3]

Mr. Davy tells us of a king in Ceylon who frequently
had his band playing for his delectation; the musicians
had to sing at the same time.[4]

I have been able to find but one example of an orchestra
among Indians, and that in a description of an Indian
festival in Patagonia. The band consisted of drums, fifes,
and bows only. The drum was a shell or bowl over which
a skin was stretched; the fife was a thigh bone of a guanaco
pierced with several holes, and either placed to the mouth
and played, or "stroked" with a short bow with horsehair.[5]

That the primitive orchestra recognised a conductor
has already been stated; indeed the *báton* is known as well,
but is always used with an audible stroke, which custom,
I am sorry to say, occurs also in Europe sometimes. For
conducting the Indians use a notched stick drawn over a
resisting medium.[6] The king of the Monbuttu himself beats
time with all the dignity of a musical director; his *báton* is

[1] Bickmore, *l. c.*, p. 191 (illus.).
[2] Raffles, *l. c.*, i. p. 471; *Javese Instrum.*, by Veth, *l. c.*, i. pp. 470-480.
[3] Jukes, *l. c.*, ii. p. 48.   [4] Davy, *l. c.*, p. 156.
[5] Musters, *l. c.*, p. 81.   [6] Schoolcraft, *l. c.*, ii. p. 514.

a kind of child's rattle.[1]   On the Andaman Islands a board
is used upon which time is struck with the feet.   This
board is made from the trunk of a *Pterocarpus dalbergioides*,
is shield-shaped, and often five feet long and two feet
broad.   The convex side is turned outwards, and the pointed
end fixed in the ground, a stone laid under it and the
whole board is struck with the heel only.[2]   In Australia
dances are led by a man who, following the time of
the music, directs the movements with a crescent-shaped
instrument.[3]   At any rate Mr. Daniel errs in saying that
the first conductor was the successor of an oyster-shell
(thus pointing to its use for marking the time) and that
the composer Lully (1633-1687) was the first bandmaster.[4]

(*q*) INSTRUMENTS OF THE MOST ANCIENT PERIODS OF CULTURE.

Although it is no part of my task to attempt to follow
up the development of musical instruments from the
earliest to the present times, yet I may be allowed to say
a word or two about those periods at which the construction of instruments experienced special development,
either in connection with the progress of a nation's own
culture or through European influence.

The majority of instruments in Sumatra has been
copied from the Chinese and other civilised nations of
the East,[5] while in Ceylon Portuguese influence is
obvious.[6]   Unfortunately Mr. Davy does not mention to
which specimens of instruments (which he illustrates)
this remark appeals.   He speaks of drums, tomtoms,
trumpets, and bows.   It is unnecessary to say anything
further here about Chinese and Japanese instruments,
the artistic manufacture of which has long been known
and appreciated; the influence of their art makes itself

---

[1] Elson, *l. c.*, p. 269.
[2] Man, *l. c.*, p. 399.
[3] Eyre, *l. c.*, ii. p. 235.
[4] Daniel, *Transf. des Instr.*, pp. 266-267.
[5] Marsden, *l. c.*, p. 195.
[6] Davy, *l. c.*, p. 156 (illus., p. 240).

felt in Burmah. Especial mention has been made of a harp "soum," of a violin "turr," with three strings, of a bow (said to be a perfectly original invention of the Burmese), of a flageolet "pullaway," of a collection of cymbals "kyezoup," of a guitar "patola," of a drum "boundaw," and of a pan-pipe "heem".[1] A speciality of the East is the drums arranged in a circle in the midst of which the player sits so that he can easily produce a variety of tones from them. Very similar are the Siamese instruments, which are frequently arranged in two stereotyped kinds of orchestras—Pepat (consisting of six instruments) and Mahari (of eight); these titles are translated by Bowring into "common band" and "singing band".[2] The peculiar mixture in the East of primitiveness and culture, originality and progress is also found in the instruments common in Tonkin : drums, bassoons made of copper, oboes, guitars, and violins.[3]

A vast number of really beautiful musical instruments once existed during the time of ancient civilisation in Mexico. Ruined by Spanish invasion, and to-day much under-estimated, we find here the remains of so high a state of culture that a short notice of it even in this place seems not out of place. Music seems to have been as it were a step-child. But what was it in the days of the Greeks and Romans? Regarded from the present-day point of view, did the musical art work of the Greeks stand as high as the poetic or plastic? By no means; so in Mexico the inferior condition of music, which in the case of Rome and Athens appears to us quite natural, should not be thought too little of. The most frequently mentioned instruments are two kettle-drums : hue-huetl (huehuilt, vevtl, tlapanhuehuetl), and teponaztli ; the

---

[1] Symes, *l. c.*, p. 508; Yule, *l. c.*, p. 13 *seq.;* illus. by Malcom, *l. c.*, i. p. 204 *seq.*

[2] Bowring, *l. c.*, i. p. 147.

[3] Baron, *l. c.*, p. 672; Richard, *l. c.*, p. 726.

former was capable of being tuned and accompanied the song; the latter was a sort of double kettle-drum with two different tones.[1] In Malinalco, near Toluca, there was a kettle-drum called the tlamalhuilili;[2] the Aztecs had a host of most characteristic wind and percussion instruments, the former being shaped like animals[3] (birds, snakes, or the like). In Yucatan there were nose-flutes, bamboo tubes, mussel trumpets,[4] and also a kettle-drum, tunkul.[5] Among the antiquities of Chiriqui (Panama) there are wind instruments made on the same principle as the above-mentioned Aztec instruments, in the shape of an animal, with two openings (two to six notes of the octave), the mouthpiece being in the tail, or in the elbow if shaped like a human figure. Sometimes a ball was placed inside, the tone varying with the position of this ball.[6] Scherzer found in Central America a primitive fife " el pito," a drum " el atambor," an instrument " el tan," consisting of a piece of wood, eighteen inches in length, and struck with a stick, another, "la tortuga," made of a tortoise-shell and also struck with a stick. With these instruments the monotonous music of a pantomime was played.[7]

During the reign of Tutul Xuis at Uxmal (Maya nation) a dwarf found two musical instruments, the silver Tunkul and the Zoot. An old prophecy said that when the music of that instrument was heard in the land the monarch must abdicate in favour of the being who played it. And so it happened, for in the fight between king and dwarf the latter came off victorious.[8]

[1] Clavigero, l. c., vol. i. book vii. § 44, p. 398 (illus.); Torquemada, l. c., lib. xiv. cap. xi.; Th. Backer, l. c., pp. 51, 52; Nebel, l. c., plate 6 (counting from behind).

[2] Bancroft, l. c., iv. p. 504; Mexico, Anales del Min. de Fomento, 1854, i. p. 241.

[3] Bancroft, l. c., iv. pp. 519, 561 (illus.); Prescott, Hist. Conqu. Mexico, iii. pp. 103-108.

[4] Landa, l. c., pp. 125-126, § xxii.   [5] Baker, l. c., p. 54.

[6] Bancroft, iv. p. 19.   [7] Scherzer, l. c., p. 153.

[8] Bancroft, l. c., v. p. 632.

CHAPTER IV.

THE BASIS OF OUR MUSICAL SYSTEM.

1. HARMONY.

WHEN at the beginning of the last century Kolbe travelled among the Hottentots he found them playing different gom-goms in harmony. They also sang the notes of the common chord down to the lower octave, each one beginning with the phrase whenever the former had already come to the second or third tone, thus producing a harmonious effect.[1] The words to this song were simply " ho, ho, ho ". Burchell, who repeatedly assures us that he probably was the first European who ever touched the African soil in that part where he travelled, describes the harmonious singing of the Bachapin boys [Mus. Ex. 14]: sometimes one of them led the band and the rest joined in at different intervals, and, guided only by the ear, attuned their notes in correct harmony. The elder boys, whose voices were of a lower pitch, sang the bass, while the younger produced, in their turn, the higher tones of the treble.[2] The Bechuana also sing in harmony. The melody of their songs is simple enough, consisting chiefly of descending and ascending by thirds, while the singers have a sufficient appreciation of harmony to sing in two parts.[3] Moodie tells us that he very often heard the Hottentot servant girls singing in two parts; they even sang European tunes which were quite new to them with

[1] Kolbe, *l. c.*, p. 528.   [2] Burchell, *l. c.*, ii. p. 438.
[3] *Ibid.*

(139)

the accompaniment of a second of their own.[1]   The same
is said by Soyaux of the negro girls in Sierra Leone.[2]
We need not trace European influence in these instances,
for the girls had neither been taught to sing the second
voice nor had they heard it, but made it of their own
accord.   Many peoples (*e.g.*, the Oriental nations) have
every opportunity of hearing European harmonic music
but none of them understand it, and much less would they
be able to invent a second voice to a new tune.   This
shows that the capacity of singing in different parts
requires a peculiar gift, a natural talent and original
feeling for harmony, which cannot be acquired by mere
hearing harmonic music.   Another still more striking
example of Hottentots' musical talent was related to
Moodie by a German officer.   When the latter happened
to play that beautifully pathetic air of Gluck's, "Che faro
senza Euridice," on his violin, "he was surprised to observe
that he was listened to by some Hottentot women with
the deepest attention, and that some of them were even
affected to tears.   In a day or two afterwards he heard
his favourite melody with accompaniments all over the
country, wherever his wandering led him."[3]   At first
it seems astonishing that there should be Hottentots
apparently endowed with so great a musical gift; it is
especially surprising to hear of their repeating the air
with accompaniments, since the German officer was
certainly not able to play both on his violin at the same
time.   This statement, however, will no longer appear to
us incredible if compared with similar examples in the
accounts of some other travellers.   Theophilus Hahn, who
lived in Africa for fifteen years, tells us that his father,
the missionary, used to play some hymns before the tribe
of the Nama Hottentots to the accompaniment of a con-

---

[1] Moodie, *l. c.*, ii. p. 227.   [2] Soyaux, *l. c.*, ii. p. 174.
[3] Moodie, i. p. 228.

certina.   Some days after they would repeat the hymns *with the Dutch words* which they could not understand. Hahn says "they drawl the grave sounds of the hymns such as 'O Haupt voll Blut und Wunden,' 'Ein Lämmlein geht und trägt die Schuld,' with the same ardour as 'O du mein lieber Augustin,' 'My heart is in the Highlands,' or 'Long, long ago'".[1]   These tribes have not only an admirable talent for music but for general imitation as well.   They imitate so faithfully the approach of the lion, the fright of the different animals, and capture of its prey, that they can make themselves intelligible even to a person who does not understand their words. Although this dramatic talent is peculiar to Hottentots and Bushmen, other savage tribes display an equally great talent for music and admirable feeling for harmony.   The Ashantis play their instruments in two parts,[2] [Mus. Ex. 18], the Asaba people (Niger) frequently sing in sequences of thirds,[3] the Maoris sang in thirds when Cook visited New Zealand for the first time.[4]   [Mus. Ex. 15.]   On Samoa the natives had some songs for two voices long before any European influence could have existed.[5]   Mr. Zimmermann heard on the Solomon Islands the women singing in a chorus with a sort of harmony ; the melody was very simple, partly resting on one tone, partly rising and falling in a chord, out of which the third and fifth could easily be distinguished.[6]   Again, Mr. Williams tells us that he heard on the Fiji Islands a song where the bass alternated with the air; then the singers sounded one of the common chords in the bass clef without the alternation.[7]   On Java numerous orchestras play elaborate music in different parts ; the harmony is said to be rather barbarian ; the scores, however, which Mr. Land

---

[1] Globus, vol. xviii. p. 120.

[2] Bowdich, *l. c.*, p. 138.

[3] Day, *Niger*, p. 272.

[4] Forster, *l. c.*, ii. pp. 477-478.

[5] Wilkes, *l. c.*, pp. 135 and 145.

[6] Zimmermann, *l. c.*, i. p. 234.

[7] Williams, *l. c.*, p. 142.

lately published [1] undoubtedly show the germ of counterpoint in so many cases that these examples are interesting at least from this point of view.   [Mus. Ex. 25.]
Whether harmony was known in ancient India is, to say
the least, doubtful.   In Sanskrit harmony is termed sruti,
and melody raga,[2] but it is not certain whether sruti
means harmony in our sense.   At present the Hindu
harmony is merely a continuation of the tonic or dominant similar to the Scotch bagpipe music.[3]   A similar
"harmony" occurs in examples of music in Tongatabu
and among the Bushmen.   [Mus. Ex. 20, 21.]   On the
Andaman Islands men sing in unison ; some women sing
with the children in falsetto, an octave above ; the
remainder of the women sing in what seems to be intended for a perfect fifth, but what is occasionally a minor
sixth above the men.   Difference of pitch in the voices
introduces other notes which—according to Portman—
can only be called " out of tune ".   Be that as it may,
they sing at times in intervals which are intended to be
harmonious.[4]   In the Siamese the perception of concords
in notes is as acute as that of a European musician : they
are just as long in tuning an instrument as we, but they
do not seem practically to introduce such concords into
their music.[5]   The North American Indians sing in unison
as a rule, harmony being seldom employed, and when it
is, it is always altered every time the song is performed.[6]
The Keres in New Mexico sing in three voices.[7]   From
the west coast of America La Perouse quotes a song in
two voices.[8]   [Mus. Ex. 19.]
     Thus neither harmony nor the germs of counterpoint

---

[1] Land, *l. c.*   [2] E. Balfour, *Cycl. of India*, ii. p. 1019.
[3] Saurîndramohana Thákura, *Hind. Mus.*, p. 54 ; Day, *Mus. Hind.*, pp.
11-12.
[4] Portman, *l. c.*, p. 184.   [5] Bowring, *l. c.*, i. p. 150.
[6] Th. Baker, *l. c.*, p. 18.   [7] Davis, *El Gringo*, p. 119.
[8] La Perouse, *l. c.*, ii. p. 150.

are entirely unknown to primitive nations, and it would seem from all the examples I was able to collect that the principle of tonality is in most cases unmistakable. Baker in his monograph on Indian music expressly calls attention to the fact that the songs of the Iroquois start from a fundamental tone to which the melody finally returns.[1] The same has been remarked by Stumpf in his essay on the songs of the Bellacula Indians.[2] They themselves said they knew these songs before they ever saw the white man.[3]

The numerous examples of a primitive orchestra, indeed the frequent occurrence of the quartette form systematically arranged according to four separate voices, also points to the existence of harmony and tonality, and their appreciation by savage races. A quartette of marimbas seems to be especially favoured by the Angola.[4] Livingstone found a marimba quartette and four drums playing together,[5] in other cases two marimbas, two cassutos, and one guilando (bass) were played in *ensemble.*[6] In Guatemala several marimbas accompany the songs in correct harmony.[7] It is a well-known fact that African and Malayan players understand European music so well as to be able to accompany by ear with their whole orchestra a simple European tune, and to play our dance music from memory without having ever seen the notes.

People who know how to accompany a song and how to play in *ensemble* cannot be without a certain feeling for harmony and tonality.

With these ethnological facts to hand we may oppose the widespread theory of harmony and counterpoint being musical inventions of modern times. Some thirty years

---

[1] Baker, *l. c.*, p. 19.   [2] Stumpf, *Bellac. Ind.*, p. 416.

[3] Helmholtz said (*l. c.*, p. 342): "The ancient world developed this principle of tonality in homophonic music, the modern in harmonic" (?).

[4] Merolla, *l. c.*, p. 244.   [5] Livingstone, *l. c.*, p. 293.

[6] Carli, *l. c.*, i. p. 695.   [7] Bancroft, *l. c.*, i. p. 705.

ago Westphal took great pains to prove that the ancient
Greeks at least knew harmony and made use of it in their
instrumental music.[1]   He would probably have been much
more credited if it had been known that this supposed
modern invention was in use among savage tribes in
ancient times.   Rousseau called harmony " une invention
Gothique et barbare.   Les Europeens sont les seuls qui
aient une Harmonie des Accords.   Harmonie étoit réservé
à des peuples du Nord."   A somewhat similar opinion
has since been expressed by several authors.[2]

Now we have seen that even uncivilised races know
how to accompany a simple song by ear, while some of
the more civilised ones, as the Chinese and other Oriental
people, do not understand our harmony, although they
have every opportunity of hearing our music.   Thus the
difference between people with and without harmonic
music is not *a historical but a racial one*.   There is of
course no doubt that our feeling for and comprehension
of harmony have been developed by time, but so also has
our feeling for melody. . If we compare a modern song
with an air of savage races, we find the latter very short,
restricted to two to three tones and the same phrase
constantly repeated, while our musical themes are worked
out, built up, prolonged and varied so as to form a
coherent, elaborate melody.   So it is not harmony alone
which has been developed in course of time.   Therefore
I do not think that our ideas of the structure and formation of melody are completed before our ideas of harmony
begin, but that both originate at the same time, and going
hand in hand in their respective development mutually
influence each other.   It is impossible to work out a
melody without harmonic changes, and the development
of a melody is entirely dependent upon the harmony.   It
is true there were periods in the history of music when

[1] Westphal, *l. c.*, p. 24.   [2] Willard, *l. c.*, p. 40.

melody seems to have gone its own way and when the whole music seemed to develop in a melodious direction only, but this is the case with harmony and counterpoint as well. Is it not significant that nations without any feeling for harmony would not have developed their music, nor even their melody to the same degree as we have done, and that their airs would have remained melancholic and monotonous unless they had been taken up by European composers, who harmonised them and worked them out to accomplished works of art? On the other hand, the most primitive germ of harmony and counterpoint is the continuation of the key-note throughout the piece; the same method, but intended only instead of actually sung, gives the principle of tonality: the essence of melody. This shows their common origin. Thus, after all, Rameau was not so wrong when he said: " La melodie n'est qu'une suite de l'Harmonie,"[1] and "il poroît que la melodie provient de l'Harmonie ".[2] Primitive harmony is no doubt very rude, but primitive melody is precisely of the same kind.

It may still be objected that those savages who know harmony now may have acquired it in the course of time (even without foreign influence), and may have been ignorant of it centuries ago. I think, however, I can take it for granted that there are still savage tribes, whose culture has remained stationary ever since the stone age. If this is so, it seems — to say the least — extremely improbable that such tribes (as Bushmen, Australians) should at the same time have made any progress in music alone.

2. MAJOR AND MINOR KEY.

It is surprising how often savages sing in the minor key. The music of Australian tribes is to a great extent

---

[1] Rameau, *l. c.*, p. 23.   [2] *Ibid.*, p. 138.

minor, and so was the music of the Tasmanians.[1] The
songs of the former are marked throughout by sudden,
frequent, and ever-varying inflections of voice, in compass
rarely exceeding the distance of a third, and minor intervals predominating. In Tonga the songs begin in a slow
and solemn style; gradually other voices and instruments
join in, and then the performers begin to quicken their
time both in music and dancing to the loudest pitch and
quickest possible movement. The whole mostly in the
minor key.[2] Music in Nukahiwa (Washington Islands)
dwells principally upon quarter tones, not going beyond
the minor third from E to G, except that it sometimes sinks
into D. The rising from E to G and sinking *vice versâ* takes
place by successive quarter tones, the minor third[3] being
always preferred. [Mus. Ex. 24.]

The negroes in Sierra Leone always sing in minor.[4]
The Bongo negroes also sing sometimes in the minor
key.[5] The inhabitants of the lake district of East Africa
appear to affect the major rather than the interminable
minor key of the Asiatics.[6] Again, in Fiji singing is
invariably in the major key.[7] The examples of African
music show a preference for the major key to the minor,
and therefore we cannot say that as a rule the minor key
occurs more frequently among uncivilised people as a
whole;[8] it depends upon the race or perhaps upon the
country.

It has been said that there exists an internal connection between the major and minor key and our feelings of
pleasure and pain. If this were so, savages ought to sing

---

[1] Bonwick, *l. c.*, p. 32; Rev. G. W. Torrance, *l. c.*, p. 355; Howitt,
l. c., p. 327; Topinard, *Austral.*, p. 72.

[2] Turner, *l. c.*, p. 135.   [3] Langsdorf, *l. c.*, i. p. 160.

[4] Soyaux, *l. c.*, ii. p. 174.

[5] Ratzel, *l. c.*, i. p. 516. (So also in Dar Fertit, N.W. of Albert
Nyanza).

[6] Burton, *Lake Reg., East Africa*, ii. p. 291.

[7] Williams, *l. c.*, p. 141.   [8] Marsden, *l. c.*, p. 196.

mostly in the major key, as they sing more frequently on merry occasions, and they ought to sing invariably in minor on sad occasions.   This, however, is not the case. Bancroft says of the natives of South Mexico that their jolly songs are sad and the merriest music melancholic.[1] I confess I cannot fancy how jolly music can be at the same time sad ; it evidently only appears to *us* sad, and that proves that an objective opinion as to the character of this music can hardly be given.   In Australia, says Lumholtz, women and men sing mostly in the wood, but hardly in the camp.   They are gay and happy, but their songs are melancholy and in excellent harmony with the sombre nature of Australia.[2]   [Mus. Ex. 22 and 23.] Now, this statement does not point to a connection with the mood and disposition of our mind, but with external nature.   This external nature as such, however, cannot be sad or merry ; it only appears so to *us*, *i.e.*, *we* are sad or merry, and the Australians themselves evidently are merry, as the author says, so I cannot see any correspondence between a certain key with a certain disposition of our mind.   The Tasmanians were a merry people before the war with the English began, yet they sang in minor. The Bahama negroes have the strange custom of singing at night in front of the hut of a dying friend.   Men, women and children, each one taking some part in the harmony, sing it in a full chorus.[3]   [Mus. Ex. 9.]

The melody, apart from the words and the scenery, seems to me rather a merry one, although it is certainly not intended to be so.   As soon as I imagine the whole scenery and the occasion on which it is sung, the same melody at once assumes a sadder character.   At any rate it is intended to be sad, but it is in major.   Baker in his above-mentioned monograph tried to show that Indian songs are invariably in minor if the subject is a sad one,

---

[1] Bancroft, *l. c.*, i. p. 665.   [2] Lumholtz, *l. c.*, p. 156.

[3] Edwards, *l. c.*, p. 525.

and in major if it is a merry one.   In most cases, however,
he could only guess at the mood of mind from the words,
and it was not at all certain whether they did not admit
of more than one interpretation according to the mood of
the people for whom they were destined.

In the face of these facts we may say primitive men
are equally familiar with the minor and the major key,
without using them in a manner corresponding to the mood
or disposition of the mind.   They also know and use
harmonies in minor.   In the song of the Asaba (Niger)
people, who sing in thirds, a preference for the minor
third is rather noticeable, *especially at the conclusions*.[1]   The
natives on the islands Amsterdam and Middleburgh,
where it is the custom to sing in two parts, had a song in
A minor.   At times they concluded this song with the
A minor chord.[2]   [Mus. Ex. 17.]   This occurrence of
minor chords in savage music is no doubt of the greatest
importance, and will have to be taken into consideration
in further researches on the physiology and psychology of
music, this the more so, as Helmholtz still thought it was
not until in the first half of the eighteenth century that
people began to use minor chords in concluding a song.

We have refused to accept the theory that the minor
mode necessarily corresponds to a sad frame of mind.   On
the other hand, it is certain that the effect of the minor
is different from that of the major.   Why is it ?   It is
questionable whether savage tribes notice any peculiar
difference.   They will sing the mode best fitting to their
voice, and will stick to this mode in their songs without
changing it in any striking degree, *i.e.*, if the melody has
advanced so far as to being fixed and settled at all.   One
mode, once in use, remains so, as a rule, with very few
exceptions.   In music, taken as modern art, the case is
very different.   In works of art the minor mode has been

---

[1] Day, *Niger*, p. 272.   [2] Forster, *l. c.*, i. p. 429.

the more seldom used up to the beginning of this century and is no doubt later developed. Therefore, we may connect with it the idea of the unusual and may use it on occasions where something extraordinary is intended. But why is it that it came in use so late and was formerly so seldom to be met with? The reason of this is to be found in the construction of our instruments. On the old flutes (even at Handel's time) it was impossible to play in minor; the trumpets and horns—at that time without valves—had only the so-called natural tones, i.e., the harmonic upper tones, which are all in major. Of course, if instruments of different pitch were employed it was possible by a clever combination of tones to have minor melodies performed; but this was too complicated an arrangement to allow of frequent use as a rule. With the introduction of valves the melody in minor ceased to be difficult, and the minor key became as frequent in modern compositions as the major. But the old compositions are still in use as well, and with them the minor mode still retained something of its unusual characters which is thence transferred to each single chord of the same mode. But this only appeals to the accomplished musician.

There is still one question to be answered: *Why* do primitive men sing in different modes at all? To this Dr. Carter Blake said:[1] "Minor tunes are easier than tunes in major keys. The cries of children and street cries are proofs."[2] I do not think that this proof holds good. If children cry, it is, I am sorry to say, neither in major nor in minor. The street cries for which towns like

[1] *Journ. Anth. Inst.*, vol. i. p. xxviii.

[2] Joseph Kaines (*ibid.*) corrects this opinion by saying: "The child feels pain, and it awakens attention to itself by crying out; the street crier utters his burthen for the same end. The fact of pain or deprivation in both cases is expressed in the only natural way—by the minor key." This theory has been already objected to. Moreover, both children and street criers cry in the same way if they are happy. I never noticed that they changed the key in such cases.

London and Paris are still famous do not allow of any
musical annotation in many cases because the tones are
not distinct enough.   In other cases they are distinct, but
the musical phrase is *too* short (two to three tones) to
allow of one harmonisation only.   The remaining instances
of street cries are collected in W. Gardiner's book *Music
in Nature*.   Of seventeen quoted examples only one is in
minor.

Dr. Müller was of opinion that among nearly all
nations the popular songs sound as if they were in the
minor key.[1]   Helmholtz, however, was told by an experienced teacher of singing that pupils of only moderate
musical talent have much more difficulty in hitting the
minor than the major third.[2]   Again, Spohr says that
country people intone the third rather sharp, the fourth
still sharper, and the seventh rather flat.[3]   This divergency
of opinion is only explicable if we bear in mind that the
different authors spoke of different races, and I think,
indeed, that a peculiar mode of singing depends upon a
peculiar quality of the organ of voice ; I mean originally,
as with little training we are, as a rule, equally fitted to
sing either of the two modes.   It is with the voice as with
the lips in playing a wind instrument : weak lips intone
each interval rather flat.   It is also the uncertainty of
intonation and the constant fluctuation of the voice which
give us the impression of the minor key rather than of the
major.   Mr. Gilman noticed that in the Zuñi melodies the
indecision of the singer between the minor and major third
was a striking feature of all the Zuñi music[4] (Mexico).
Mr. Stumpf says of the Bellacula Indians that they raised
the pitch to half-a-tone when the excitement increased,
while the intervals of the minor third were widened to

---

[1] Müller, *l. c.*, p. 161 ; he says : " Die Terz klingt unbestimmt zwischen
der grossen und kleinen Terz ".

[2] Helmholtz, *l. c.*, p. 302.   [3] Spohr, *l. c.*, i. p. 257.

[4] Gilman, *l. c.*, p. 91.

major thirds.[1] This shows that the two keys do not
correspond to two different qualities of feeling (of pleasure
and pain), but merely to the increasing and decreasing of
it, quite independent of its quality.   Mr. Lichtenstein also
noticed the indecision between the major and minor third
(neutrale Terz) in the singing of the Hottentots,[2] and Day
says that the neuter third *perhaps* occurs in the songs of
the Asaba (Niger) people.[3]

3. THE SCALE.

The scale is a melodious type of a peculiar mode.
Long before we are able to speak of a regular scale,
peculiar intervals seem to be especially chosen in singing
and in instruments in preference to others, and yet we
are by no means justified in regarding every succession
of tones or intervals as a systematic scale.   This was
especially the case in primitive times, when the melody
was too fluctuating to allow of distinct tones and a
systematic order.   Still, in some examples of primitive
songs, and above all in instruments, we may notice that
some intervals were more in favour than others, and thus
the frequent use of a certain succession of tones may have
influenced the formation of a regular scale.   Which were
these intervals ?

An ancient pipe from the stone age (illustrated by
Fétis) shows the first four tones (*i.e.*, one of the equal
halves) of the diatonic scale.   An instrument from ancient
Mexico, called by Baker " Schalmei," has the first five
tones of the diatonic scale in major ;[4] the ancient flutes of
the Iroquois had the first five to six tones of the diatonic
scale in minor ; in some instances it was possible to play
their higher octave as well.[5]   The guitar, nanga, of the

---

[1] Stumpf, *Bel. Ind.*, p. 408.   [2] Lichtenstein (Germ. ed., ii. p. 550).
[3] Day, *Niger*, p. 272.   [4] Baker, *l. c.*, p. 57.
[5] *Ibid.*, p. 55.

Karagwe tribe is described by Grant as having seven strings, six of which form a " perfect scale ".[1]   I suggest diatonic scale, as otherwise a different meaning of the word scale would have been mentioned.   A syrinx of stone from ancient Peru had the following succession of tones : [2] E, F sharp, G, A, D, C sharp, F, A.   The Balafong in Senegambia had, according to Engel, fourteen key-boards on which the minor scale could be played through two octaves and a half.   Mr. Ellis, however, measured the bars again, and found that bars five to six gave a very fairly correct minor scale without the leading note.[3]   The tamul in Ceylon had the diatonic scale,[4] perhaps influenced by the heptatonic scales of ancient Hindu music.[5]   The Ongé tribes appear to have our diatonic intervals, but we know little of them.   The songs conclude in what Portman assumes to be the tonic, but which is in reality the second note of the scale.[6]   The songs of the Bellacula Indians Stumpf quoted[7] are founded partly on the pentatonic, partly on the heptatonic system.   Finally, the old Egyptian flutes which were brought to London two years ago, and which have been calculated to date from the year 3000 B.C., had a complete diatonic scale.[8]

Let us first settle the fact that a succession of tones exactly corresponding to our diatonic scale (or a part of it) occurs in instruments in the stone age, and that we have no reason to conclude that a period of pentatonic scales necessarily preceded the period of heptatonic ones.[9]

[1] Grant, l. c., p. 183.   [2] Traill, l. c., p. 128.

[3] Engel, Mus. Anc. Nat., p. 13 ; Ellis, Var. Sc., l. c., p. 507.

[4] Nell, l. c., p. 201 ; Joinville, l. c., p. 440.

[5] Chrysander, l. c., p. 28.   [6] Portman, l. c., p. 185.

[7] Stumpf, l. c., p. 425.

[8] Wilkinson also mentions that the diatonic as well as the pentatonic scale was in use in ancient Egypt (l. c., i. p. 487).   An Egyptian pipe of the British Museum has the tones C, D, E, F, F sharp.

[9] Engel said in his Mus. Anc. Nat., p. 16, that the diatonic scale is to be found at the time of the most primitive culture ; it is not the only one,

Helmholtz was of opinion "that not merely the composition of perfect musical works of art, but even the construction of our system of scales, keys, chords, etc., is the work of artistic invention, and hence must be subject to the laws of artistic beauty ".[1] He bases this assertion upon the historical presumption that " mankind has been at work on the diatonic system for more than 2500 years, since the days of Terpander and Pythagoras, and that the same properties of the human ear could serve as the foundation of very different musical systems ". But when Helmholtz wrote these lines some of the most important discoveries were not made, and the old Egyptian flutes having a diatonic scale (2000 B.C.) completely surprised the musical world. In face of these facts, I think, we shall have to modify our theories accordingly, and may say : It was this diatonic succession of tones which, as the most practical, has remained stationary up to the present time, and has been the constant basis in the development of music to the high standard it reached in the seventeenth to nineteenth centuries. All the other systematic attempts at a scale either made a successful development of music impossible, or they degraded it from its rank as an art to a mere intellectual trifle.[2]

Another theory according to which men in constructing the scale gradually proceeded from a succession of larger intervals (chiefly the pentatonic scale) to the comparatively small ones of the diatonic scale is not in accordance with

---

" but less artificial than theorists have frequently declared it to be ". Hipkins says (in Day, *Hind. Mus.*, p. x.): " In the present state of our knowledge it is impossible to affirm that a pentatonic scale is of greater antiquity than a heptatonic, or that a chromatic scale preceded an enharmonic composed of quarter tones ". Stumpf (*l. c.*, p. 426): " Es scheint, dass geradezu in allen Welttheilen und *zu allen Zeiten* solche 5 stufige Leitern in verchiedener Form sich finden ". Compare Ellis's statement, *Var. Sc.*, p. 19.

[1] Helmholtz, *l. c.*, p. 366.

[2] Chinese music stands in the same relation to ours as writing does to drawing.

ethnological facts.   On the contrary, many savages constantly use smaller intervals than we do.   According to Davis Australian savages and Maoris use quarter tones, and I may add that Davis was very careful in obtaining the correct notes, inasmuch as he used a monochord especially constructed for this purpose.[1]   The natives of Nukahiwa also sing in quarter tones.[2]   The Arabs seem to be still more particular in distinguishing sharps and flats than we are.   The equal third and quarter tones of the Arabs, Villoteau mentions, are no doubt a mistake. Kosegarten[3] affirms that Villoteau constantly mixes up the Arabian and Persian musical system, and so does Kiesewetter in his treatise on Arabian music.[4]   According to Fleischer, however,[5] the Persian and Arabic music system cannot possibly be separated, while Arabic and Egyptian music have nothing in common.   All these questions were at last settled by Land (*Gamme Arabe, l. c.*).   He says Arabe lutenists had seventeen notes within the octave, strictly distinguishing between flats and sharps. Out of this mass of tones they formed diatonic scales according to our principle with flats only or with sharps only; thus they distinguished the C sharp major scale from the D flat major scale in practice, while we distinguish it merely in theory.   The equal division of equal quarter tones (twenty-four altogether) is of later date and still to be met with.[6]   In Sumatra the interval of an octave is divided into six tones without intermediate half tones.[7] The melodies similar to those of Ireland generally have

---

[1] Grey, *l. c.* (musical examples).   [2] Langsdorf, i. p. 160.
[3] *l. c.*, p. 142.   [4] Kosegarten, p. 145.
[5] Fleischer, *l. c.*, p. 501.
[6] Compare E. Smith, *l. c.*, p. 177; mus. exampl., Christianowitch, *l. c.* Salvador Daniel (*l. c.*, pp. 48-49): "Les tiers et des quarts de ton dans la musique des Arabes ont entièrement erronnée et due à l'emploi des certain gammes.   Ces gammes ont un des modes d'ornamentation les plus usités, surtout par les chanteurs et les violonistes."
[7] Marsden, *l. c.*, p. 195.

the minor third instead of the major. On their primitive
violin the natives play in our division. The Chinese
know and practically use the pentatonic *and* heptatonic
scale. The southern and rural people use the former, the
northern and more cultivated circles the latter.[1] This has
been pointed out lately in an excellent paper of Mr.
Gilman's. To his researches we also owe the most important statement, that just as the Pythagorean use of the
progression of fifths did not *create* the scale, but was the
result of the Greek scale of his time, so in China the same
progression became the foundation of theory through the
fact that by its use an accurately determinate form could
be given to the scale which was already in use among
them.[2] In Java the instruments have the pentatonic
scale,[3] but Dr. Crotch asserts that all the real native
music of Java is composed in a common enharmonic
scale.[4] Mr. Ellis, in his excellent paper on *The Scale
of Various Nations*, sufficiently proved that pentatonic
scales do not necessarily arise from inability to appreciate
semitones, and that some of the existing pentatonic scales
may be formed by omission from scales of seven tones[5]
In consequence of all these facts we have to abandon the
theory that a period of pentatonic scales preceded the
present period of diatonic scales. Mr. Helmholtz himself
seems to be in favour of this modification of his former
theory, as the new English edition of his celebrated book
on *The Sensation of Tones* contains all the valuable material
that Mr. Ellis brought together to support the new theory
of the scale.

The above-mentioned facts also show the impossibility
of founding the structure of the scale entirely upon any
natural properties of the ear, or on the laws of the con-

---

[1] Gilman, *Chin. Mus.*, p. 62 ; Williams, *Middl. Kgdm.*, 2nd edit., ii.
p. 95.

[2] Gilman, *l. c.*, pp. 157-158.   [3] Crawfurd, i. p. 339.

[4] *Ibid.*   [5] Ellis, *Scale of Var. Nat.*, p. 526.

stitution of musical sound. Therefore some other authors tried to found the scale upon the natural structure of our organ of voice. Thus Engel considered the pentatonic scale as being easier for children (and primitive people) than the diatonic. Others, as Waterhouse, went as far back as to the animal kingdom, and there they found the *hylobates agilis* singing the chromatic scale.[1] This gibbon (it was a female) achieved the chromatic scale admirably, effecting especially the descent with great precision. This is the more remarkable " as the chromatic scale is not an easy task even to the human vocalist ". The gibbon started from an E, ascending to the upper octave and descending again, always sounding the lower E almost simultaneously with the upper note, whatever that note might have been. Mr. Claude Trevelyan assures us that the pentatonic scale is not only "natural" to some men but also to some animals, such as a Scotch terrier, Persian cats, and cuckoos.[2] Not being a zoologist I may be excused for taking the humorous side of this latter statement without considering it as in any way important from a scientific point of view.[3]

I think that the human voice equally admits of any pentatonic or heptatonic intervals, and very likely we should never have got regular scales if we had depended upon the ear and voice only. The first and unique cause to settle the type of a regular scale is the instrument.[4]

---

[1] Darwin, *l. c.*, ii. pp. 299 and 358: " Professor Owen, who is a musician, confirms the foregoing statement ". Notes given by W. C. L. Martin, *Gen. Intro. to Nat. Hist. Mamm.*, 1841, p. 432.

[2] *Journ. Soc. Arts*, 3rd April, 1885, p. 555.

[3] I entirely agree with Stumpf's criticism of this statement : " Als Satire auf neutrale Terzen könnte einer diese Bemerkungen geistreich finden. Ich fürchte aber, sie sind ernsthaft gemeint, und dann sind sie erst recht zum Lachen " (*Viertelj. Musikw.*, ii. p. 523).

[4] " Whenever an instrument is made, there must always be established something more of certainty than belongs to such vague, wandering sounds " (Chorley, *l. c.*, p. 15). Attempts to found the structure of the scale on the

To obtain a scale the oldest instrument we know (the bone, or reed-pipe) is at the same time best fitted, as it does not admit of any change in the intervals. This heptatonic and diatonic succession of tones is indeed the most practicable and most simple for playing instruments, always bearing in mind that the oldest instrument is the pipe. On a pipe the player cannot possibly make reasonable use of more than eight holes, as he has not more fingers free to handle them, and he will very likely not be skilled enough to handle them with all four fingers of each hand, but with three only. Now, if on a short pipe six holes are pierced at equal distances within the limit of one octave, the result will always be the diatonic scale. This limit of an octave is a natural one (not for the sound, the ear or the voice, but for the player), as every player notices that he gets the higher octave of each tone without any fingering, simply by blowing with greater force of breath. In speaking of equal distances of the *holes* (not of the *intervals*) I am quite aware that in a modern flute the piercing and arrangement of the holes for the diatonic scale is not at all as easy as one might think. But in a primitive pipe this difficulty does not exist. For the same reason, *i.e.*, the simplicity of the construction, the use of smaller intervals than half-tones would be impossible even in more refined instruments, such as the modern violin. I should like to see the fingering of a modern violinist if he had to play quarter or third tones. He can play them, but his hand would not be able to execute a very complicated composition. Even the chromatic system, with its

---

construction of instruments were made on several occasions : P. Amiot and later on Wagener (*l. c.*, pp. 48-52) founded the pentatonic scale upon the panpipe. Stumpf once arrived at the conclusion : " Die meisten Leitern sind nicht auf das Gehör, sondern auf eine mathematisch-mechanische Saiteneintheilung gegründet " (*Viert. Mus.*, ii. p. 523). I myself brought forward the theory that the construction of the scale is founded on the construction of instruments in *Allg. Mus. Wochenschrift*, Dez., 1890.

distinction of sharps and flats, was too complicated for
instruments, and it has been made possible only by a
compromise between the physicist and the practical player.
*The chromatic intervals in our equal temperament are indeed
the smallest possible intervals, not for the ear, or the voice, or
the laws of sounds, but for a practicable instrument.*

We owe the scale not to nature (voice, ear, laws of
sound or animals), and not to science or artificial systems
that were worked upon and thought out for centuries, but
to the practical player and the qualities of his instrument.
Definite successions of tones were in use long before they
became regular systematic scales. The Shi-vo-la song, *e.g.*,
is composed just within the major diatonic scale, while the
Du-me-chim-chee may be viewed as composed exactly to
cover a pentatonic scale, although both may be said to
embody a stage in the development of the art before the
appearance of scales.[1]

That the simplicity and practicability of the diatonic
system for instruments is not the result of my speculation
only, is clear from the fact that this construction occurred
to the primitive mind of the man of the stone period. Since
then many other attempts have been made, and we find
sometimes in primitive flutes and pipes the most extraordinary arrangements of holes; nevertheless, from the time
of the stone age up to the present day, the diatonic division
has remained triumphant over all queer experiments of
instrument makers, and all too minute and detailed specu-
lations of the theorists.

To our modern musical feeling it seems appropriate
to begin from below in playing the scale, then to gradually
proceed to the higher octave, whence we go down again
to the original key-note to finish up the musical picture.
This manner of beginning and ending a piece does not
seem to be innate in our mind, nor is it the only natural

[1] Gilman, *Zuñi Melod.*, p. 91.

way. The Australians for instance begin from above, as
we have seen, and leave off in a deep, scarcely audible
note,[1] even in examples where the principle of tonality is
unmistakable. Considering this, our feeling seems to be
the outcome of a mere habit probably originating from
playing instruments (wind and stringed), where the deep
tones are always easier to produce than the high ones and
therefore easier to begin with. After all, it is not at all
offensive, even to our musical feeling, to begin the scale
from above, if we only try to get a little used to it.

4. MUSIC NOTES AND RHYTHMIC DIVISION.

It has often been supposed that the music of savage
races is all in regular duple time. The quoted examples,
however, prove the contrary. It is of course difficult to
say whether the triple or the duple time is the more
frequent, as we can never say by hearing a song whether
it has, *e.g.*, four $\frac{3}{4}$ bars or one $\frac{4}{4}$ bar with trioles. However
this may be, primitive music can be committed to notes
in duple as well as in triple time. In many instances the
change between those two divisions is so sudden and
frequent that we have to note down the $\frac{5}{4}$ time. Thus a
war-song of the Sudanese, sung before they go off to
battle, is noted down by Mr. Zöllner in $\frac{5}{4}$ time.[2] Mr.
Stumpf, in his as usual very careful observations on some
songs of the Bellacula Indians, suggests that a notation
in $\frac{5}{8}$ time would at times probably be the most appropriate.[3]
Some songs of the Kwakiutl Indians (British Columbia)
are sung in a five-part bar, which—according to Boas—
frequently occurs in the music of these tribes.[4] Several
of the melodies of the Asaba people Capt. Day collected
employ a mixed time of alternate bars of triple and common

---

[1] Schürmann, *l. c.*, p. 242.   [2] Zöllner, *l. c.*, p. 447.
[3] Stumpf, *Bellac. Ind.*, p. 409.
[4] Boas, *l. c.*, p. 51, mus. exampl., p. 59.

time.[1] Mr. Baker noticed that the Indians in singing never marked the beginning of a bar but only the rhythm in general. On the other hand, he said that only five of thirty-two collected examples were in triple time.[2] As the bars, however, are not marked in singing, his division is either a mere voluntary one or the first-named observation is not quite correct.

Mr. C. Engel in his days expressed the opinion that the North American Indians had music notes.[3] The two examples he quotes [4] do not, however, contain any music notes but only signs for the words to the songs—in one word, they are a kind of rough picture writing. He evidently mistook the general poetical sense of the word song for the specific musical one, while he did not seem to have thoroughly examined the signs themselves, in spite of his illustrating them too. Mr. Kohl himself says he believes he can show that the Indians have discovered something which may be called notes.[5] The way he obtained these notes is so peculiar that it may be well to give his investigation with all the accompanying details. He asked an old Indian, whose name was Kitagignan, or the " spotted feather," to show the Indian birch bark books and songs and to sing them to him. Upon this the Indian went away from the wigwam with Mr. Kohl, sat down at a lonely place, laid the birch bark on his lap, and pointing with the finger to the signs he began to explain them. This sign, he said, signifies that the same voice and the same tune continue, that one is a kind of note that the voice shall go up, others mean nothing further than that they show me how I shall go on singing. Up to this time the Indian had only *spoken*, and on Mr. Kohl's insisting upon an actual song, the Indian began to mutter

[1] Day, *Niger*, p. 274, fn.　　　[2] Th. Baker, *l. c.*, pp. 42-43.
[3] C. Engel, *Mus. of Anc. Nat.*, p. 179.
[4] Kohl, *l. c.*, i. p. 216 ; Catlin, *l. c.*, ii. p. 248.
[5] Kohl, *l. c.*, ii. p. 84.

in a trembling voice apparently frightened and finally bathed in perspiration. All this while his finger pointed to the notes, and he raised and lowered it in accord with his voice so as to give Mr. Kohl the impression "that there could not possibly be notes for every tone" (p. 91). How Mr. Kohl, nevertheless, came to tell us he obtained the Indian music notes I could not make out at all, the related story proving anything but this. Mr. Schoolcraft speaks still more expressly of "Mnemonic symbols for music" and "musical annotation";[1] he illustrates the signs and yet overlooks their being a sort of picture writing that indicates the text only. Mr. Engel, too, illustrates the same signs[2] without noticing what they actually contain. Mr. Tylor alone recognises that these signs of Schoolcraft's merely serve "to suggest to the mind the successive *verses*".[3]

In a private letter to Th. Baker[4] Mr. Eugène Vetromile stated that the Indians had no musical annotation nor any signs to indicate definite tones, the singers easily remembering all the songs. One of them (A-ō-dōn-wĕ) assured him that he without difficulty retained in memory eighty-nine different songs which he used to sing always in the same order at the harvest festival.

Messrs. David and Lussy also say: "Il n'est pas admissible, que, dans le temps préhistoriques . . . les hommes aient conçu l'idée d'un arrangement systématique des sons à plus forte raison d'une écriture phonétique". Unlike the majority of music writers, they go so far as to say that not even the Egyptians, Chaldeans, Phœnicians and Hebrews had music notes. " C'est l'alphabet qui a fourni aux premiers peuples les éléments graphiques servant à la représantation des sons. Nous le voyonz chez les Hindous, les Chinois et les Grecs. Nous ne trouvons

---

[1] Schoolcraft, *l. c.*, ii. p. 226.   [2] Engel, *Nat. Mus.*, p. 337.
[3] Tylor, *Res. Earl. Hist.*, p. 85.
[4] Th. Baker, *l. c.*, p. 49; Fewkes, *Sum. Cer.*, p. 277.

rien de semblable chez les Égyptiens, les Assyriens, les Babyloniens, qui pourtant ne leur étaient pas inférrieurs en civilisation." [1]   Mr. Engel, nevertheless, holds that "judging from analogy we may conjecture that Assyrians, Egyptians and Hebrews had musical signs".[2]   This "analogy" is, however, quite inappropriate, for Mr. Niebuhr, who travelled·in the east at the end of the last century, remarks : " Neither in Egypt, nor in Arabia or India did they understand how to commit music to writing. Although it was said that the great artists in Constantinople had secret musical signs, I did not come across anybody there who knew music notes, not even among the dervishes of the order Mevlaui, who were known for the greatest composers of the Turks." [3]

---

[1] David and Lussy, *l. c.*, p. 2.   [2] Engel, *Nat. Mus.*, p. 179.

[3] Niebuhr, *l. c.*, i. p. 175.

CHAPTER V.

PHYSICAL AND PSYCHICAL INFLUENCE OF MUSIC.

AMONG savages the influence of music is far more distinctly noticeable than among people in a higher state of civilisation. We cannot say that it is always stronger and deeper, nor does it seem to last for a long time, but it is brought to light in a more naïve and natural way, and is therefore a more suitable and welcome object of psychological observation.

It is certainly not a mere accidental coincidence of circumstances when some African tribes dance and sing more frequently at the time of the "palm wine season," or when the Ainu on the island of Yezo dance more at the opening of the hunting and fishing season.[1] The Bechuanas indulge in singing more especially at the time of the rains and of the harvest.[2] Burchell supposes that this custom has its origin in those feelings of gladness which would be so naturally excited by the fall of copious and frequent showers in a land where all hopes of an abundant crop of corn depend wholly on the quantity of rain. The Lincoln tribes in Australia do not allow a single evening to pass without singing; on these occasions their features show such unmistakable signs of joy and happiness that one would scarcely believe how these good-natured countenances could be capable of the highest expression of rage and fury.[3] It is remarkable that we sing as a rule more frequently in consequence of plea-

[1] H. v. Siebold, *l. c.*, p. 48.   [2] Burchell, *l. c.*, ii. p. 599.
[3] Schürmann, *l. c.*, p. 243.
(163)

surable feelings, than of feelings of sadness, although in
the latter case the lamentations and outcries may be more
striking than the harmless humming of a man in good
humour. At any rate, music is the direct and immediate
effect of the feelings of the moment, and this may be seen
with " savages " as well as with " civilised people ". I
therefore cannot agree with Mr. Barrow's opinion that
dancing and singing are the immediate effect of pleasurable
feelings, only in the state of very primitive culture, while
among civilised people they are arts which, " acquired by
study (?) and practised at certain times, have no relation
to our feeling ". I am almost afraid that Mr. Barrow
mistook the typical piano lesson for the art of music.[1]

A very graphic description of the part that music
plays among the natives of Australia is given by G. Grey:
To a sulky old native, his song is what a quid of tobacco
is to a sailor ; if he is angry, he sings ; if glad, he sings ;
if hungry, he sings ; if full, provided he is not so full as to
be in a state of stupor, he sings more lustily than ever.[2]
The peculiar character of their songs renders them under
all circumstances most solacing to the natives. The songs
are short, generally containing only one or two ideas,
constantly repeated over and over again, producing much
the same effect that the singing of a nurse does upon a
child. To us these songs seem barbarian and unmelodious, but the Australians like them and have in turn no
appreciation of European music. Should a European
endeavour to perform his music before them, it would be
laughed at " as a combination of silly and effeminate
notes," and for weeks afterwards the natives would
entertain their friends by mimicking the tone and attitude
of the white man, an exhibition which never fails to draw
down loud shouts of applause. Sometimes, however, even
they seem to be moved sympathetically by our music.

[1] Barrow, *l. c.*, i. p. 148.
[2] Grey, *Two Exp. to Austr.*, ii. p. 300.

Thus one of the natives burst into tears when he heard "God save the Queen". On another occasion Mr. Grey observed during a funeral the great effect of music upon the natives. Even those infants who sat passively on their mothers' shoulders, not understanding the cause of lament, seemed to be affected as the involuntary tears rolled down the cheeks.[1] This, of course, may be mere reflective imitation, for if all people in a company cry, children will always cry too, even without music; still the grown-up persons, at least, seemed to express their sadness by music, and then, again, to be more deeply moved by hearing it. I may mention that the Australians are accustomed to quiet their children by music if they cry.[2] Another example of the influence of music is given in a narrative of Mr. Peron: While an Australian family were taking their simple meal Mr. Peron's company began to sing the "Marseillaise". At first the natives seemed more confused than surprised, but soon listened attentively. The meal was forgotten and their satisfaction was manifested by contortions and gestures, so "whimsical" that the Europeans could hardly refrain from laughing, while it was equally difficult to the aborigines to hide their enthusiasm. But scarcely was the first strophe ended before exclamations of rapture were uttered by every one. A young man, especially, was almost frenzied; he tore his hair, scratched his head with both hands, agitated himself in a hundred different ways, and repeatedly iterated his approving clamour. After this vigorous and warlike song the Europeans sang some "light and tender airs" but soon perceived that they affected the natives but in a slight degree.[3]

A similar exciting influence was often observed when the tamtam was sounded, of whose effect we gave a few examples on p. 106. Mr. Du Chaillu noticed this among

---

[1] Grey, *Two Exp. to Austr.*, ii. p. 331. [2] Gerland-Waitz, *l. c.*, vi. p. 782.
[3] Peron, *l. c.*, p. 840.

savages on his travels in Equatorial Africa. No sooner
do they hear the tamtam than they lose all control over
themselves, and the louder and more energetically the
instrument is beaten the wilder are the jumps of the male
African, and the more disgustingly indecent the contortions
of the women.[1] Mr. Reade observed that his people
always began to sing when he compelled them to overcome their natural laziness and to continue rowing.[2]

Skilled singers in Greenland well know how to
express different passions by soft or animated tones of the
drum and the motions of their body. This they do during
a banquet which lasts for several nights, until all pro-
visions are consumed and the participants too exhausted
to articulate any longer. He who can make the drollest
contortions of the *body* passes for the master-*singer*.[3]

The Indians have special songs for the time of mourning as well as for the time of pleasure, for leisure hours
as well as for the hour of triumph. Simple and rude as
they may be, they have always a definite character. The
required expression is, however, attained by variety of
time rather than of cadence.[4]

When, on his third voyage, Columbus landed on
Trinidad, he ordered his sailors to dance on board a ship
to the sound of a tambourine, thinking he would decoy the
Indians. They however put down the oars, seized their
shield and bows, shooting at the ship with arrows. Possibly they mistook the whole affair for a war-dance and
feared mischief.[5]

The savages themselves are quite aware of the great
power of music, and try to make use of it whenever a
peculiar emotional effect is intended, and especially so in
the case of diseases. The primitive physician performs
his duty—strange to say—with musical accompaniment.

[1] Du Chaillu, *Equ. Afr.*, p. 201.   [2] Reade, *Sketch B*, ii. p. 313.
[3] Cranz, *l. c.*, i. p. 163.   [4] Sproat, *l. c.*, p. 63.
[5] Columbus, *l. c.*, p. 111.

There are, it is true, some cases where it seems to me doubtful whether an emotional effect is really intended, or whether the doctor simply uses a well-thought-out bit of humbug which he is able to express in a more naïve way than his European colleague.

When among the negroes a rich man calls in the doctor, all musicians are called together, surround the patient, and play on instruments day and night.[1] The negroes do not think this is worse than the actual disease. Among the Wasambara in East Africa the doctor comes with a small bell in hand, which he rings from time to time. The patient sits before him on the ground, and the doctor begins in a singing tone: "Dabre, dabre," which he repeats several times, to which the patient answers: "Eh".[2] The Benguela call their musical doctor Kimbunda,[3] the Lomami call him Tawuli, and the Zanzibaris Mganga.[4] The Kafirs, too, have their musical doctor.[5] It is especially the ceremony of circumcision, which among some tribes is seldom passed over without singing and dancing. The Banshaka decorate themselves on such occasions in the most funny way with leaves, amulets, and fetishes, roar and caper all the time, clapping hands and making altogether an infernal noise.[6] In Madagascar, too, the circumcision is celebrated with general merry-making, during which the "happy fathers" amuse themselves with singing, dancing, eating and drinking.[7] In South Africa even the first menstruation of a girl is made a general festival, celebrated with music.[8]

In Australia the doctor shakes a bundle of reeds,[9] an

[1] Proyart, l. c., p. 574.
[2] Krapf, l. c., ii. p. 116 (German edition; in the English edition this remark is left out).
[3] Magyar, l. c., i. p. 26.   [4] Shooter, l. c., p. 173 (edition, 1853).
[5] Doehne, l. c., p. 44.
[6] Lenz, Skizzen, p. 301. (Upper Ogowe River.)
[7] Pfeiffer, Madag., p. 187.   [8] Macdonald, l. c., p. 116.
[9] Schurmann and Teichelmann, l. c. (1840), part ii.

action otherwise used during a song to mark the time. At Port Jackson Mr. Hunter saw a physician who did not speak or sing to the spirit of the disease, but only put his mouth near the sick part of the body.[1] In Borneo the natives perform recitatives, songs, dances and processions in order to catch the soul of the patient, which is supposed to have ran away before the evil spirit.[2] In Tanna (New Hebrides) the natives believe that the doctor sends the illness; consequently they are very much afraid of him, and quite overload him with presents when they think he ceased to send the illness.[3] The obeah or medicine man of the negroes in Jamaica commences his cure with a dance, which he himself performs, not the patient, as in the case of the tarantella.[4] Surely, very few European colleagues would be a match for him in this respect.

Among the North American Indians the doctor is a very important person. He is in the most cases an old woman, not in a figurative sense, but in reality. With the Wallawalla Indians a medicine woman tries to expel the illness through her actions. She stands over the patient singing under great excitement accompanied by a dozen men and boys. She is constantly in motion, making all kinds of grimaces, falls on her knees and pretends to draw out the bad spirit with both hands, blowing into them, and, as it were, tossing the spirit into the air.[5] These Indians believe that singing influences the cure of a patient, so that all convalescent sick are directed to sing for several hours during the day. Thus we have many reasons for wishing those Indians good health.[6] The Mandans (Missouri) and Minetaris (Fall Indians of the Hudson Bay) have a medicine woman who dances, the Moluches (Chili) and Puelches in Patagonia male and female doctors; the former wear women's dress,

---

[1] Hunter, *l. c.*, p. 476. [2] Hein, *l. c.*, p. 29.
[3] Engel, *Mus. Myths*, pp. 84-144. [4] Lewis, *l. c.*, p. 158.
[5] Wilkes, *l. c.*, iv. p. 399. [6] Wied-Neuwied, *North Am.*, ii. p. 190.

and both cure the patient by singing, beating a drum, and shaking a rattle.[1]   The same is the case with the medicine man of the Araucanians, who call him Gligna or Dugol.[2] In British Columbia the doctor sings when he visits the patient, while a chorus of other people intones a song outside the house, and beats time on the roof of the house with long sticks.[3]   The Manchi or medicine man of the Pehuenches (Indians in the Argentine provinces) used a sort of drum in his musical invocation, with which he hoped to expel the evil spirit.[4]   If only the good spirits too would not be frightened away !

One of the most important occasions on which music is employed is during childbirth.   It is hoped that by this either the evil spirit is expelled or the patient encouraged.   Fortunately this event passes off very easily in the savage world.   Should, however, this not be the case, the poor woman, who is maltreated and bothered in the most incredible manner and suffers considerably, must allow herself to be also treated by the most noisy and discordant music.   It is, of course, not our task to follow the different phases of this act, although from the point of view of ethnological medicine some interesting facts might be brought to light.[5]   As is well known music is employed for medical purposes up to this time, when, however, some involuntary humour can scarcely be avoided.[6]   In spite of this we can say music has an emotional influence, and this fact remains true however funny the attempts may be which " savage " or " civilised " doctors and laymen at times make in employing music for medical purposes.

---

[1] Falkner, *l. c.*, p. 115.   [2] Molina, *l. c.*, ii. p. 105.
[3] Mayne, *l. c.*, p. 261.   [4] M'Cann, *l. c.*, i. p. iii.
[5] I refer for further particulars to Ploss, *Das Weib* and *Das Kind*.
[6] Bibliography by Engel, *Mus. Myths*, ii. pp. 84-144.

CHAPTER VI.

TEXT AND MUSIC.

IN the relation of text and music there seems to have been little change from time immemorial. It would be just as difficult to characterise in general the mutual position of both in the songs of savages, as it is to-day to arrive at a satisfactory solution of the question as to the rank of poetry and music when united in a single art-work. All depends upon the quality of the text, and in primitive times upon the development of language as well.

The most striking feature of all the savage songs is the frequent occurrence of words with no meaning whatever. This we have found in the choral songs of the Bushmen,[1] and sometimes in those of the Kafirs,[2] although the latter also possess some solo songs with a definite subject.

The songs of the Todas (Nilgiri Hills) are unlike those of other hill tribes usually devoid of any signification, or if they have a meaning at all they refer merely to events of recent occurrence.[3] The Todas speak a peculiar dialect that has given rise to all sorts of mysterious hypotheses as to their origin. According to Mr. Metz, however, they do not speak a language peculiar to themselves; it is only their pectoral pronunciation which produces that apparent dialect. The great national songs of the Kamchadales are called Bachia, a word the constant repetition of which constitutes the whole of the song. The melody is not devoid of expression, although Mr. Langsdorf, from whom

---

[1] Wood, *l. c.*, i. p. 258.　　　　[2] *Ibid.*, p. 153.

[3] Metz, *l. c.*, p. 30.

I borrow this remark, could not discover any meaning in
it whatever.[1]

Many Papuans in New Guinea have no regularly developed language at all, and therefore not much can be
expected of their vocal music, at least not of the text.
These texts contain words that never occur in the current
language, and therefore the meaning is very difficult to be
found out, if there should be one at all.[2] On the Tonga
Islands the words of songs are in the Hamoa language,
which the natives do not understand (comp. chap. i.).

In Australia a short song of one or two lines easily
spreads from tribe to tribe until the last, which may speak
a quite different language, does not in the least understand
what it is really singing.[3] The songs lose a good deal
of their popularity if in use for a long time. Thus we
Europeans do not seem to be the only ones who get blunt
in musical matters. The Narrinyeri tribes are skilful in
the utterance of emotions by sounds. They will admire
a " foreign " corrobberree simply for the sound of it, not
understanding a word of the meaning. They may not be
able to define the feelings which the corrobberree expresses,
but yet they will learn it with great appreciation if it seems
to express something which their own composition does
not.[4] The Port Lincoln tribes have a variety of songs, all
consisting of only two or three verses each. If the proper
metre or number of cadences be but observed, they care
little or nothing for the meaning of the words of the song,
which they generally do not understand.[5]

Among the Indians of N. America meaningless words are
especially in use. Of course this is not alike with all the
tribes, but in trying to give a general description of their
songs we may combine the statements of the numerous
writers on this subject in the following sketch : Dances and

[1] Langsdorf, *l. c.*, ii. p. 303.   [2] Schelling, *l. c.*, p. 81.
[3] Lumholtz, *l. c.*, pp. 156, 238; Oldfield, *l. c.*, pp. 256-258.
[4] Taplin, in Wood, *l. c.*, p. 143.   [5] *Ibid.*

songs seem merely a succession of sounds and motions without any fixed system. Pounding on rude drums of hide accompanies the songs, which are sung *without words,* and in which some travellers pretend to have detected some savage melody.[1] In singing some tribes use the sounds "hi, ah," no intelligible words being uttered.[2] They commence in a low tone and gradually swell to a full, round, and beautifully modulated chorus.[3] Among other tribes the songs are monotonous chants,[4] extending over but few notes, varied by occasional howls and whoops in some of the more spirited melodies.[5] Choruses are always executed with great exactness in spite of the large number of singers.[6] The words are often borrowed from other tribes without being understood; [7] the songs themselves are "not deficient in harmony,"[8] while they have no melody.[9] Chinook songs (Chinook proper is spoken on the Lower Columbia River) have a text which the natives mostly do not understand.[10] The meaning of the serpent song of the Passamaquoddy Indians is unknown, as the words belong to an obsolete or to a secret language.[11] The Sioux Indians commenced their singing in a low tone, gradually raising it for a few minutes, then closing it suddenly with a shrill yell; after a slight interruption they recommenced the same air, which they sang without any variation for nearly three-quarters of an hour. This was accompanied by a few unmeaning words.[12]

Side by side with these meaningless songs there are also solo songs with a definite subject, and these sometimes occur among the natives of one and the same tribe.

[1] Bancroft, *l. c.*, i. p. 281.   [2] Parker, *Explor. Tour.*, p. 241.
[3] Townsend, *Narr.*, p. 106.   [4] Sproat, *Scenes*, p. 64.
[5] Bancroft, *l. c.*, i. p. 201.   [6] Cook, *Voy. to Pac.*, ii. p. 310.
[7] Jewitt, *Nar.*, p. 87 ; text of a war-song, *l. c.*, p. 97.
[8] *Ibid.*   [9] C. Grant, *l. c.*, p. 306.
[10] Boas, *Chinook Songs*, *l. c.*, p. 244.
[11] Fewkes, *l. c.*, p. 263 (mus. example).
[12] Keating, *l. c.*, i. p. 438.

Many travellers, Catlin in particular, have been puzzled by the occurrence of the word "Hallelujah" in Indian songs, and made use of it as one of the reasons for the Indians originating from the ten lost tribes of Israel (comp. p. 51). Mr. de Monts, who accurately observed the text, says about it : At first they sang "halvet ho ho he," then the general outcry followed " E," then again " Egrigna han he hu," and at last the ominous " Tameia allelujah tameia don veni han han he he". From this Mr. de Monts draws the conclusion—unintelligible to me—that this song was sung in praise of the devil.[1] Mr. Adair also heard the word, and adds that the Indians never repeat at any other time the words they sing in their religious dances. He concludes, therefore, that the meaning of this divine hymn must have got lost.[2] The most probable suggestion, however, is that of Mr. Tylor, who calls our attention to the fact that the word is combined of such syllables as frequently occur in so many similar words of the most different nations of the globe.[3]

The Macusi Indians in Guiana amuse themselves for hours with singing a monotonous song, whose words, hai-a, hai-a, have no further significance.[4]

Speaking of the Iroquois Mr. Morgan says that their war-songs are in a dead language, or, at all events, they are unable to interpret them. "They are in regular verses or measured sentences, and are learned by them with the dance originally."[5] Mr. Baker, too, observed the meaninglessness of the Indian songs, making the additional remark that primitive man could only be satisfied with such simple utterances as long as his mind was too little developed.[6] I think, however, this fact must have a deeper psychological source, for even we sing our meaning-

---

[1] Monts, *l. c.*, chap. vi. p. 861. [2] Adair, *l. c.*, p. 97.
[3] Tylor, *Prim. Cult.*, 2nd edit., i. p. 189. [4] Schomburgk, *l. c.*, p. 274.
[5] Morgan, *l. c.*, p. 2 ff. [6] Th. Baker, *l. c.*, p. 7.

less tra la la, etc., without being in the least disturbed by
its having no signification whatever.

For the present the above facts may serve to prove the
following conclusions :—

1. In primitive times vocal music is not at all a union
of poetry and music.   We find, on the contrary, vocal
music among tribes which owing to the insufficient development of language cannot possibly have any kind of poetry.
Thus the position of vocal music is quite independent of
any other art.

2. It is impossible that in these cases music arose as
a direct imitation of the natural accent ready made in
speech, because these texts are neither themselves a
language, nor could the melody *alone* have been taken
from a developed language, for in such a case the words
would have been borrowed together with the music.
Entirely meaningless words simply serve to facilitate the
vocalisation.

Another striking feature of these savage songs is the
liberty with which the composer treats the grammatical
structure of the sentence and the logical order of words.
Thus in most of the Andamanese songs the words in their
poetic form are so mutilated to suit the metre as to be
scarcely recognisable ; indeed, it not unfrequently happens
that the composer of a new song has to explain its meaning
in the ordinary vernacular to his chorus as well as to the
audience in general.[1]   I am afraid that modern composers,
too, would do well to take the same trouble in explaining
their songs to the public as the Andamanese composer, for
they treat the words with the same carelessness.   It may
be allowed to ask, how in such cases the composer can
have followed the natural modulation of the words, how
from this can music have arisen if the composer had to
change the words, their form, sense, etc., in order to adapt

[1] E. H. Man, *l. c.*, p. 119 ; Portman, *l. c.*, pp. 185, 193.

them to his music? Evidently the musical modulation (the tune) was an accomplished fact in this case, originating elsewhere, before the composition of the poem began.

In Australia many of the natives cannot even give an interpretation of the songs of their own districts—not to say of others—and most of the explanations they give are very imperfect, as "the measures or quantities of the syllables appear to be more attended to than the sense ".[1] If negroes sing they keep strict time and do not allow themselves to be hindered by any obstacle in the use of words. The most obstinate Scripture texts and well-known passages in hymns must be adapted to any melody.[2] Now, even in Bach's, Handel's, Haydn's, and Mozart's time the Bible text had to undergo similar treatment.

As a rule savages do not understand how to invent and to compose a long connected story or a complete poem; they simply take up any current event, put it into two or three strophes and repeat this several times. Mr. Lumholtz relates this of the natives on Herbert River in Australia,[3] and it is elucidated by many examples of Grey's.[4] Europeans, and their whole behaviour and appearance, are frequently the subject of these songs. They are usually performed in the form of question and answer, the chorus being a mere repetition of one or two words.[5] Music in Samoa was a monotonous chant of a line or two repeated over and over again, with no variety beyond two or three notes. "They sought variety rather in time. The singers began slow and gradually increased until, at the end of ten or twenty minutes, they were full of excitement, the perspiration streaming down, and their tongues galloping over the rhyme at breathless speed." [6] Speaking of the Ainu, Mr. Siebold says he heard them

---

[1] Eyre, *l. c.*, ii. p. 229 ; Catlin, i. p. 216; Dieffenbach, *l. c.*, ii. p. 57.
[2] Allen, War, etc., *l. c.*, p. iv.   [3] Lumholtz, *l. c.*, pp. 156, 238.
[4] Grey, *Austr.*, p. 310.   [5] Eyre, *l. c.*, ii. pp. 239-240.
[6] Turner, *Samoa*, p. 125 ; *Poly.*, p. 211.

singing in a hoarse voice while they were paddling, or at
night on horseback. Their songs were of a plaintive
character, very short, and repeated several times.[1] Mr.
Lesseps tells us of a Kamchadales song whose words
were : " Daria (a Russian female name) sings and dances
still ". The eight bars of which it consisted were repeated
almost without ceasing.[2] Mr. Burckhart heard a national
song of the Arabian women whose first line was repeated five
or six times by the leading chorus and then echoed by the
other parties. In the same manner the second line was
sung ; but the third, which always contained the name of
some distinguished warrior, was repeated as often as fifty
times. The ladies, however, pronounced that name in
such a manner as to render it difficult for the men, who
listened, to know who was the happy mortal.[3] The most
of the Kafirs' songs consist of only a few words which they
repeat over and over again, with such musical variation
as their national task or individual fancy may dictate.[4]
The songs in Kamerun are but a constant repetition of
the same sentence, provided they have an actual text with
some meaning in it.[5] Mr. Poole heard on Queen Charlotte
Islands (the northern of the two groups in the Pacific
Ocean) two favourite songs, of which the first—kept within
the compass of five tones—was repeated four times and
ended in a chorus ; the second was a mere repetition of the
tone " B," while the words of both had no meaning.[6]

If we ask for the reasons of these constant repetitions
in primitive poetry and music, we shall have to answer
that primitive man lacks the power of elaborating the
outcome of his fancy to a complete work of art. The
circle of ideas he has is too limited in comparison with

---

[1] Siebold, *l. c.*, p. 48.

[2] Lesseps, *l. c.*, i. p. 104. Daria is also the usual Central Asian term for
a river.

[3] Burckhart, *l. c.*, p. 47.　　　[4] Grout, *l. c.*, p. 193, with examples.

[5] Buchner, *Kamer.*, p. 29.　　　[6] F. Poole, *l. c.*, p. 322.

the abundance of feelings. The child is in precisely the same position; as soon as it produces a rhyme on the spur of the moment, it begins to repeat it several times; by this it works itself up to the necessary mood or disposition of mind which its limited intelligence cannot supply with sufficient variety of ideas. After all, every lyric poet gives us one idea only, but always repeating it in other words and new combinations.

Still, even savages attain the higher forms of poetry at times, and this quite apart from dramatic representations, which are to them, from the very beginning, the natural example of a complete work of art. Thus some songs of the Australians have texts of a comparatively advanced kind, and although monotonous repetitions are not at all avoided, there is still a definite idea clearly expressed.[1] Topinard says of these songs : " Les paroles en roulent sur des sentiments doux, plus souvent sur des idées de vengeance et de représailles, et se transmettent de père en fils et de tribus en tribus verbalement ".[2] Many of the original Maori songs, too, contain very beautiful ideas ; the metre is difficult to describe, there being no regular measure of verse ; the chief object is to make the lines suit their tunes. They have songs on every subject, love, war, as well as incantations, laments, traditions,[3] nursery and boat songs.[4] Night is the favourite time for the Maori orator to make speeches ; he waits until all is still in the " pa," and then stepping forth from his house and marching in front of it sings in a loud, shrill tone some old song which bears on the subject he is going to speak upon. His speeches are generally answered by another, and thus the discussion is kept up during the best part of the night.[5]

Among the Hottentots the mother praises her child in

---

[1] The best collection of Australian songs (words) by Grey, *Austr.*, p. 310 *seq.*

[2] Topinard, *L'Austr.*, p. 72. [3] R. Taylor, *l. c.*, p. 306.

[4] Dieffenbach, *l. c.*, ii. p. 27. [5] R. Taylor, *l. c.*, p. 343.

a song, touching and kissing all the parts she is going to sing about.[1] Bushmen, Hottentots, and Waganda have animal fables that betray no little talent for close observation.[2] Mr. Gardiner mentions some hunting- and war-songs of the Kafirs. Every song, he says, has a different air; a few are humorous and colloquial, the women being asked questions to which they respond. Others are danced by the men and directed by the king himself, while the women in the centre raise their voices to the highest pitch. At the end of a song the king s heralds run along the lines always shouting O, O, O, to indicate its conclusion.[3] So simple, not to say vulgar, are the words to the songs of many tribes that one might doubt how from so primitive a beginning our highest poetical ideals could have arisen. And yet they did so arise, although even so natural a subject as love seems to indicate a higher state of progress in poetry. At all events we have not found sufficient examples for Mr. Engel's assertion "that love-songs should be found all over the world is only what might be expected".[4] For, contrary to all expectations, we find some tribes which do not know this kind-of poetry; those on the Lower Congo have it, but they sing equally frequently on war, hunting, and palm-wine.[5] The songs of the Hassanyeh tribes on the White Nile are sung in praise of a favourite member of the tribe, or they are narrations of a love adventure, or they praise one of the present European-visitors.[6] The Haussa have songs with beautiful texts, recited "extempore" by a singer, the burden being sung by the chorus.[7] When the Joruba of the Sudan are beaten in battle by the Haussa, they at once make a poem in which they sing of their own power, the dread of the enemy, and their victory, while in reality

---

[1] Hahn, *l. c.*, p. 2; Ploss, *Das Kind*, ii. p. 76.
[2] Ratzel, *l. c.*, i. p. 466.   [3] A. Gardiner, *l. c.*, p. 59.
[4] Engel, *Nat. Mus.*, p. 304.   [5] Tuckey, *l. c.*, p. 373.
[6] Petherick, *l. c.*, p. 139.   [7] Lander, *Rec. Clapp.*, i. p. 296.

the Haussa were the victors.[1] The Badagrians sing during
the human sacrifices. The victim is given a bottle of rum,
and while he drinks it he is slain from behind. Then his
heart is cut out of the body, and while still warm and
bleeding is presented to the king, who, as well as his chief
wives, bite into it. Then it is carried about in the village
and the following song sung by the people :—

> As we gaze upon the slain
> Courage mounts in every vein :
> Hearts of iron, breasts of steel,
> Bold Badagrians reveal.[2]

The songs of the Murzuk (Sahara), played by women
on the erbab, or by young Arabs, are all pretty and of
plaintive character ; the language of the Sudanese, on the
whole, sounds very musical, while the words are long
connected stories.[3]

Among the Sioux Indians of North America lullabies
are in use.[4] On Nukahiva Mr. Langsdorf heard a typical
representation of a warlike scene. One of the people saw
at night a fire upon an enemy's island and asked, Where
is the fire? The others answered, Upon Tanata. This
excited the idea of battle and revenge on one hand, and of
pity and melancholy on the other, ending with the thought
of the time they would be able to feed on human flesh.[5]
On Samoa, too, some songs have the form of question and
answer sung by two parties ; and thus they go on singing
as they walk along the road, or paddle the canoe, or do
any other piece of work. These songs often contain
sarcastic remarks, and in passing the house or village of
parties with whom they are displeased they strike up a
chant embodying some offensive ideas. " Their bitter,

[1] Lander, *Rec. Clapp.*, i. pp. 289-290.   [2] *Ibid.*, ii. pp. 260-263.
[3] Lyon, *l. c.*, p. 173.
[4] Greenwood, *l. c.*, p. 17 ; Ploss, *Das Kind*, ii. p. 76.
[5] Langsdorf, *l. c.*, i. p. 164 *seq.*

venomous songs lead even to war." [1]   The natives on
Tahiti have historical ballads; the children are early
taught the "ubus," songs referring to the legends or
achievements of the gods.   Their traditionary ballads are
a kind of standard or classical authority, to which they
refer for the purpose of determining any disputed fact in
their history. [2]   Speaking of the negritos on Philippine
Islands Mr. Schadenberg mentions a song whose words
were: "We are poor men, and lead a miserable life". [3]   It
is very seldom that savages are aware of the miserable
condition they are living in.

The songs of the Kamchadales do not celebrate the
death of heroic ancestors, nor the adventures of hunt and
war; they are ballads of a melancholic, fanciful character,
apparently inspired by sadness, love, and domestic feelings.
The music has a wild, strange sound, reminding us of woe
and sorrow, and as if it would contain the memory of a
happy past that has gone by for ever. [4]   I do not know
whether Mr. Kennan, who made this remark, did not put
more feeling into the music than it actually contained,
but he expressly assures us that the song "Penjinski," as
sung by the inhabitants of Lesnoi, more particularly expressed the above character.   Their dance melodies, however, are said to be very jolly, containing some "staccato"
passages, which are repeated many times without any
variety.

The union of words and music assumes at times a
quite different form, resembling our "recitative".   Upon
the fact that this recitative does not occur in the *most*
primitive state of culture I have to lay special emphasis,
if for no other reason than that it requires a comparatively
developed language.   When it occurs, however, the more
primitive form of choral dances is to be found at the same

---

[1] Turner, *Polyn.*, p. 345. [2] Ellis, *Pol. Res.*, i. p. 286.
[3] Schadenberg, *l. c.*, p. 145. [4] Kennan, *l. c.*, p. 161.

time. These two distinct classes of songs, the choral
dance song and the solo song (recitative), we have been
able to follow throughout the book. Among some tribes
the recitative form is in itself impossible : " The Barea
and Bazena (in the Kunáma country, Abyssinia), who
possess a large number of wise laws, have many songs,
and more melodies than all their neighbours. Their night
song, ' Goila,' is renowned far and wide. The recitative
which is peculiar to the Tigré and Tóbedauie is entirely
unfit for the character of the language." [1] An important
statement as to the "recitative" is also made by Mr.
Portman in his treatise on Andamanese music. " The
singing of the Andamanese is in regular duple time. This
is more particularly marked in the choruses, when you
have the rhythmical accompaniment. The continuance
of one note, or of a sequence of notes a little distance
apart, which is an attribute of Oriental music, often leads
persons *who do not know the meaning of the word* to call
Andamanese solos ' recitative,' which term, as meaning
musical declamation, *does not in the least apply*." Examples
like this form one of the strongest arguments against Mr.
Spencer's speech-theory, according to which music arose
from emotional speech, and the recitative was its most
primitive form. As to the subjects of the Andamanese
songs, Mr. Portman says they had no religious, no nursery,
and no love-songs, the principal subject being pig hunting,
fish shooting, turtle and dugong spearing, fighting, making
boats, bows, etc. " The music, rhythm, accent, and intonation, is no clue to the sense of the song, and a person
not knowing the language would be ignorant as to whether
a fight, hunt, or the making of a boat was being described." [2]

Thomson explicitly mentions the recitative. His

---

[1] Munzinger, *l. c.*, p. 535 ; Tigré is one of the chief languages of Abyssinia, consequently highly developed (*ibid.*, p. 539); so also is the Bedouin
language Tóbedauie (*ibid.*, p. 341).

[2] Portman, *l. c.*, p. 184.

Zanzibar porters were distinguished by a wonderful " elasticity of spirits"; they danced, sang, and beat time with their hands, and they also performed recitatives accompanied by cheery shouts.[1]   Guessfeldt describes a festival at Nkondo which consisted of dances, rhythmic songs, and beating of drums.   During this an individual arose and improvised a few lines, which the chorus answered.[2]   The social and domestic songs of the Joruba and Borghus are recitatives and the exact opposite of their public and national songs.[3]   At Katafungi (West Africa) Lander heard the natives sing : " It appeared to be something comical, in the form of a recitative, to which they kept time by clapping their hands ". [4]

The Malays of Sumatra ("the Italians of the Orient ") amuse themselves during their leisure hours with songs which are a sort of proverb, a description of events in their daily life.   Many of these are carefully practised ; they are recitatives and are produced at festivals, while others are extemporised.[5]   Such extemporisations by individual singers are repeated during pauses in a regular choral song, with which, indeed, they alternate ; they are therefore neither the only kind of music they possess nor the most primitive, but are merely a certain connection between music and a more coherent and developed speech and poetry.   This difference in the two forms of music found among so many savage tribes is clearly preserved in later periods of culture where the kind of recitative, as is usual during religious service, is taken by so many writers for the most primitive form of music.   This is quite an error.   Even the ancient Armenians recognise a

---

[1] Thomson, *Centr. Afr. Lak.*, i. p. 96.

[2] Guessfeldt, *Loango*, p. 76.   Nkondo Ndindshi in Mayombe, West Africa.

[3] Lander, *Rec. of Clapp.*, i. p. 290.

[4] *Ibid.*, p. 256.

[5] Marsden, *l. c.*, p. 197.

difference between the recitation of the Psalms and the singing of them, and both of these systems were in use in divine service.[1] Ibn Khaldun, an Arabian writer in the final period of Arabian rule in Spain ("the Montesquieu of the Orient"), says that the Arabs were in former days well acquainted with the art of improvisation, while song and music generally were in a very rude state. Later only, when they learned more of foreign culture, did they designate modulation of the voice " Song," and distinguish it from the declamation of the Koran and their prayers, which they called "Taghjir".[2] I would here remark that they read the Koran in a sort of recitative, and that they made a difference between this and real song, which at all times has been something other than recitatival improvisation.

It sometimes happens that in speaking the excitement of passion leads to rising modulations of the voice. An example of this is given by Martius. " When the Botocudo longs for and passionately demands anything he raises his voice to a monotonous song. It is as though the poverty of his expression would be retrieved by the increased power of sound."[3] Guessfeldt, too, says : " Negroes are excellent orators and speak for hours together without tiring. At times their speech becomes a sort of singing recitative, in which sounds of a plaintive melody may be remarked, and in which those around join."[4] These examples, however, demonstrate but the truth of what they themselves say, that when excited we modulate our voices more under certain circumstances ; but not until music has arisen from other sources is this modulation of speech recognised as being akin to musical

[1] Petermann, *l. c.*, p. 366 ; Armenian musical annotation (alphabet) by Schröder, *l. c.*, p. 243 ; mus exampl., *ibid.*, pp. 370-371.
[2] Kiesewetter, *l. c.*, p. 10.
[3] Martius, *l. c.*, p. 330 note.
[4] Guessfeldt, *Loango*, p. 84.

modulation, and transformed into melody and song.   That
this transformation of speech into song is no proof of the
origin of music and of language is made clear by the fact
that there are equally good examples to the contrary in
existence, from which, however, no one has drawn any
definite conclusion as to the origin of language from music.
How often does a composer sink himself deeply into the
mood which governs him, until he at length finds words
which enable him to exactly express his intention !   (Beethoven's 9th symphony.)   Examples in musical history are
both so numerous and so generally known that I need not
give any here.   Moreover, it sometimes happens that the
singer, too, allows the melody to drop, as it were, in order
to *speak* a certain word or even a sentence, because the
effect points to a definite idea, and it is just in this definiteness that the acme of expression lies.   The one is
psychologically as correct as the other, for all depends upon
one's object.   From an artistic standpoint one can say that
music must always remain music, speech remain speech,
but as a matter of fact, in every-day life, ordinary speech
changes to musical modulation as often as musical modulation to ordinary speech.   In the Indian drama, which
was originally sung, song has later on been replaced by
speech ;[1] *there we have an example of song changing to speech.*
A kind of *spoken song*—in *ordinary*, and not only in that of
passionate conversation—was much more common in primitive culture than is now the case.   Oddly enough, those
people among whom speech-song was most common—the
Indo-Chinese (Japanese)—have not progressed in the
development of music ; the emotional element of speech
being laid in subjection by the intellectual.   Their music
is for them nothing but a trifle.   *Thither then has this song-
speech led them, historically, and in fact : to Scholasticism, to
a surrogate of Science, not to Art,* least of all to Music in our
meaning of the word.

[1] Lassen, *l. c.*, ii. p. 504.

Cadence and accent are characteristic signs of the Chinese tongue, and all Indo-Chinese races have embodied them in their own language. That of the Siamese is the richest in cadence, that of the Burmese has less, while the Cambodian languages and the spoken tongues of the Laos have none at all. In the native Hokken (Fo-kiëen) pronouncing dictionaries, the Chinese characters are divided into eight classes to correspond with the number of tones. In Burma or Siam mere modulation of the voice may completely alter the meaning of a word.[1] Japanese ambassadors used to sing at the receptions at European courts.[2] The Dahomian language, called Ffou by the people, and Lingoageral by the Portuguese, is, like the Popo, one of the poorest and least developed tongues of the great and rich Joruban family; and it is just this poor tongue that, like the Chinese, largely depends upon the cadence: the word which we write " so " means there " to-day," " to-morrow," " a horse," " bring " (imp. verb and root), " thunder," " a stick," according to the modulation of the voice. One and the same word " do " has a dozen different meanings.[3] It is significant that the importance of the cadence in more developed languages is lost. Even originally the connection between cadence and meaning was not intuitive, in the sense that a certain inflection " belonged directly and of itself to particular emotions " ; the comprehension of it rested both ontogenetically and phylogenetically on experience and reciprocal agreement.[4] Mr. Foster noticed this singing in speech (without, however, mentioning if it influenced the meaning of the word) on the islands Amsterdam and Middleburgh,[5] as did Wilkes in

---

[1] Bastian, *On the Ind.-Chin. Alph.*, *l. c.*   [2] Billert, *l. c.*

[3] R. F. Burton, *Notes on Dahom.*, p. 313.

[4] On the importance of cadence in primitive languages, the musicians especially ought to compare Mr. Tylor's most valuable researches in *Prim. Cult.*, i. p. 151.

[5] Foster, *l. c.*, p. 425 ; *Pink. Collect.*, vol. xi. p. 678.

Tierra del Fuego.[1]   This, however, is less surprising on solemn occasions, such as, for instance, the announcement of a victory in a wrestling match.[2]   The Fiji islanders explain by a humorous legend their practice of tattooing *among men instead of among women*, as in Tonga.   The messenger who reported the custom from Tonga got it by heart and repeated it in his *singing tone ;* but on the journey he struck his foot against a stump, and in consequence sang the message exactly reversed.[3]   May we then conclude that in this place a singing tone in the speech was usual in the case of ordinary announcements ?   The Narrinyeri tribes in Australia have, in the place of " yes," a kind of guttural grunt, and the same sound with a different inflection means " no ".   In addition, they have many unarticulated tones which take the place of our interjections.   Thus " kai-hai " is an expression of surprise ; the women say " kaw-kah-kah " when they greet their friends—it sounds " like an old crow ".[4]

Baker has shown by numerous musical examples the existence among North American Indians of two different forms of music : the recitative, and the rhythmic choral song.   In his opinion the latter is the older form of the two for the following reasons :

1. The characteristic feature of primitive song was the collectiveness of amusement.   2. We find an unbroken line beginning with simple rhythmic songs up to accomplished strictly measured airs (he quotes thirty-two examples written down by himself, and eleven quoted by other writers).   3. The rhythmic form has been mentioned by almost every writer upon the subject of North American Indians.   4. Such recitatives have a flow of words and a clearness of expression which are both incompatible with primitive song.[5]

---

[1] Wilkes, *l. c.*, i. p. 125.   [2] *Pink. Collect.*, vol. xi. p. 680.
[3] Williams, *l. c.*, p. 138.   [4] Taplin, in Wood, *l. c.*, p. 143.
[5] Th. Baker, *l. c.*, p. 47.

CHAPTER VII.

DANCE AND MUSIC.

It is scarcely possible to speak of the beginning of music without at the same time thinking of the dances with which it was so intimately connected. This is, moreover, no accidental connection that can under certain circumstances be omitted as in the case of poetry and music; it is more than a mere connection, it is a unified organism which later led to an independent musical branch, so unified that it is neither possible to treat of the subject of primitive dance without primitive music, nor to make it even probable by means of ethnological examples that they ever were separated.[1] In regard to this, Richard Wagner was undoubtedly on the right track—as he always was when following the bent of his genius—when he traced the original form of music to the dance. But I believe that he erred in his further investigations of this idea in placing the art of poetry third in the order of original art-forms (he even suggested the spelling " Tichtkunst " instead " Dichtkunst " for the sake of analogy with " Tanzkunst " and " Tonkunst ").[2] Later arisen, and in spite of emotional influences always depending upon our intellect, poetry preserved an independent position, which afforded all sorts of connecting links but admitted of no organic unity. So in primitive culture there existed

---

[1] " In Africa dancing cannot be separated from singing, just as it is impossible to separate the colour from the skin. An African would not live for a week without this amusement." (Lander, *Rec. of Clapp.*, i. p. 293.)

[2] R. Wagner, *l. c.*, iii. p. 122.

not only poetry without music (which in the case of the dance would be quite inconceivable) but also *vocal* music without poetry, without even words, while the recitative and "speech-song," which was a hybrid of comparatively late date, had been proved to be incapable of further development.   It was, too, only later that vocal music became a combination of two different arts, while dance music is and remains a whole, and as such is subject to the common fate of all development.   We must not think of "dance" always in the exclusively modern sense, but in the sense of regular ordered movements, not rarely coupled with pantomime, even in the most primitive state. By way of explaining this we will give a few general ethnological observations on the subject of the dance.

Mr. Corry relates that in Africa dancing takes place every night, and that every village resounds again with song and music after sunset.   Villages situated a league apart often sing alternately the same song for hours together, and the youth of both sexes listen to the far-reaching sounds with rapt attention and manifest pleasure.   On every occasion of joy or sadness dancing is indulged in.   There are monotone songs, at times tender and pleasing, at others wild and stormy, but always accompanied by slow movements.[1]   Mr. Webster describes the Hottentot dance as a "ludicrous shuffling," and the music of the gourah as being like "Neil Gow's fiddle," which "made the Scottish maidens beat with their heels".[2] A few dancers, grasping the doorposts, beat time, while others lean on chairs and stamp with their feet, both being an expression arising from the necessity for regular movements.   When the Bechuana wish to dance they arrange themselves in a circle; each dancer blows his reed-pipe at any interval that may seem most agreeable to him. Around the dancers is an outer circle of women and

---

[1] Corry, *l. c.*, p. 153.   [2] Foster, *l. c.*, i. pp. 275-276.

girls who follow each movement and beat time by clapping their hands.[1] This same desire for regular rhythm we find, too, among the Makalaka, who accompany their dances with drums and songs, the performance itself reminding one strongly of a European quadrille.[2] The Makololo dance with so much excitement and wildness that their dance resembles a scene in a lunatic asylum. They frequently asked if the whites also dance, and Livingstone gave them such an account as did not leave them to form a very high opinion of Europeans.[3] The natives of Obbo began their dance by all singing together a wild but pleasant-sounding melody in chorus. Time was marked by a big drum, and all the small drums entered so precisely at the right moment that the effect was that of a single instrument.[4] The Wanyamwezi (East Africa) accompany their wild springs and foot-stamping—which they call "a dance"—with songs and the beating of drums, the Sidis with hand-clapping, foot-stamping, and sing in strict time and with unmistakable gratification.[5] In this matter the Ovambo are more easily satisfied, for their dance is a mere procession.[6] The dances of the Sudanese soldiers so closely resembled the *can can* of the "Jardin Mabille" as to make Mr. Long suggest that the latter may have originated in Africa.[7] The Barâbras in Upper Egypt are quite artists in the elaboration of new striking, rhythmical effects. At their dances they simultaneously beat a different rhythm with their hands and with their feet.[8] At Katunga (in the Joruba country, Western Sudan) the natives make such extraordinary jumps into the air during their dances that one might almost believe they had no bones.[9] At Wowo ninety to a hundred

[1] Wood, *l. c.*, i. p. 329.
[2] Mauch, *l. c.*, p. 43.
[3] Livingstone, *l. c.*, p. 225.
[4] Baker, *Albert Nyanza*, i. p. 314.
[5] Grant, *l. c.*, p. 66.
[6] Ratzel, *l. c.*, i. p. 356.
[7] Ch. Long, *l. c.*, p. 71.
[8] Villoteau, *l. c.*, p. 128.
[9] Lander, *Rec. of Clapp.*, i. p. 115.

women arranged some religious processions in which they
marched in time to the music of the drums and fifes and
sang with their shrill voices.   They went in pairs, carrying
boughs which they waved in time; it is said to have been
a grotesque spectacle.[1]   Mr. Moore relates that the
negresses are always very pleased when a white man
will dance and drink with them, but if the drink is mixed
by a European whom they do not know they will always
make him take the first draught in fear of poison.[2]   The
dances on the Canary Islands are in some respects of
the greatest importance for us.   The original population
(Guanches) were the only savages who danced " deux a
deux " as we do in our dances.[3]

From the above facts we may once more conclude that
all the dances depend upon time, and this is quite as much
a psychological as a physical requirement; the psychological need, like everything psychical in man, is a product
of social character, and as all dances are of a social nature
these compel the individual to introduce the necessary
order and arrangement for a number of onlookers and
participants.   The physical requirement arises from the
necessity of dissipating our surplus energy by some self-
selected activity.   Necessity of time and movement, music
and dance, are, like interior and exterior, two different
sides of one and the same thing.

Examples from primitive people of all continents con-
firm what has already been said.   In a rich and complete
collection of Australian dances Mr. B. Smyth has drawn
attention to the accord of the regular dances with the
music.[4]   The most interesting ones take place when one
tribe invites another.   " It is surprising to see the perfect
time that is kept in this way, and the admirable manner

[1] Lander, *Rec. of Clapp.*, ii. p. 121.   [2] *Astley Coll.*, ii. p. 280.
[3] Barker and Berthelot, *Hist. Nat. Can.*, vol. i. part i. p. 155;
Berthelot, *Memoir*, p. 202.
[4] B. Smyth, *l. c.*, pp. 166-176.

in which the motions of the dancers accord with the
music. There is no confusion, irregularity, or mistake." [1]
When some gifted individual has invented a new dance or
song a grand merry-making is resolved on. Friends and
enemies are alike welcome, and all animosity is buried
during the festivities.[2] Primitive art thus brings about
easily what no other power can do, and so strikingly
exemplifies the fact that art, quite unconsciously and
unintentionally, is the noblest and most effective source
of moral impulse.

We have already (in chap. i.) spoken of the great
rhythmic effect of the Maori war-dance. It looks so
terrible that the peaceable natives of Tahiti who witnessed
it on board ship ran away in terror.[3]

Cook mentions a dance in Tongatabu to which a chorus
of forty to sixty men made up the musical accompaniment, reciting sentences while dancing, and with such
precision as to give the impression of a performance of a
single man.[4] Cook speaks in a similar strain of a dance
in Hapai, where numerous dancers seemed to act as if
they were one huge machine.[5] On the Marquesas Islands
song and dance were accompanied by hand-clapping;[6]
here too it was remarked that time was most strictly kept.
On Hawaii there were some troops of singers and dancers
who performed their art for payment.[7] Mr. A. B. Meyer
relates of the dances and songs of the negritos in the
Philippines, " that they are confined to mere jumping in a
circle round a girl and stamping with the feet. The same
meaningless phrase is repeated in a monotonous manner
in the same way as is usual with other savage tribes, as,
e.g., in Celebes and in the Bay of Tomini." [8]

[1] Eyre, *l. c.*, ii. pp. 229-241.   [2] Oldfield, *l. c.*, pp. 256-258.
[3] Beechey, *l. c.*, i. p. 222.
[4] Cook, *Third Voyage*, iii. p. 295 ; *Pink. Coll.*, xi. pp. 678-679.
[5] Cook, *ibid.*, i. p. 248; *Pink. Coll.*, xi. p. 667.   [6] Meinicke, *l. c.*, p. 255.
[7] *Ibid.*, ii. p. 306.   [8] A. B. Meyer, *Negritos*, p. 21.

One of the commonest dances on the Caroline Islands strongly resembles the French *branle de Capucins*, and it too is accompanied by a monotonous song;[1] the melody quoted by Freycinet is more French than native. The inhabitants of Radak perform their song-dance in the evening while sitting in a circle round a brightly burning fire. Great delight is manifested by every one, and all voices unite in a chorus. Such songs resemble those of the people on Owaihi, but are ruder and more distorted, as it were, the ever-increasing sounds of the song eventually degenerating into a howl.[2] The most popular, and in fact the sole, property of these people is their "boats and drums, which also serve as playthings for their children". When the natives of Batavia perform their "missari" dance they arrange themselves in two rows, move their bodies from right to left while swinging their arms in circles in opposite directions. Then they sing a slow, plaintive song accompanied by a number of gongs of various sizes.[3] In speaking of the Papuan dances in New Guinea, Mr. Rosenberg says: "*De dans beteekent bitter weinig en heeft veel van bokkesprongen, waarbij men achteruit huppelt*".[4] Among the Dyaks of Borneo Mr. Bock found dances and songs performed together when a child was born;[5] their sword dance, to which the strictest time was kept, was also accompanied by music.[6] In Ceylon Mr. Davy witnessed a dance at which the natives clapped their hands as they jumped and nodded their heads, throwing their long entangled forelocks from behind over their faces. This strange dance was accompanied by a rude kind of song.[7]

[1] Freycinet, *l. c.*, ii. p. 121 ; mus. exampl., ii. p. 398.

[2] Chamisso, *l. c.*, p. 115 ; I am sorry I cannot explain to the reader how one can dance while sitting, but Chamisso is express in saying: "sitzender Liedertanz".

[3] Bickmoore, *l. c.*, p. 190.   [4] Rosenberg, *l. c.*, p. 93.

[5] Bock, *l. c.*, p. 78.   [6] Keppel, *l. c.*, i. p. 63.

[7] Davy, *l. c.*, p. 118.

In describing the dances of the South Sea Islanders the Tahiti myth of the cocoa-nut tree may, perhaps, be mentioned. According to it, Tiniran, "the king of all fish," decoyed all the fish of the sea to him, which changed their forms into a partial resemblance to human beings and gladly united in their dance with him, who was himself in his true attribute half man and half fish. Koro, his son, secretly listened to his father's invocation, attracted the fish, danced with them, and then taught the natives of Mangaia the mysteries of dancing.[1]

The hill tribes of Assam (India) have dances that are quite typical for the primitive state of this art. The musicians are placed in the midst of a circle, the dancers leap around and at intervals drink a sort of rice beer. The longer the dance lasts the wilder it becomes, until one musician after another drops off and finally sleeps the sleep of the intoxicated until daybreak.[2] The Kachénzes (Tatars in Siberia, governments of Tomsk and Yeniseisk, on the right bank of the Abakan River) have dances like those of the Kalmuks, consisting of simple bodily movements kept in strict time.[3]

The dances of the North American Indians are united with songs or instrumental music of the simplest kind. At such entertainments the Indians of the Upper Missouri assume very grave faces that bear such a decided contrast to their rapid movements and burlesque appearance, that a stranger is unable to discover by what sentiments the dances are actuated.[4] This play of the features among Indians has almost invariably puzzled Europeans, and has often given rise to the idea that the Indians are entirely without feeling, a view which close examination has always refuted. Mr. Charlroix described as early as 1721 the war and fire dance of the Mississagas at Cataraqui:

---

[1] Wyatt, *l. c.*, p. 100.   [2] Murray-Ansley, *l. c.*, p. 275.
[3] Georgi, *l. c.*, p. 238.   [4] Perrin du Lac, *l. c.*, p. 75.

The performance lasted all night long by the light of the
fire and the accompaniment of drums and the chichikone.
When the fire was put out one of the dancers danced with
a coal of fire in his mouth, an effect only lately introduced
into modern ballet dances by the aid of electric light.   At
present, Mr. Chamberlain says, these Indians have forgotten all about their dances, and their talent for singing
has been directed to the church, while a short time ago
the Salvation Army " charmed away some of the Indians
into their ranks ".[1]   The Indian dances in New California
are wild and different in every tribe.   The song which is
sung or whistled during the dance is for the most part
without words.   The natives are fond of gambling with
sticks, the number of which is to be guessed ("odd or
even ").[2]

While leaving for another part of this chapter the task
of giving the characteristics of some peculiar Indian
dances, I will continue to describe their general character
by adding a few examples from Central and South America.
The dance of the Klarheywey (Zuñian, South Mexico)
consists of two parts, distinguished by different songs
and different movements.   Both parts are danced to vocal
music, which is in the first part accompanied by a drum,
in the second by a number of horns.[3]   The Iroquois had
thirty-two different dances, twenty-six of which were
entirely original, while only twenty-one are still in use.[4]
They were all accompanied with music, song and dance
alternating.   During a war-dance a war-whoop was given
by the leader and answered by the entire company.   It was
a prolonged sound upon a high note, with a decadence near
the end, followed by an abrupt explosive conclusion, in
which the voice was raised again to the original pitch.[5]
The frequency with which the Iroquois danced in a circle

[1] Chamberlain, *l. c.*, p. 159.   [2] Chamisso, *l. c.*, p. 20.
[3] Fewkes, *Sum. Cem.*, p. 47.   [4] Morgan, *l. c.*, p. 291.
[5] *Ibid.*, p. 272.

caused Baker to think it was meant to represent the course of the sun, which the Indians worship;[1] but we have seen this circular dance among so many tribes and on all continents where the sun is not worshipped, that this conclusion does not necessarily follow. It appears to me rather that the circular form is adopted (if intentionally adopted at all) for the same reason that we have adopted it in our games: to keep the company together, and to concentrate in an equal degree the interest of all participants on the object of the play. Moreover, many kinds of birds dance thus in circles[2] (*e.g.*, *Tetrao phasianellus*) without worshipping the sun.

In ancient Mexico the dances were accompanied by songs and instruments; both began with deep notes which constantly rose in pitch and were accelerated as the pleasure increased.[3]

At Huacho (a town in Peru) the Indians dance in the street in time to the music of a pipe and tabor, to which time is given by small bells tied to the legs. They become so passionately absorbed in their dance that when a second troop of dancers comes up neither will give way to the other to pass until cudgels are brought into requisition.[4] During an Indian festival on the Rio Chico (in Patagonia) the men and women sat down on the grass at different spots, a few old hags singing the while in their melodious way; the music began and four Indians would set off in a quiet march round the fire in strict time with the music. The *tempo* gradually quickened, the men threw off their mantles and exhibited themselves adorned with white paint daubed all over their bodies, each having a girdle of bells (reaching from the shoulder to the hips) which jingled in time to the music.[5]

When preparing for their dances the Caribs and

[1] Th. Baker, *l. c.*, p. 3. [2] On dances of birds *cf.* Darwin, *l. c.*, ii. p. 74.
[3] Clavigero, *l. c.*, p. 400. [4] Stevenson, *l. c.*, i. p. 403.
[5] Musters, *l. c.*, p. 81.

Arawaks paint their whole bodies with figures of snakes, birds, and other animals, while their hair is powdered red, this being done by the women, an occupation which sometimes keeps them busy for days together. The face is covered with carmine, white and yellow stripes.[1] The dances in Guiana are described as being a sort of *carousel* at which those who take part wander round and round in a circle keeping time with monotonous songs, the meaningless text of which is generally " hia-hia-hia ". This movement is now and again interrupted by copious libations which alternate with a round or two of the dance.[2] On the same principle—but minus the drink—is the Warau dance in Guiana.[3]

The Bahama negro dance is full of uncultured grace. A dancer begins accompanied by a tambourine and triangle, while various individuals in the crowd keep time by beating of feet upon the rough floor, and slapping of hands against their legs.[4]

The importance of time and the consequent unity of dance and music is unmistakable among all primitive people. I am almost afraid that my readers will be already wearied by the numerous examples of this kind quoted in this and in other chapters. I cannot, however, alter the facts, and think I am justified in maintaining once more its importance as one of the most weighty results of our ethnological researches.

There are, too, some tribes which have neither original dances nor original music—for instance, the Copper Indians. They borrow their dances from the Dog-ribs Indians (North America), who accompany them with songs. These Indians are in point of fact the dancing masters of the country.[5] Another example of danceless and musicless Indians in South America (chap. i. p. 54) probably rests

---

[1] C. Quandt, *l. c.*, p. 2. [2] Im Thurn, *l. c.*, p. 309.
[3] Wood, *l. c.*, ii. p. 619. [4] Edwards, *l. c.*, p. 524.
[5] Franklin, *l. c.*, p. 291.

upon insufficient investigation or rather on the reticence of the race in expression of their feelings, for even among them, as has already been said, a modest attempt at a dance was noticed. Unfortunately original, harmless, and even useful pleasure of savage dances has often been partially suppressed by the misdirected efforts of culture. Fritsch, at any rate, says that the majority of those Africans who have come in contact with missionaries have been taught to detest dance music.[1] It is hardly possible to attempt the civilisation of those tribes in a more inappropriate way. It is as if a child were forbidden to be a child; by this it would at the same time be deprived of the possibility of becoming a man. Again and again travellers have spoken in most praiseworthy terms of these dances and of the good feeling aroused by their means—thus Burchell (chap. i.). Lander says "the nightly moon-dances in Africa are the most beautiful, most harmless, most peaceful of pleasures possible"; in fact he could not speak too highly of them.[2]

So important and so honourable is participation in the dance considered by many African tribes that even the king himself will take a chief part. He will come out before his subjects and lead a dance, e.g., in Dahomey,[3] among the Kanima,[4] at Wowow and Bussang (Niger).[5] In Manyéma (E. Africa) the dance is the king's prerogative. When he chooses a good-looking woman for a partner the royal invitation to the dance is equivalent to an offer of marriage, and the consequence of such an arrangement is that innumerable complications arise.[6]

"In some cases dances are considered a part of religious rite, just as smoking and intoxication. And this is by no means confined to mere savages. In the middle ages

---

[1] Fritsch, *Die Eingeb.*, p. 191.   [2] Lander, *Rec. of Clapp.*, i. pp. 294-298.
[3] Wood, *l. c.*, i. p. 645.   [4] *Ibid.*, p. 567.
[5] Lander, *Niger*, ii. pp. 175-177.   Cameron, *l. c.*, p. 268.

there were several sacred dances in the Catholic church,"[1]
and processions are still customary. In Nubia songs
and dances resembling those of the dervishes but of
livelier rhythm than that of the Arabs form part of a
religious ceremony.[2] In its intensity of excitement it
creates an almost terrible impression. The religious
purpose is, however, neither a necessary part of the
dance festivals nor is dancing obligatory to the religious
solemnities. The Australian corrobberree has nothing
whatever to do with religion,[3] and in the Temple of Eap
in the Carolines songs and dances do not occur.[4] On the
other hand, mysteries are so closely connected with dancing
among savages that " to dance this or that means to be
acquainted with this or that myth, which is represented
in a dance or *ballet d'action* ".[5]

The dance in Africa also forms part of the funeral
ceremonies, a fact which is in direct opposition to our
modern view. The Sulima (West Africa, east of the
Sierra Leone coast) bury their dead in perfect silence.
Within a month after this they assemble again round the
grave, the men dancing and shouting, the " Jelle " playing
and singing, the women dancing. Only on these occasions the dancing women are allowed to make indecent
gestures.[6] Baker witnessed a funeral dance of the Latuka:
the dancers were decorated with ostrich feathers, monkey
or leopard skins, and carried iron bells covered in leather
and tied round the waist. These bells they rang " by
jerking their posteriors in the most absurd manner ". The
indescribable noise was increased by the beating of seven
nogaras tuned differently and by blowing the antilope
horns which each dancer wore round his neck. The
women remained outside the row of dancers dancing a

---

[1] Lubbock, *Orig. Civ.*, pp. 260 and 527, with numerous examples.
[2] Brugsch, *l. c.*, p. 254.　　　[3] Wood, *l. c.*, p. 38.
[4] Chamisso, *l. c.*, p. 12;.　　　[5] A. Lang, *Myth. Rel. Rit.*, i. p. 283.
[6] Laing, *l. c.*, p. 368.

slow, stupid step, and screaming a wild and most inharmonious chant, whilst boys and girls in another row
beat time with their feet.[1]   A dance at the grave of a
deceased person is still common in Nubia, the entire
ceremony appearing in the highest degree barbarous and
artificial.   Miss Edwards, who was a frequent witness of
the scene, propounded the query as to whether this was a
custom originated in " savage Africa " or an old Egyptian
tradition.   For herself she decided that its origin was most
probably Ethiopian.[2]   To judge from already mentioned
examples, I believe that we can trace back these funeral
dances to a custom which prevailed among the original
population of Africa before the time of Egyptian civilisation, which might have been handed down from these
tribes to ancient civilised Egypt.   The lamentation itself
is a definite musical phrase executed by women who,
beginning on a high note, proceed down the scale in third-
tones to the lower octave or even the twelfth.   It is taught,
like the zaghareet, or cry of joy, by mothers to their young
daughters in their earliest years.   Perhaps, Miss Edwards
suggests, it may be the identical phrase which formerly
was sung over the Pharaohs in the royal tombs.[3]

   That which exercises the most powerful inducement to
men to dance seems to be the same as that in the animal
kingdom.   I need not mention, however, the numerous
examples in the animal kingdom, for I can refer to the
interesting chapter of Darwin's on the subject in his
Descent of Man.[4]   The frequent occurrence of indecent
dances among men points to the same idea.   It is, however, a matter of difficulty to speak of decent or indecent
dances, for each people must be judged from the point of
view of its own customs, and such judgments can only be

---

[1] S. W. Baker, *Albert Nyanza*, *l. c.*, i. p. 243.
[2] A. B. Edwards, *l. c.*, p. 251.   [3] *Ibid.*, p. 252.
[4] Darwin, *l. c.*, ii. p. 74.

formed after many years of observation, and above all by an open unprejudiced mind.

The natives of Timbuktu, who played both at chess and draughts at a time when the Europeans scarcely knew of the place, have among them also jugglers, conjurers, and ventriloquists. Their music, of which they have twenty-four different kinds, pleased Mr. Shabeeny very much; some of their dances were highly improper.[1] Of the West African negroes Mr. Corry relates: On changing a dance "the originator delivers a solemn oration about musical instruments, into which he generally introduces a description of some warlike undertaking"; after this the dance is renewed, especially by the women, who as a rule totally disregard decorum. The men express their satisfaction by applauding, but sometimes feelings of shame arise in the young women, who flee for protection to the elders of their sex.[2] The Kimbunda tribes in Africa have numerous dances, songs, and entertainments of all sorts; both sexes dance, and very indecently too. The chief begins and is followed by the warriors. Next the captives are killed, roasted well and eaten, and then the women are allowed to appear, who, although their part is to represent the "lady of the house," are often more shameless than the men. The entire company becomes intoxicated at last and continues dancing and singing all night until the morning.[3] The wedding dance *Batuk* is forbidden in the streets of Loando on account of the many improper gestures which attend it. Men and women place themselves in a circle at the sound of the *kipuita* (a sort of drum); those standing round begin a short monotonous song. It is repeated for hours together, the dancers also taking part. They all turn and wind round on one spot, gesticulating and rubbing their backs one against the other until one falls exhausted, whereupon another immediately

---

[1] Shabeeny, *l. c.*, p. 25.   [2] Corry, *l. c.*, pp. 67-68.
[3] Magyar, *l. c.*, i. pp. 312-314.

takes his place. At times a man and a woman will jump into the middle of the circle from opposite directions and bump their stomachs against one another. At times the man raises the girl up in the air, who leaps up from behind on his shoulders.[1] Mrs. Ida Pfeiffer describes a dance in Madagascar at which the dancer, whenever he approached any of the women, made expressive gestures without being in the least deterred by the presence of the Europeans. His actions aroused shouts of laughter and obstreperous applause from the audience.[2]

The Narrinyeri tribes in Australia (at the Lakes Alexandrina and Albert, and the Lower Murray River) have various descriptions of corrobberrees which are usually danced by the men only, while the women sit on the ground and sing. Their songs are sometimes harmless and their dances not indecent; at other times (according to the Rev. Geo. Taplin's account) they are obscene. The women's dances are altogether " immodest and lewd," and when they take place the men sit on the ground and sing. Mr. Taplin says: " Although I stood in the dark alone and nobody knew that I was there, I felt ashamed to look upon such abominations ".[3] Nevertheless he compares these " immodest and lewd " dances to the dance of Egyptian women, as illustrated in Cobbin's *Family Bible* at St. Luke vii. 32. The resemblances, he adds, " could not have been more exact ". The dances of the Tasmanians were " no more renowned for their purity than were those of civilised people ".[4]

Most New Zealand dances, of which the natives are particularly fond, are, according to Rev. R. Taylor, very indecorous; [5] Lubbock mentions two kinds, " warlike and amorous," [6] while Meinicke declares them to be lascivious.[7]

---

[1] Lux, *l. c.*, p. 38.
[2] Pfeiffer, *Madag.*, p. 186.
[3] Taplin, *l. c.*, p. 38.
[4] Bonwick, *l. c.*, p. 36.
[5] R. Taylor, *l. c.*, p. 349.
[6] Lubbock, *Preh. Times*, p. 467.
[7] Meinicke, *l. c.*, i. p. 330.

The dances in Fiji are anything but decorous.[1] Song
and dance at Nukahiva consist of a continuous hop in one
spot, during which the dancers occasionally raise their
arms, making a rapid tremulous movement with their
fingers. To this time is beaten with the hands. The
song is more of a howl than a regular concert of voices, but
the inhabitants seem satisfied with this so much as to
make Mr. Krusenstern doubt whether the natives of Nukahiva would be affected at all by the best European music.[2]
At the night dances in Samoa all kinds of obscenity in
looks, language, and gesture prevailed.[3] Langsdorf relates
that in Nukahiva and Tahiti the women appear entirely
naked at the dance festivals, "a fact which gives rise to
much indecency".[4] Speaking of Polynesian dances, the
hula-hula had the worst reputation of all; the melody
which accompanied it was somewhat complicated, although
the text consisted of only two constantly repeated sentences.[5]
Buchner heard some Polynesian youths singing a four-
part male chorus which, it is true, had been taught them
by missionaries, but which nevertheless testified to their
musical talent. The Polynesian haka, borrowed from the
Maoris, originally had the same object as the hula-hula.
The song connected with it was composed of two or three
notes which rose to a veritable howl and ended in a sharp,
short note, the effect of a sudden silence which immediately
followed being most surprising.[6] This kind of passionate
and indecent dance, very common in Polynesia, seems to
be somewhat idealised by the more civilised Malays of
Java, where Mr. Bock witnessed a dance at the end of
which the male dancer kissed his partner.[7]

Hindus and Mohammedans in India consider it un-
dignified for an honest man or an honourable woman to

---

[1] Lubbock, *Preh. Times*, p. 456.
[2] Krusenstern, *l. c.*, p. 333.
[3] Turner, *Samoa*, p. 125; *Polyn.*, p. 211.
[4] Langsdorf, p. 132.
[5] Buchner, *Still. Oz.*, p. 354.
[6] *Ibid.*, p. 143.
[7] Bock, *l. c.*, p. 12.

dance. The Brahmins, who allow no European nor Hindu of a lower caste to enter their temples, permit dancing girls who are of lower caste and lead immoral lives to do so, because, as they say, professional dancers are required for their religious feasts.[1] Nevertheless both Hindus and Mohammedans look on at a dance with great delight, and also listen to their own noisy music while hating that of Europeans.[2] Mr. Niebuhr tells us: For an honest Mohammedan it is taken amiss if he were to show his ability in dancing.[3] The same is the case with the Turks and Arabs.[4] Mohammedans have a very low opinion of our ladies because they dance with strange men; but they are allowed to dance before the men and among themselves in ladies' parties. On such occasions each lady appears as beautifully dressed as possible, dances with her slaves, and changes her dresses eight to ten times in the evening.[5] Mr. Niebuhr tells us of à Greek lady—the Greeks are particularly fond of dancing—who during an evening party changed her dress and furred coat five times within two hours. Speaking of the Ostiak dances (animal pantomimes) Mr. Georgi says: "One can easily imagine that the gestures in them are not rarely immodest ".[6] It is significant that in the language of the Omawhaws (North American Indians) the word " watche " means both " dance" and " sexual intercourse ".[7]

Very much rarer are the examples of dances which in no way wound the European sense of propriety; at the same time it must be observed that both classes of dances, decent and indecent, may occur among one and the same

---

[1] Haafner, l. c., pp. 372-373.

[2] Ibid., l. c., p. 172; the dancing girls are concubines of the Brahmins and of other high caste men, that they might not be obliged to have intercourse with girls of a lower rank. Details about Indian dancing girls, ibid., pp. 177-178, 244-248, 309-312.

[3] Niebuhr, l. c., i. p. 182. [4] Ibid., p. 175.

[5] Ibid., pp. 182-184. [6] Georgi, l. c., p. 80.

[7] Long, Rock. Mount., i. p. 338.

tribe. The dances on Bornabi (Caroline Islands) are by
no means indecorous, and are performed by unmarried
men and girls, who keep time to the music by graceful
movements of the arms, legs, and indeed of the whole
body.[1] In Tahiti pregnant women are debarred (for the
time being) from dancing the Timorodee.[2] In Java Mr.
Jukes witnessed a pantomime performed by four young
maidens who in no way behaved improperly, yet they were
considered courtesans by profession. Into their songs
were introduced notes of such shrillness and harshness
as he had never previously heard.[3] The quietness and
modesty of the Bushmen and Hottentots during their
dances have been frequently remarked, and the great
decorum observed in those of the Mandingoes is at times
striking.[4] The dance in Murzuk performed by men and
women is in no way indecent; on the contrary, the
slowness and regularity of the movements is both elegant
and pleasing.[5] The Fiji dance, Meke-meke, is performed
by boys and girls, for whom an old musician plays; the
melody, which is sung simultaneously, always repeats the
same rhythmical movement, $-\smile\smile$, within the compass of
a few tones. The girls display considerable grace and
coquet. like Europeans with " their accursed large black
eyes ". Despite this, however, they are not immodest, but
enjoy pure pleasure in the rhythmical movements and
songs.[6] Mrs. Wallis, too, holds the opinion that at Fiji
dances one may learn at least modesty.[7] The Abipones
(South American Indians) always have decent dances.[8]

The part taken by the two sexes in the dance is worthy
of note. To judge by the experience one can gain in
civilised countries, it is not surprising that among savages
the women, both quantitatively and qualitatively, busy

---

[1] Angas, *Polyn.*, p. 384.　　[2] Cook, *First Voyage*, in *Pink. Coll.*, xi. p. 520.
[3] Jukes, *l. c.*, ii. p. 50.　　[4] Caillie, *l. c.*, ii. p. 73.
[5] Lyon, *l. c.*, p. 174.　　[6] Buchner, *Still. Oz.*, p. 273.
[7] Bonwick, *l. c.*, p. 36.　　[8] Dobrizhoffer, *l. c.*, i. p. 66.

themselves most with the dance, a fact which is the more remarkable as the dances of savages are much more exhausting than ours.

The Fans in Africa, who have an excellent musical ear, are passionate dancers, the endurance of the women being almost incredible. (*Toute comme chez nous.*) " Never did I see female endurance equal this," says Mr. Reade.[1] Among the Bagirmi the women are mentioned as being exceptionally good dancers,[2] and they sing heartily while dancing. A popular national dance of the women in Logon consisted in their moving to musical accompaniments round in a circle from which they attempted to eject each other by pushing with their posteriors. The victor continued dancing in triumph until she too was finally ejected.[3] Similar " jokes" frequently occur in Africa. The beautiful women of the Shuas (Sudan) in a similar dance come together with such violence as to burst the belt of beads which they carry round their hips and which represents a value of fifteen to twenty dollars.[4] The Sura women, too, in India, dance a wedding dance on the same lines.[5] C. Long describes a dance of twelve girls in Khartum, who, with a peculiar clucking sound made by compression of the lips against the teeth, moved in concert with the tambourine, while their jingling bracelets marked the time of the music.[6] A women's dance at Kordofan was accompanied by a monotonous song and hand-clapping, time being beaten " with the right *fore* foot "[7] (" mit dem rechten Vorderfuss," as Mr. Heuglin literally says). Speaking of the women in Madagascar Mr. Rochon relates the following custom : " While the Malagasy are at war their wives continue singing and dancing during the day, and even through a great part of the night ; they believe

---

[1] Wood, *l. c.*, i. p. 603.   [2] *Ibid.*, p. 711.

[3] Nachtigal, *l. c.*, ii. p. 521.   [4] Wood, *l. c.*, i. p. 702.

[5] *Ibid.*, ii. p. 750 (with illustr.).   [6] Ch. Long, *l. c.*, p. 19.

[7] Heuglin, *l. c.*, p. 37.

that such continual dancing inspires their husbands and augments both their strength and courage ".[1]   When the war is over they all assemble at sunset and begin to dance and sing in a most noisy manner with instrumental accompaniment.   During these dances a good deed is as much praised as a wrong one is ironised, so that Mr. Rochon says of them : " Les jeux sont des leçons *utiles ;* on y célèbre les belles actions, et on s'y moque des ridicules ".   In some sense this may remain true for games of all sorts, times and countries.

Among the Australians the wildness of the women, when excited, surpasses that of the men.[2]   In the time of a popular tumult the same may be observed among us ; the women are always in the foremost rank.   In Australia when an old woman has begun to sing she will not cease until completely exhausted, then another will take up the burthen and continue the song.   The effect of these songs is immense ; they are in fact the causes of most disturbances.[3]   Among the aborigines of Victoria the women generally are the musicians, and their performance is led by a leader (usually an elderly man) who beats time with the corrobberree sticks.   The time kept by the performers and the women who beat the opossum skins, and the accuracy with which the movements are executed, is astonishing.[4]

In Magindanao (Philipp.) the women indulged in a dance of their own ; fifteen of them formed a semicircle in which they moved backwards and forwards.   The first sang for three or four minutes, then dropped off and the next took the song exactly as the first had done, the entire performance lasting about an hour.   At such festivals (in the Sultan's palace) the men pay no attention to the women.[5] On Amsterdam and Middleburgh Islands the women sing

---

[1] Rochon, *l. c.*, pp. 37-38.   [2] Grey, *Austr.*, p. 314.
[3] *Ibid.*, p. 316.   [4] Br. Smyth, *l. c.*, i. p. 168.
[5] Th. Forrest, *New Guinea*, pp. 245-246.

and accompany themselves by snapping with their fingers.[1]
On the Sandwich Islands the women are the principal
dancers and keep in time to the sounds of a drum accompanied by a song in which they all join. On these
occasions the women display all their finery, particularly
in European clothes if they are so fortunate as to possess
any.[2] With us they seem to display the gifts of nature
rather, if they are so fortunate as to possess any. The
Dyaks of Borneo have public dancing girls (Bolian or
Blian);[3] to most women is known the art of powdering
the face.[4] Malay women in Sumatra never dance, but in
Java both sexes do.[5]

At Sagar, in the Central Provinces of India, the women
dance while the men look on;[6] in Southern India the
native dancing women are generally better dressed and
wear more clothes than the others. Men make their own
clothes and women their own jackets.[7] The often-praised
dance of the Bajadirs in India did not call forth any
praise from Mr. Sainte Croix. They still have clappers
on their ankles and accompany their own songs themselves, only making use of semitones.[8] [The author
may mean the notes of the so-called black keys which
may point to a pentatonic scale.] In Tonking only
women dance, and they have to sing at the same time.[9]

The women of the Apache Indians " do the principal
part of the dancing ".[10] On Queen Charlotte Island
women dance at the festivals while the men stand in a
circle beating time with sticks, which, with tambourines,
are their sole instruments. Their songs are simple and

---

[1] Cook, *Second Voyage*, in *Pink. Coll.*, xi. p. 594.

[2] Campbell, *l. c.*, p. 203.   [3] Hein, *l. c.*, p. 28.

[4] Bock, *l. c.*, p. 13.   [5] *Ibid.*, p. 12.

[6] Murray-Ansley, *l. c.*, p. 253.   [7] Shortt, *l. c.*, p. 392.

[8] Sainte Croix, *l. c.*, p. 258.

[9] Baron, *l. c.*, p. 672 ; Richard, *l. c.*, p. 726.

[10] Henry, in Schoolcraft's *Arch.*, vol. v. p. 212.

monotonous and accompany most of their dances and ceremonies. On this island Mr. Mackenzie heard soft plaintive tones which sounded like church music.[1] The Iroquois have special dances for women side by side with dances for men only; this is often the case with many Indian tribes, and therefore we will describe such dances later on together with the men's dances. For the present we may state that the women's share in the dance is still greater than in the music (*cf.* chap. ii.), and as the most primitive music is only that of a choral dance, primitive music owes more to women than to men. It is a pity that this excellent womanly attribute has been so suppressed in the course of civilisation, and that this fact and the regard for women generally did not begin to be recognised and shown until in the very youngest phase of culture, and this only gradually.

With the above-mentioned ethnological facts in hand we shall be in a position to meet a widely promulgated error. A certain doctor once wrote to a lady who wished to go on the stage : " The genius of musical composition is ' *homme*,' and accept it as a compliment when I say that you are essentially ' *femme* ' ". To this Upton questioningly replies : " Is there any instance in modern times, perhaps in any times, of a female composer who attains even to the eminence of a third-rate opera writer ? " [2] It is true there are very few female composers at present and they are not first-rate either. In primitive times, however, women did incomparably more for the *reproduction* as well as for the *production* of music. Donovan seems to think otherwise, for he says : " Woman did nothing whatever for the first steps of musical development, because she could have felt none of that strong impulse to listen again. But who dare deny that women of to-day possess deep appreciation of music ? " [3] This impulse,

[1] Bancroft, *l. c.*, i. p. 170.   [2] Upton, *l. c.*, p. 21.
[3] Donovan, *Mus. Act.*, p. 117.

in his opinion, lay with the man in the connection of primitive music with action of the body, or dramatic action. Unfortunately Donovan did not turn this excellent remark to further account, for he probably overlooked the fact that it is just for this very " action of the body " that the woman has a stronger impulse than the man, because she who as a rule neither fights nor hunts stores up a greater " surplus of vigour ". This is the peculiar character that woman possessed in primitive time as proved by ethnological examples, and this is as a rule the same character she possesses to-day ; she is still the one who dances more frequently and energetically than men. Mr. Donovan's further question, however, contains no doubt some truth : " Who dare deny that women of to-day possess deep appreciation of music ? " " Appreciation " certainly ; this, however, is not the question, but musical activity in the form of composition, and this is less to-day than in primitive times.

There are a few tribes in which only the men dance, or at any rate there are certain dances in which only they are allowed to take part. But it is characteristic that sometimes dances would not be complete without the women's part, and consequently their *rôles* have to be played by men. This occurs in the Keche dance in the Marotse Kingdom (Africa) which is performed by two men, one of whom represents a woman.[1] In the cor-robberrec at Darling Downs in Queensland only men dance.[2] Among the Lincoln tribes in Australia only two or three women may join in the dance at the same time, although they all sing.[3] In Tahiti, however, the men rarely dance,[4] while among the Papuans men are generally the dancers, and perform as well as possible for they know that the women like it. Their movements are of such

[1] Ratzel, *l. c.*, i. p. 382.　　　[2] Beckler, *l. c.*, p. 82.
[3] Schürmann, *l. c.*, p. 243.　　　[4] Meinicke, *l. c.*, ii. p. 189.

grace as to be almost an ideal for our ballet dancers.[1]
Mr. Miklukha Maklay, who was the first to visit certain
parts of New Guinea, saw only men dancing. Some of
the men went round a fire in one circle, while others
stood in a second, women and children in a third. The
entire company moved in time to the music, which was
kept up almost all night, and only after becoming completely exhausted did they cease and take their meal.[2]
Among the Arabs of Hyderabad only the men dance while
the women look on, the female *rôles* being played by boys
who wear on such occasions the native female dress.[3]
The Orinoco Indians, too, have only male dancers, who,
young and old, form a circle holding each other's hand,
and turn sometimes to the right, sometimes to the left
for whole hours in silent gravity. Most frequently the
dancers themselves are the musicians as well.[4] The
women of the Kalushians of Norfolk Sound sit upon the
ground while the men dance and sing a " not inharmonious
melody which supplies the place of music ".[5] Among the
Iroquois the Buffalo dance " Dageyagovanno " is designed
for men only, but the women may take part in the " feather
dance " if they are disposed. Out of thirty-two dances
fourteen were for both sexes, seven for women only, and
eleven for men ; of the first fourteen three were costume
dances and three no longer in use ; of the second class
three were costume dances and six obsolete.[6]

It has often been observed in savage dances how
frequently the sexes dance apart from each other. In
Hisinene (east of Tanganyika) the women never dance
together with the men, but sometimes they arrange a
dance among themselves in which their actions and
gestures are even more immoral and indecent than are
those of the men, although they too are in bad enough

[1] Schelling, *l. c.*　　　　　　　[2] Miklukha Maklay, *l. c.*, p. 845.
[3] C. Murray-Ansley, *l. c.*, p. 251.　　[4] Humboldt, *l. c.*, p. 465.
[5] Langsdorf, *l. c.*, ii. p. 114.　　　[6] Morgan, *l. c.*, p. 290.

form.[1] The fact that the dances of both sexes are kept separate is no proof that the dance is thereby rendered less indecorous, and the reverse. Gurney remarks à propos of Richard Wagner's statement that primitive dance is in most cases a love scene: " The original people's dance has nothing to do with lovers. It is curious how often among uncivilised peoples the dances of the men and women are kept separate " (*l. c.*, p. 159). It is true, primitive dance is not a love scene, as a rule, but an animal pantomime, nevertheless it has to do with the sexual instinct, the separation of the sexes being no proof to the contrary, as may be seen in the above examples. Among the Moresco (W. Barbary) men are not allowed to dance with married women, but girls may with bachelors; the former are so closely veiled that not any part of their bodies is seen naked. At their wedding festivals the married dance during the day, the single at night.[2] In Australia it occurs here and there that men and women dance separately,[3] but they also dance together sometimes.[4] Frequently the women are mere onlookers, singing and beating time on rolled-up opossum skins.[5] Sometimes Mr. Oldfield observed the women, when apart from the men, perform a kind of waltz among themselves, far more graceful in its measure and figures than the violent dances of the men. Both sexes decorate themselves for these festive occasions with the greatest pains, uttering loud cries of admiration when they have the opportunity of seeing themselves in a mirror.

Among the Tasmanians the dance was the chief pleasure of the men, and only on very exceptional occasions women were allowed to dance with them, though indulging at times in a merry dance among themselves at home. Now

---

[1] Cameron, *l. c.*, p. 40.
[2] Addison, *l. c.*, p. 439.
[3] Eyre, *Austr.*, ii. p. 232.
[4] *Ibid.*, p. 236.
[5] Oldfield, *l. c.*, pp. 256-258.

and then they were permitted to dance before their masters, " and they then became very mirthful ".[1]

Among the Tatars of Kazan " the men and women dance for themselves only ".[2]

In America similar cases occur; thus among the Abenakis, Chactas, and Comanches the women dance the same dance as the men, but *after* them and always out of their sight.[3]

The Sioux Indians are so fond of singing and dancing that Catlin called them the " Dancing Indians," as they had dances for every occasion and for every hour of the day. In them the women are rarely allowed to take part, but they have some of their own, *e.g.*, the *scalp dance*, in which they stand in a circle round a scalp, jumping from the ground in time to the beating of drums, and continually singing and keeping time all together admirably.[4] The women of the Californian Indians are rarely permitted to dance with the men, but when this honour is granted them they play a very subordinate *rôle*, merely swaying their bodies to and fro in silence.[5] Even when dancing *at the same time* as the men they do not dance with them.[6] In some tribes, however, men and women unite in dancing.[7] At the mission station St. Joseph in California the natives represent in dancing battles or scenes of domestic life. Their music consists in singing and clapping with a stick which is split at one end. The women have their own particular songs and their own style of dancing. They hop about near the men but never in concert with them.[8]

That it is just among the Indians that the sexes are so often separated is due to the fact that they are not

---

[1] Bonwick, *l. c.*, p. 36. Bonwick's further remark that most savages keep the monopoly of dancing " for the masculine feet " is no doubt an error.

[2] Georgi, *l. c.*, p. 105.   [3] Domenech, *l. c.*, ii. pp. 199, 214.
[4] Waitz, *l. c.*, iii. p. 211.   [5] Bancroft, *l. c.*, i. p. 393.
[6] *Ibid.*, p. 416.   [7] Schoolcraft, *Arch.*, v. pp. 214-215.
[8] Langsdorf, *l. c.*, ii. p. 196.

accustomed openly to express their feelings, and this more particularly in the intercourse of the sexes. In Yucatan ballets were performed in which as many as 800 dancers took part, but " it was not customary for the men and women to dance together ".[1]

It is, however, the rule among savages that both sexes dance together. This is the case among the New Zealanders, who, moreover, have dances for men or women only;[2] and this is the case in the Gilbert and Marshall Islands,[3] and at times in Samoa;[4] in these dances the feeling for symmetry is quite unmistakable. On the Caroline Islands many kinds of festivities take place which are shared in by the two sexes separately or by both together.[5]

On a journey from Spiti to Lahul through the Sutlej valley in the Himalaya Mrs. Murray-Ansley saw dances performed by both sexes, the accompaniment being a melodious song, of which at times four bars were sung and four whistled alternately.[6] Among the Chukchi both sexes dance together.[7] In New Mexico the dance is performed either by a single dancer or by a very large number of both sexes,[8] and music is their invariable accompaniment. The dance of the Indians in Guiana was not much more than a measured series of steps by men and women. A monotonous chant sung in unison, the jingling of bracelets and anklets made of hard seeds, and the wings of beetles was the accompaniment.[9]

---

[1] Landa, *l. c.*, p. 129. [2] R. Taylor, *l. c.*, p. 349.

[3] Meinicke, *l. c.*, ii. p. 342. [4] Turner, *Sam.*, p. 124; *Polyn.*, p. 210.

[5] Chamisso, *l. c.*, p. 133. [6] Murray-Ansley, *l. c.*, p. 281.

[7] Merck, *l. c.*, p. 65. [8] Bancroft, *l. c.*, i. p. 515.

[9] Brett, *l. c.*, p. 320.

CHAPTER VIII.

PRIMITIVE DRAMA AND PANTOMIME.

WE have seen in the former chapters how intimately music and dancing are connected. Primitive dances have in the most cases a special meaning: they have to represent something and have therefore a position among the other arts quite different from the modern dances. At such representations no words are spoken, but mimicry and gestures are not less a language, far better fitted to explain the action than the primitive language of words. These pantomimes, as we may call them, are indeed a primitive drama, and as music is always connected with dances one may judge how great the importance was that music had on these occasions. Dramatic music, or musical drama, if you like, is not an occasional union of two different arts, it is originally one organism, and at the same time the earliest manifestation of human art in general. Therefore, Richard Wagner's artistic genius again correctly defined the essential character of the drama when he said: "Long before the epic songs of Homer had become a matter of literary concern they had flourished among the people as actually represented works of art, supported by the voice and gesture, so to speak, as concentrated, fixed, lyric, dancing songs ("ver-dichtete, gefestigte, lyrische Gesangstänze"), in which the poets' fondness of resting with the description of the action and the repetition of heroic dialogues prevailed".[1] In

[1] Wagner, *l. c.*, iii. p. 124.

(214)

one word, the historical order of all the branches of poetry does not begin with the epos—as frequently taught—but with the drama, lyric coming next, the epos lastly.   This is the order the ethnologist can trace, this is at the same time the most simple and natural way in the development of poetry.   The epos requires for all its psychological details so much polish of language, so much grammar and refined style to follow all the different shades of expression as to render very difficult our expecting this from very primitive people.   For the dramatic representation mimicry and gestures are not only quite sufficient but the only effective means for explaining the action to an audience of different tribes, which sometimes do not understand their respective dialects and are accustomed to converse in gesture language.

Unfortunately Richard Wagner lost his advantageous position (just as in speaking of dance and music) when elaborating his intuitive idea.   Then he called those dancing songs "a middleway station from the ancient lyric to the drama," although the pantomime cannot possibly be the very beginning of poetry and a middleway station at the same time.   Wagner constantly overlooks the fact that the primitive drama is pantomime only, not poetry as well, no words being spoken in it.   It is not until later on that other arts, poetry among them, begin to show their germs, which they unfold and develop in the same proportion as they become independent and separate themselves from the common trunk.   This done it would be contrary to all laws of development that the accomplished arts should once more form an organic union as they might have formed in their primitive state.   Therefore, the attempt to unite the accomplished arts in equal rank to a single art work is theoretically a contradiction and practically an impossibility.   The result of such an attempt was always that the composer either spoiled his art by a theoretical prejudice or practically acted contrary

to his rules.   Wagner's artistic genius was never in doubt
for a single moment which way to go, and therefore his
theory has remained an intolerable chaos, while his art
has flourished in unrivalled splendour.

Thus we have reached the most recent phase of the
drama before speaking a single word of the original
pantomime, a proof how far-reaching and important it
is to settle its character, of which we are now going to
give a few examples.

The dances of the Damaras consist mostly of mimic
representations of the movements of oxen and sheep.
The dancers accompany their gesticulations by monotonous tunes, and keep time by clapping the hands and
striking the ground with their feet.[1]   In the Ngumbi
forest in Africa the gorilla is the object of mimic representations, during which an iron bell is rung and a hoarse
rattle mingled with the other sounds.   Then the measure
grows quicker and quicker, a drum is beaten, sticks
thundered on the log, until the whole hunting and rolling
of the gorilla is performed with great truth to nature.[2]

Among the Fans, who are cannibals, the dancers are
fond of all sorts of mummery, in which a man disguises
himself as any animal by putting on some cloth and
mats, performing all kinds of grotesque movements amidst
the jubilating shouts of his fellow-tribesmen.[3]   Such
mummeries as occur on all the continents seem to be
the origin of our masques, which are in great favour with
savages and occur in very characteristic shapes.   Thus
the primitive animal pantomime is in some sense the
original of our fancy-dress balls.   Another kind of pantomimes is that in which the dancers closely imitate all the
movements they are accustomed to perform in a real war,
as do the natives of Mahenge.[4]   These representations are

---

[1] C. J. Andersson, *l. c.*, p. 230.   [2] Reade, *Sav. Afr.*, p. 195.
[3] Lenz, *l. c.*, p. 88.   [4] Thomson, *Centr. Afr. Lak.*, i. p. 186.

evidently based on the principle of employing that over-
flow of vigour and energy which is necessary for the
struggle of life (war, hunt, work), without, however,
being in appropriate use for a time. Mr. Lander saw at
Katunga a pantomimic performance in three acts. The
first was a dance of twenty men wrapped up in sacks;
the second represented the capture of a boa constrictor,
which was imitated by one of the dancers as well as
circumstances permitted it; the third, which caused the
most laughter, was a caricature of the white man, who
was, however, very badly represented by a white-painted
dancer. During the "entr'act," which was very short,
there was a concert of drums and pipes and national songs
of the women, whose choruses were joined by the whole
people.[1]

In Australia, too, there are pantomimic gestures connected with some songs which are passed on from performer to performer, as the song is carried from tribe to
tribe.[2] The aborigines of Victoria have their war dances
before and after fights, dances appropriate to occasion of
"making young men," dances in which the women only
take part, and dances in which the movements of the
kangaroo, the emu, the frog, the butterfly are imitated.[3]
Mr. B. Smyth tells us that the perceptive faculties of the
natives are very clear, and their power of observation and
imitation sometimes quite extraordinary. Monotonous
and harsh as their chants may be, the natives are by no
means unsusceptible of the power of music. The young
people readily learn how to sing and how to play on instruments.[4] The natives at the Lake Albert imitate in
their dances the actions and movements of a frog, the
hunting of the emu, the voice of a bird.[5]

The New Zealanders, too, invariably accompany their

[1] Lander, *Rec. Clapp.*, i. pp. 116-121.   [2] Howitt, *l. c.*, p. 327.
[3] R. B. Smyth, *l. c.*, i. p. 166.   [4] *Ibid.*, p. 266.
[5] G. F. Angas, *Savage Life*, i. p. 63.

dances with gesticulations. Their most exciting dance is the war dance, performed before a battle commences with the purpose to excite their warriors to the highest pitch of fury.[1] The dances of the ancient Tasmanians were imitations of animal movements.[2]

The dance Hewa (in the South Sea Islands) is an accomplished pantomime in which the abduction of a girl or the birth of a boy is represented.[3] The Dyaks of Borneo have different kinds of dances representing the movements of animals, or a pantomime representing the hunting. All these dances are opened with music, to which excellent time is kept, and not seldom concluded in drunkenness.[4] One of their pantomimes represented a sham fight in which one of the warriors was apparently killed, while the victor discovered too late that he had killed a friend, whereupon he showed unmistakable signs of regret and sorrow. Suddenly the slain warrior got up and began a frantic dance.[5] Thus even in this state of culture there seems to be a general desire for the story to end well. The Papuans imitate in their dance the minstrelsy of birds, and always like to display some symmetry in their movements. Of two dancers standing next to each other, the one is always anxious to make the same movement with the right leg or arm which the other is performing with the left.[6]

The dances of the Chukchi closely resemble those of the Indians. The men dance quite nude, having only the feet covered and the hair ornamented with feathers. Their movements consist of wild imitations of hunt and fight. The women sing to this and again imitate the movements of their own daily occupations, such as carrying water, collecting berries. Thus these dances become

---

[1] Angas, *Savage Life*, i. pp. 328-329. [2] Bonwick, *l. c.*, p. 35.
[3] Meinicke, *l. c.*, ii. p. 189. [4] Boyle, *l. c.*, p. 82 *seq*.
[5] St. John, *l. c.*, i. p. 55. [6] Schelling, *l. c.*

natural mimic ballets.[1] The dances of the Kamchadales are
pantomimic, while the music to them is sung with always
increasing passion. The rhythm is a system of six trochees
(bachia-a).[2] The fish-Tunguses have the same rhythm
but without the division into strophes. With unvaried
monotony it is repeated to perfect exhaustion. The
Ostiaks on the Ob (main river of W. Siberia) have similar
dances at their religious feasts, whence Mr. Swan concludes
that a religious purpose must have formerly existed in the
dances of the Kamchadales as well.

Besides these dances of the Kamchadales Mr. Langsdorf mentions the sea-dog dance and the bear dance, at
which they go from the gentlest, softest motion of the
head and shoulders to the most violent motions of the
whole body. Mr. Lesseps mentions the partridge dance.
Of course they are all accompanied with music, and it is
almost painful to see with what great exertion, especially
of the lungs, they are carried on.[3] Mr. Krebs saw similar
dances on the Island of Spierken (Kurile group, south of
Kamchatka, formerly belonging to Russia, since 1875 to
Japan). The inhabitants are Ainus.[4]

The dances and games of the Indians in California
represent scenes of war, hunting, and private life.[5] In
the Rocky Mountains the natives have the calumet
dance, lasting from two to three days and always performed with the expectation of receiving presents ; another
dance represents the discovering of the enemy ; again,
others are repeatedly described by travellers as the bear
dance, beggar dance, bison dance,[6] ox dance, sun dance.[7]
Speaking of the Sioux Indians Mr. Keating mentions the
dog dance and the Chippewa scalp dance, of which the

[1] Merck, l. c., p. 65.　　　[2] Erman, l. c., i. 3, p. 189.
[3] Lesseps, l. c., i. pp. 105-106 ; Langsdorf, l. c., ii. p. 302.
[4] Krebs, l. c., pp. 379-391.　　　[5] Bancroft, l. c., i. p. 393.
[6] Long, Exp. Rock. M., i. pp. 332-337.
[7] Perrin du Lac, l. c., pp. 120-123.

music is low and melancholic but not unpleasant. The
performers stand in a circle each with the wing of a bird
in his hand (origin of the fan?), with which he beats
time on his gun, arrow, or something that would give a
sound.[1] The Indians in Guiana also have animal dances
at which they keep up a monotonous chant, every dancer
stamping the ground in strict time with the others.[2] As
they danced they uttered alternate cries which resembled
the note of a certain bird often heard in the forests. Two
pieces of wood, rudely carved, had to resemble the bird
itself, others to represent infants.[3]

It is no doubt a sign of further progress in those performances when the spoken word comes to the aid of the
representation, and from this moment we may speak of
the drama proper.

At Zleetun (or Zuletin, or Ziliten, or Sliten, North
Africa) Mr. Lyon heard the negro women singing a
national song in a chorus while pounding wheat, always
in time with the music. One of the songs, sung by three
girls, dealt with the return of the warriors, when suddenly
they beat without measure and sang as if for one who was
dead, endeavouring to comfort the girl who was supposed
to have lost her lover. Then a goat was supposed to be
killed and the entrails examined until a happy sign was
discovered which indicated that the lost lover died nobly.
They then resumed their pestles, winding up with a
beautiful chorus. The master of the girls, however,
forbade their singing any more, saying it was unholy and
displeasing to their Lord Mohammed, the Prophet of God.[4]

The dramatic narratives of the negroes are on the whole
remarkable. So true to nature is their action that they
even indicate the space of time which elapsed between two

---

[1] Keating, *l. c.*, i. p. 438, with mus. example.
[2] Im Thurn, *l. c.*, p. 309.
[3] Brett, *l. c.*, pp. 154-156.
[4] Lyon, *l. c.*, p. 336.

events by producing a sound like *r-r-r-r*.[1]   In ancient Egypt
there was, however, no public show which would resemble
a theatre, nor pantomimic exhibitions nor scenic representation.   The priests succeeded in forbidding this noblest and
highest outcome of the human mind in order to use the
mere rudiments of art for their own religious purposes.
In consequence of the absence of a drama in Egypt, Mr.
Wilkinson came to the conclusion that the stage was a
purely Greek invention, and the pantomime a Roman.[2]   I
think that the ethnological examples sufficiently prove a
much earlier origin.

One of the most interesting forms of a primitive drama
is the Australian corrobberree.   The performers decorate
themselves in some grotesque style, marking each rib by
a broad stripe of white paint over the black skin, thus
making the chorus look like a number of skeletons " endued
with life by magic powers ".[3]

The festivities began by the dancers intoning a plaintive song, to which the old men and women joined in at
times.   The words to this were simply: " Junger a bia,
mati, mati," which they always repeated.   They commenced in a loud, shrill tone, gradually sinking in pitch
and decreasing in force until the tones were so soft as to
be scarcely distinguishable from a gentle breath of air that
rustled in the bush.   During the song the dancers remained
in a bent position, and marked the time with their feet,
lifting them from the ground in short movements.   At the
same time plucking the long ends of their beards, they
suddenly changed the music to a loud " ha hei, ha hei,"
striking their spears and wameras against each other and
stamping the ground vigorously with their feet.   Then
they got up with a sudden jerk, shouting a terrific " garra
wai ".   Again they assumed the first motion, but in twice as

[1] M. Buchner, *Kunst der Neger*, p. 13.

[2] Wilkinson, *l. c.*, i. p. 455.

[3] *Illustr. Lond. News*, 1863 (illustr.).

quick time ; now the whole row moved sideways up and down, shoulder on shoulder ; now they danced in a circle, all with the same music and the same stamping of feet.[1]

In another corrobberree, which Mr. Lumholtz saw, the music was performed by one man only, the others dancing in a chorus. A single woman was allowed to take part in dancing, which was considered a great honour to her. The music, in strict time with the movements, was quick and not very melancholy. The monotonous clattering, the hollow accompaniment of the women, the grunting of the male dancers and the heavy footfall of the men, reminded Mr. Lumholtz, especially when he was some distance away. from the scene, of a steam engine at work. While all took great pleasure in the performance, the musician only apparently had no interest in what was going on, and, beating time, he sang with his hoarse tenor voice without looking up. He had already been watching the exercises for weeks, and knew them all by heart ; but even he sometimes seemed to be amused.[2] However primitive a córrobberree may appear to us, it is a well-prepared and elaborated dance, which it takes both time and practice to excel in.[3]

Speaking of the tribes on Mary River or of the Bunja Bunja Country, Mr. Edward Curr mentions two kinds of corrobberree, the dramatic and the lyric. The intelligence that a new corrobberree had been composed was received with pleasurable excitement by the surrounding tribes. The poet having introduced his work to the neighbouring tribes, these in turn invited their allies to witness it and aid in the performance. In this manner a corrobberree travelled, and was sung with great enthusiasm where not a word of it was intelligible. The story of the drama appears to have been exceedingly short and simple, and rarely free from obscenity. Besides, there was an

---

[1] Browne, *l. c.*, p. 445.   [2] Lumholtz, *l. c.*, p. 240.
[3] Sturt, *l. c.*, i. p. 84.

amazing simultaneousness of action, and excellent time was beaten by the women.

The corrobberree music—says Curr—is much like a chant. A string of words often runs to the one note. All the parts are variations of one tune, sung in different kinds of time, and at various rates of speed. There is a peculiar tendency to slide in semitones from one key into another, and the effect of the music is almost invariably minor. A favourite practice is to raise the pitch suddenly an octave, and in order to effect this it is sometimes necessary to allow it to slide to a low pitch before. Instead of intimating the conclusion of one part of the piece by two or three yells, as the singers do at times, a more musical practice is often followed of trilling the sound of *r* at a high pitch.[1]

The Kuri dance is another kind of primitive drama. Mr. Angas described one that was performed by five different classes of actors:[2] 1. A body of about twenty-five young men, including five or six boys, the dancers. 2. Two groups of women, merely taking the part of supernumeraries, and beating time with their feet during the whole performance. 3. Two remarkable characters of the play. 4. A performer distinguished by a long spear. 5. Two singers—two elderly men in their usual habiliments.

The man in group four commenced a part which called forth unbounded applause; with his head and body inclined on one side, his spear and feathers behind his back, standing on the left leg, he beat time with the right foot, twitching his body and eyes, and stamping with the greatest precision; he remained a few minutes in this position, and then suddenly turned round, stood on his right leg, and did the same over with his left foot.

Mr. Bonwick heard at Port Jackson what he called a " speaking pantomime "; it dealt with the courtship

---

[1] Curr, *l. c.*, iii. p. 167; other descriptions of corrobberrees by G. F. Angas, *Sav. Life*, i. p. 102.

[2] Angas, *l. c.*, i. pp. 103-107.

between the sexes, and was performed with very expressive actions.[1]

On Cook's second voyage Mr. Foster saw a "comic opera" on the Society Islands, the first act of which concluded with a burlesque beating of three of the participants.[2] The performance of the Hurra, the festival dances on O-Waihi, called forth Mr. Chamisso's admiration. The singing of the dancers, accompanied by the drum, begins slowly and softly, gradually quickening and increasing, while the dancers proceed and play in a more lively manner.[3] At Gresek in Java Mr. Tombe saw a Malayan comedy. "It was precisely what we call a Chinese shadow-play" and had to represent a war. The music to it consisted of kettle-drums, gom-goms, and the Javese violoncello, while the manager and thirty young dancing girls sang the praise of the emperor and his ancestors.[4] Mrs. Ida Pfeiffer witnessed at Bandong the performance of a Javese pantomime in three movements, representing a fight, where the noisy and discordant music changed to a soft, plaintive melody as soon as one party was defeated. The whole performance was really pretty and expressive. The dancers kept their eyes constantly fixed on the ground, as is customary among most non-European nations, to express profound respect for the spectators.[5]

The most complete description of the Javese national drama is given by Mr. Raffles, who reports of two different kinds of it, the "topeng" (characters represented by men), and the "wayang" (represented by "shadows"). In general the performers have only to "suit the action to the words," which are spoken by the "dalang," the manager of the entertainment. The gámelan accompanies the piece and varies in expression according to the nature of the action or the kind of emotion to be excited. The

---

[1] Bonwick, *l. c.*, p. 33. [2] Elson, *l. c.*, p. 247.
[3] Chamisso, *l. c.*, p. 152. [4] Tombe, *l. c.*, p. 58.
[5] I. Pfeiffer, *l. c.*, i. p. 212.

whole of the performance has more the character of a ballet than of a regular dramatic exhibition.[1]

In Sumatra the custom prevails during their dances that a young lady ("gadis") sometimes rises and, with her back to the audience, begins a tender song which is soon answered by one of the "bujangs" in company. Professed story-tellers are sometimes raised on a little stage and attract the attention of the audience by buffoonery, or mimicry, and keep the company in laughter all night long. The young men frequent these assemblies in order to look out for wives, and Mr. Marsden remarks: "The lasses set themselves off to the best advantage".[2] From this we may see how near the Javans come to European civilisation.

A savage opera of the more advanced kind is performed by the Khyongthas, wild tribes in South Eastern India.[3] The performers, male and female, each had a cigar, which, at emotional passages, was stuck either behind the ear or through the pierced lobe thereof. The instruments were a "shawn" (a cross between the clarionet and the trumpet), "a battalion of drums" tuned up with screws in the most scientific style, and arranged in a circle in the middle of which the player was sitting. The opera, a happily ending love story, with a "primo corifeo tenore," a grumbling bass king, and a romantic soprano, was performed in the most exact style. Mr. Lewin really did like the music; it had distinct rhythm and time, while the choruses were sometimes very quaint and jolly. The drums, too, with their different and mellow tones were employed most judiciously, varying in expression and "tempo" to suit the dramatic action of the piece.

The climax of realism seems to be reached by the Chinese drama. Mr. Görtz tells us that one of his companions saw a performance where a woman actually

[1] Raffles, *l. c.*, i. pp. 335 and 469.   [2] Marsden, *l. c.*, p. 267.
[3] Lewin, *l. c.*, p. 156.

tore out the heart of her female rival and ate it before the very eyes of the audience.[1]

Speaking of the Aleutian Islanders (Indians) Mr. Choris mentions a pantomime in which a sportsman shoots a beautiful bird; it suddenly revives, however, into a beautiful woman with whom he at once falls in love.[2] The ancient Nahua, which belong to some extent to the civilised nations of the Pacific States, always had great preparations for the public dances and dramas, with music, choirs and bands generally led and instructed in many rehearsals by a priest. When one set of dancers became tired another took its place, and so the dance continued through the whole day, each song taking about one hour.[3] The drama scarcely equalled the choral dance, although in this respect, too, the Nahuas showed considerable advancement. The play generally had the character of a burlesque. The performers mostly wore masks of wood or were disguised as animals.[4] Singers appeared on the stage, but no instrumental music is mentioned. The ancient writers unite in praising the perfect unison and good time observed by the singers both in solo and quartette, and they mention particularly the little boys of from four to eight years of age who rendered the soprano in a manner that reflected great credit on the training of their priestly tutors. Each temple, and many noblemen, kept choirs and bands of professional musicians usually led by a priest, who composed odes appropriate to every occasion. The art of music was under royal protection, and singers as well as musicians were exempt from taxation; an academy of science and music was founded where the allied Kings of Mexico, Tezcuco, and Tlacopan presided and distributed prizes to the successful competitors.[5]

[1] Görtz, l. c., iii. p. 60. [2] Choris, l. c., p. 9.
[3] Bancroft, l. c., ii. p. 289. [4] Ibid., p. 291.
[5] Ibid., ii. p. 294, with bibliography on music of ancient Mexico, note 24.

The Indian singer often acts while he sings or dances, representing at the same time a certain scene from life. Sproat describes one of those dances, where a man appears with his arms tied behind his back with long cords, the ends of which are held by other natives, who drive him about. The spectators sing and beat time on their wooden dishes and bearskin drums. Suddenly the chief appears, and plunges his knife into the runner's back. Another blow is given, a third one, until the blood flows down his back, and the victim falls prostrate and lifeless. Mr. Sproat adds he never saw acting more true to the life. And yet the blood was only a mixture of red gum, resin, oil and water, the same that was used in colouring the inside of canoes.[1]   In ancient Mexico and in Guatemala there were ballets at which rarely less than 400 people, but sometimes more than 2000, performed.[2]   During the great feast of Toxcatl the music was supplied by a party of *unseen musicians*, who occupied one of the temple buildings.[3]   The Maya nations in Central America had dramatic performances under the leadership of one who was called "holpop," or master of ceremonies. Women were not allowed to take part in the mummeries, and the plays had a historical character with songs in the form of ballads founded upon local traditions and legendary tales.[4]

Messrs. Spix and Martius tell us of a pantomimic scene of the Coroados in Brazil, which was a kind of lamentation, saying: "They had attempted to pluck a flower from a tree, but had fallen down". The scene is interpreted by the above authors as the loss of Paradise.[5]

Of a peculiar character are the scenes in those theatres where the audience consists of white and black, where

---

[1] Sproat, *l. c.*, pp. 66, 67.

[2] Brasseur, *l. c.*, p. 10, with complete descriptions of those representations and musical examples.

[3] Bancroft, *l. c.*, iii. p. 427.   [4] *Ibid.*, ii. p. 712.

[5] Spix and Martius, *l. c.*, ii. p. 238.

civilisation and originality each react in its own way on
the impression of the drama.   At Quito, Indians with their
wives and babies, and negroes were admitted to the theatre,
together with a party of ladies and gentlemen in evening
dress.   At the most important moments the audience, in
its excitement, rose up and stood on the benches.   In one
of the tricks a pistol was fired, and then all the babies set
up a squall simultaneously, so that the actors had to stop
until the mothers could manage to hush the babies to sleep
again.[1]   This is perhaps a counterpart to Mr. Schlagintweit's narrative of a representation in California, where
the performance was interrupted by babies' cries, in consequence of which the male audience—there were very few
females there at that time—commanded the *actors*, not the
babies, to be silent.[2]

It has often been asked why our dramatic performances
frequently assume a tragic character, although we are at
liberty to choose any other—perhaps more satisfactory—
subject.   A desire for tragical events, however, seems to
be deeply rooted in human nature, and always points to a
freshness and originality of feeling which, not being entirely
used up in every-day life, still press to the surface to unfold
their full emotional vigour in the most precious and noblest
part of our mental life—in our fancy.   Only he, whose life
itself is a mechanism or a tragedy, has no need for serious
play of fancy.   Savages do not yet seem to be in this state
of mental decadence.   Mr. Buchner once said: " Everywhere among the so-called savages we come across the
custom to allow oneself to be shuddered at a sort of
devil ".[3]   Among the women of the Maoris the desire for
" fear and dread "—the two dramatical requirements of
Aristotle—seems to be still more prevalent.   Their chief

[1] I. Pfeiffer, *Second Voyage*, ii. p. 226.
[2] Schlagintweit, *l. c.*, pp. 303-304.
[3] Buchner, *Kamerun*, *l. c.*, p. 26.

amusement is the "tangi," or crying. The ladies do it in the most affecting way, tears are shed, hands are wrung, and the most heart-rending cries excite the sympathy of the company. Yet it is but a "mockery of woe".[1] It is scarcely possible to express a strong psychological impulse in a more simple and natural way.

[1] Taylor, R., *l. c.*, p. 349.

CHAPTER IX.

ON THE ORIGIN OF MUSIC.

WE have been told until tired of hearing it, that the one essential feature in primitive music was rhythm, melody being of accessory importance. We do not meet with a single instance among savages of melody, fixed according to musical principles; melodic cadences, where they occur, serve only as signals, or as a convenient accompaniment to certain activities, such as rowing, towing, or fighting. Even among savage tribes where some songs have in course of time become traditional, words and melody are varied after a few repetitions by different singers, or even by the same performer. Rhythm, taken in a general sense to include "keeping in time," is the essence in music, in its simplest form as well as in the most skilfully elaborated fugues of modern composers. To recall a tune the rhythm must be revived first, and the melody will easily be re-called. The latter may be suggested by the former, but never *vice versâ*. Completely to understand a musical work ceases to be difficult when once its rhythmical arrangement is mastered; and it is through rhythmical performance and rhythmical susceptibility that musical effects are produced and perceived. From these several data I conclude that the origin of music must be sought in a rhythmical impulse in man. I do not mean that musical effects consist in rhythmical movement as such; innumerable ideas and feelings become associated with it, and give rise to those emotions which we on hearing it experience.

The formalistic principle in æsthetics, according to which feelings are no essential feature in "the beautiful," has recently been excellently refuted by Sir John Stainer, who said : Music *exists* only inside the perceiving subject (only the air-waves exist outside of it, but they become music only in a perceiving mind), therefore it cannot be beautiful in itself, because it has "no objective reality or separate existence ". Stainer justly calls the theory of the "self-subsistent form of the beautiful," when applied to music, " sheer nonsense ".[1]

If it be asked whence the sense of rhythm arises, I answer, from the general appetite for exercise. That this desire occurs in rhythmical form is due to sociological as well as psychological conditions. On the one hand, there is the social character of primitive music, compelling a number of performers to act in concert. On the other, our perception of time-relations involves a process of intellection, the importance of which has been pointed out by Prof. Sully, and which I cannot better describe than in his own words : " This perception of successive or time-ordered impressions is something more than a succession of impressions or perceptions. It involves a subsequent act of reflection, by means of which the mind is able at the same time to comprehend them as a whole." [2] Now every product which is of the intellect and appeals to the intellect must contain all the particulars which follow from reflection and render it possible. And since music is produced not merely as an auditory impression and expression, but also in order to evoke reflection, it must contain the qualities above alluded to, *viz.*, time-order and rhythm. Such being the grounds for rhythmical expression the question still remains to be answered : Whence does the general desire for exercise arise ? Mr. Herbert Spencer's theory affords the most valid explanation. It is the sur-

[1] Stainer, *Music in its Relat.*, etc., p. 28.
[2] *Outlines of Psychology*, p. 206.

plus vigour in more highly evolved organisms, exceeding what is required for immediate needs, in which play of all kinds takes it rise; manifesting itself by way of imitation or repetition of all those efforts and exertions which were essential to the maintenance of life (*e.g.*, the war-dance).[1] And it has, moreover, been demonstrated by ethnological research that to bring about bodily fatigue through the manifestation of energy in a perpetually-increasing ratio up to the last degree of lassitude is an indispensable feature of primitive art.[2]

It may be objected that a mere craving for rhythm is far from amounting to a desire for tones and melody, and that, therefore, the question, as to what gives rise to our discriminative pleasure in musical intervals, is not yet satisfactorily answered.   The origin of the significance of intervals and our appreciation of them is indeed one of the utmost importance for our present purpose.   A simple example, however, will teach us that rhythm and sonant rhythm coincide.   Try to play first on a stretched, and then on an unstretched, drum or kettledrum, such as savages use, and you will see that rhythm brings us in and by itself to sound and certain tones, owing to the fact that the

---

[1] *Psychology*, § 534.

[2] It is curious, that whereas Mr. Spencer and all the other English writers who treat of the so-called *Spieltrieb* (play-impulse), *i.g.*, Messrs. Sully and Grant Allen, regard it as an entirely German idea, in Germany it has always been ascribed to English theorists.   It did indeed find embodiment in the writings of Schiller, but was, in my opinion, smothered rather than brought to light by the philosophical jargon which he learned from Kant, and by his own obscure metaphysical style.   He ran into a great labyrinth of metaphysic, whence nobody can find the way out—nor could the author himself, I should suppose.   Hence the theory remained unheeded, though committed to writing nearly a century ago.   Put in our times into intelligible form by Mr. Herbert Spencer, it has nothing in common with its earlier presentment beyond the name, the grounds being quite different. But just as Schiller was inspired by Pope and Addison in his *Anmuth und Würde* and *Briefe über die ästhetische Erziehung des Menschen*, he likewise found approximations to the *Spieltrieb* theory in Home's *Elements of Criticism*, ch. v. (see Zimmermann's *Geschichte der Aesthetik*).

rhythmical movement becomes much more distinct and better-marked on the former, than on the latter, instrument. Hence it came about that men did not stop at simply striking on deerskins as they used to do in primitive times, but proceeded to stretch them first, *i.e.*, to perform on drums and kettledrums. The same implicit principle prompted the custom, in grammar-schools on the continent, of teaching the rhythms of classic poetry in a kind of chant, not of course for musical purposes, but simply because the rhythms were rendered much more distinct when intoned. Perhaps no other illustration shows so well how a rhythmical design, in and by itself, brings us to musical tones, and, by way of these, to the appreciation of intervals and melody.

I not only affirm that rhythm is one of the main constituents, and creates the principal effect, in primitive music, a remark frequently made by composers: I also maintain that rhythm teaches us the appreciation of intervals, both as to their order and grouping. An interval as such has no musical value for us without rhythmical order in time. Even animals recognise and utter intervals, but cannot make any intelligent use of them, because they do not understand rhythmical arrangement. One of the most characteristic signs of a musical nature is, that persons so endowed very often cannot hear any noise periodically repeated without imagining it to be accompanied by music; besides which they are much fonder than unmusical persons of rhythmical movements. Again, rhythm of itself incites to a continuance of rhythmical movement, as is shown in an example given by Mr. Grant Allen:[1] " As we walk along the road, we sometimes amuse ourselves by touching every post, treading upon every second flag, or striking our stick against every lamp-post. If for any reason we are obliged to leave out one of the

[1] *Phys. Æsth.*, p. 114.

series, or to desist from want of the objects in question, a slight blank is felt, which is very faintly unpleasant. The nervous system has put itself into a position of expectancy, and is ready for the appropriate discharge at the right moment. If the opportunity for the discharge is wanting, the gathered energy has to dissipate itself by other channels, which involves a certain amount of conflict and waste." Hence arises the craving for a rhythmical succession of bars and periods.[1] Their recurrence and aggregate arrangement is much more marked and can be more easily understood by a repetition of the same tones or tunes over the same rhythmical periods; moreover, in order to give a more pronounced tone to a rhythmical period, higher notes are used, lower notes marking a decreasing movement, and so on, till we have all the elements of a complete melody. Thus we get accustomed to the interval as such, and appreciate it more than the rhythm as such, the former being the more impressive experience. That the development of a melody from detached notes is due in the first instance to a certain rhythmical movement is an obvious fact. Detached notes do not as such prompt to further development or variety. Rhythm is the initiative force which leads us on to any arrangement of notes whatever, although it must not be forgotten that the specific form assumed in any such arrangement depends a good deal upon our contingent ideas and feelings. The power exerted over us by any rhythmical movement lies in its being adjusted to the form in which ideas and feelings succeed each other in our mind. A composer may give us a direct imitation of some movement of external nature (a thunderstorm, a waterfall, or the like); but the fact holds good none the less, that the effect pro-

---

[1] Compare Guyau, *Esth.*, p. 39 : " Le rhythme ne s'explique lui-même que par la recherche du but et la tension du toutes leurs forces vers ce but unique; l'intérêt est excité par la recherche d'un but. L'intelligence est satisfaite, car nous pouvons calculer la proportion entre la grandeur du but à atteindre et l'effort dépensé " (p. 40).

duced in us even in such cases is due to our recognising, in the intensity, strength, velocity, increase and decrease of the movements, forms corresponding to the flow of our ideas and feelings, though the nature of that flow depends entirely on each individual psychical organism.

I am aware that I put forward nothing new in the assertion, that we easily connect an ascending or descending modulation with an increase or decrease of feeling, but I have always had the impression that even those writers who appreciate the importance of rhythm in music do not consider this fact a sufficient explanation to account for modulation, or for the pleasure we experience in musical intervals, but go afield for a supplementary fact. This they find in the current modulations of speech, or in the intervals used by birds in their "songs," by the perception of which, they suppose, men have come to take pleasure in intervals. I for my part think that Mr. Spencer's general theory of the origin of art is entirely adequate to explain the origin of music, and that to adduce speech and its modulations is not only unnecessary, but absolutely untenable. Men do not come to music by way of tones, but they come to tones and tunes by way of the rhythmical impulse.

It is as Guyau similarly says : " L'expression vive d'un sentiment, quand nous en sommes témoins, fait sans doute monter en nous le ton de ce sentiment mais elle fait aussi monter par sympathie le ton de tous les autres ; par cela même nous sommes portés à agir en tous sens ".[1]

To this emotional power of rhythm an intellectual element must be added. Accent and rhythm (time-division) "associates a vague multitude of sounds into a unity. This is obtained by accentuating one sound especially out of a number of sounds, thus giving them a centre round which the others group themselves."[2] " Le

---

[1] Guyau, *Esth.*, p. 30.　　　　[2] Hupfeld, *l. c.*, pp. 155, 157.

rhythme nous donne la possibilité de prévoir les sons de nous y préparer : c'est un élément connu introduit dans l'inconnu des sensations auditives." [1]　In one word, it is an intellectual element which the strict time-division introduces into the sensual perception of sounds.　In other arts (poetry, painting, sculpture), this intellectual element is introduced by the substantial object (scene) which is to be represented ; architecture claims a practical object ; music alone has its intellectual object in itself.　Every branch of art, it is true, has an emotional origin ; but in the case of music it is not until the peculiar form of time-division (bars and periods) is added to the emotional impulse that we are justified in speaking of it as music proper.

Since the above was first written (*Mind*, vol. xvi., No. 63, p. 375) I have found a good explanation of the importance of rhythm in music in Donovan's book.　I do not agree, however, with his conclusion : " Pitch relationship was from the first step in tune formation the chief formative principle in the grouping of rhythms ".[2]　I should say just the reverse : rhythm is the formative principle in the relationship of pitch, the natural tie which unites the sounds into one group, and is the cause of a certain pitch being maintained throughout the whole group, thus facilitating our perceiving it as one whole.　Pitch relationship is of no imaginable importance if the rhythmical division be not formed beforehand.[3]

Another writer, Mr. Crotti, in his *Musiconomia* seems to misinterpret the rhythmical principle by tracing it to Euler's theory of music being an unconscious counting. This appears to be a mistake from a psychological point of view.　Counting is only a substitute for our remaining

---

[1] Guyau, *l. c.*, p. 59.　　　　[2] Donovan, *From Lyre to Muse*, p. 98.

[3] Compare C. H. Parry in Grove's *Dict.*, iv. p. 605 : " Definiteness of any kind in music, whether of figure or phrase, was first arrived at through connection with dancing ".

conscious of a section of time whenever we lose the capacity of immediately perceiving the time - division. Counting is not the time-division itself.[1]

"MUSIC" IN THE ANIMAL KINGDOM.

Before passing to the discussion of Darwin's theory let us first consider the general character of the (so-called) music in the animal kingdom.

Among the protozoa no sounds are produced; among mollusca[2] and crustacea they are very rare. Among insects they are as a rule confined to the males,[3] with the exception of the Ephippigera, where both sexes produce sounds. They do not possess a true voice and produce noises rather than real tones. Many of them cannot be directly perceived by us because of the limits of our organ of hearing. "I am disposed to think," says Lubbock,[4] that ants perceive sounds which we cannot hear." On the other hand, bees produce sounds for us but seem to be insensible to ours.[5] This want of an organ of voice is the less remarkable as very few insects (only orthoptera) have an organ of hearing, viz.: gryllida, ocridida, orthoptera saltatoria.[6] Yet they attract the females by producing tones. A physiological explanation of this most curious fact is given in Mr. Graber's highly interesting experiments. While Forel thought ants were entirely deaf,[7] Lubbock came to no certain conclusion, and Galton's experiments

---

[1] I find this difference well explained in James' *Psychol.*, i. p. 613 : "Time-division is an intuitive or immediate perception, while counting is a rapid act of association with numbers ". A mistake similar to Crotti's is still more conspicuous in Preyer's paper : 'der Tonsinn,' *l. c.*

[2] See example in Tennent, *l. c.*, ii. pp. 468-470.

[3] Lubbock, *An. Intell.*, p. 61. Compare also Landois, Weismann. Simmel, however, says, *l. c.*, p. 284 : "Bei den musikalischen Insekten musiciren *nur* die Weibchen " (?).

[4] *Ants, Bees, Wasps, l. c.*, pp. 222-233.

[5] *Ibid.*, p. 290, and Preyer, *Grenz., d. Tonwahrn*, p. 24.

[6] C. Vogt, *l. c.*, i. p. 533.   [7] Forel, *Fourmis de la Suisse*.

on insects' hearing were without result,[1] Graber proved
that insects—those living in the air as well as those living
in water—react on sound-impression and run away in
consequence. His experiments further proved that this
reaction was a conscious one, not merely reflex, as the
insects got used to the sound in a comparatively short
time. It was remarkable that with blatta germanica,
or corixa, the reaction consisted in a movement of flight,
while with the orthoptera saltatoria the result was an
approaching towards the sound as in response to the call
of the males. It has been said that the sensation of
of sounds among insects was that of a mere touching,
whereby the periodical air-waves were felt but not distinguished as a peculiar sense of hearing from the sensation of touch in general (Bonnet, Haeckel, Mach). This
presumption proved to be entirely unfounded, while all
circumstances under which Graber's experiments were
made, and especially the delicacy of the sensation, pointed
to its specific character similar to our hearing.[2] Insects
may not hear exactly as we do,[3] but they do possess a
peculiar sense for receiving sounds different from all
the other sensations. This Graber proved by sounding
a bell outside a glass basin containing water, into which
the sound was transmitted along a little ivory stick with
a plate at the end, a distance of two inches from the
corixa. The insect immediately rushed off. If, however,
with this stick water-waves only were produced in the
neighbourhood of the corixa they seemed to enjoy the
undulatory movement without voluntarily moving in any
way.[4] The organ by which they perceive the sounds is
what Graber calls "die chordotonalen Sinnesorgane," *i.e.*,
nerve-ends, similar to the auditory hairs but made tense
like strings of a piano. The insects may perceive sound-
stimuli even without head and brain, their acoustic

[1] Galton, *Inquir.*, pp. 39-40.   [2] Graber, *l. c.*, vol. xxi. p. 86.
[3] *Ibid.*, p. 82.   [4] *Ibid.*, p. 71.

central organ being partly situated in the ganglia of the abdomen.[1]

I also call attention to an additional remark of Mr. Landois important for our further researches; in many cases, he says, sound productions have the purpose of preserving the individual, and some insects produce sounds in case of danger only.[2]

The birds' "song" is the song proper in the animal kingdom. Numerous examples of it, quoted in notes, have been given so many times that I scarcely need collect them. I may mention, however, some unique observations of *new* species by travellers in countries little known to European zoologists. One of the most interesting of these observations was made by Pechuël.[3] One bird sang eight to twelve notes down the chromatic scale, the last ones prolonged and softer, as if meditating. Another sang at sunrise only, others again two to three bars, or exact musical phrases. Some sang all the year round[4] except in August before the rain-season began. Mr. Byam heard in Central America a bird singing the notes of the A major chord down to the lower octave.[5] On the river of Orellana, Spaniards found a bird which followed them for miles and cried "huy, huy"; approaching a village it cried "huis," which means houses.[6] It is remarkable that notwithstanding the melodiousness of birds' song birds have no ear for time and are bound to keep every phrase they once acquire to the same key.[7]

Among the mammalia cats have the most remarkable faculty of hearing shrill sounds; next to them in sensibility

---

[1] Graber, *l. c.*, p. 142. [2] Landois, *l. c.*, p. 180.

[3] Pechuël, *l. c.*, iii. pp. 263-270.

[4] Other examples of birds, the song of which is not restricted to the love-season, by Spencer, "Orig. of Mus.," *Mind*, Oct., 1890.

[5] Byam, *Centr. Amer.*, *l. c.*, p. 159. [6] Herrara, *l. c.*, p. 37.

[7] The singing Hesperomys cognatus, observed by S. Lockwood (*l. c.*), had no ear for time, kept to the same key of B (two flats), and strictly in a major key.

are little dogs, not large ones, and sometimes ponies.[1] Thus the sense of hearing does not seem to correspond to their faculty of uttering sounds. This latter is the more difficult to be judged about as our limits of hearing are so different. When singing mice were exhibited in London some people who went to hear them could hear nothing, others a little, others again very much.[2] On the other hand, the loudest voices are not the most musical, and not every emission of sound can be called singing. In speaking of such utterances Lunn says : " It is objected by physiologists that tigers, oxen and other beasts having loud voices have neither false chords nor ventricles," and therefore their voices are unmusical. The cuckoo's call, the cat's purr, and the ass's bray are each the result of inspiration and expiration. Song-birds all sing on expiration.[3] Birds' songs alone have all the *physiological* characteristics of singing.

The monkey's tones of voice are so distinctly varied, when these animals are on duty as posts or scouts on the flanks or rear, that a person much accustomed to watch their movements will at length fancy that he can understand their signals.[4] Mr. Garner actually succeeded in understanding them, and by catching and reproducing these sounds by means of a phonograph he got the apes to do the corresponding action.[5] But this, and so many examples of the animal's *call*, proved that the vocal utterance, originally produced as emotional reflex, has been used later on with a certain intention, a special meaning, *i.e.*, in an intellectual way. All these utterances in the animal kingdom—when they once become conscious and

---

[1] Galton, *Inquir.*, pp. 39-40.

[2] *Ibid.* In his experiments with Galton's whistle Mr. Zwaardenmaker found that our limits of hearing correspond so exactly to our age that we may judge of age according to limits of hearing (*l. c.*, p. 53).

[3] Lunn, *l. c.*, p. 95.   [4] Parkyns, *l. c.*, i. p. 229.

[5] Garner, *l. c.*, p. 232. I cannot, however, sympathise with Mr. Garner's fantastic attempt to obtain an articulate speech of monkeys.

and cease to be mere emotional reflexes—have so much
more the character of a communication than of an æsthetic
product that they resemble more closely primitive speech
than primitive art. Surely a call (of females) or a cry (of
danger) is a word or a suppressed sentence, but not a composition, although the former may in its outward appearance closely resemble a musical phrase; the psychical
difference is immense nevertheless.[1] In apes especially
the intelligence for communication is highly developed.[2]

There is a remarkable peculiarity of the gorilla which
is of more importance in the question of its musical ability
than all its vocal utterances—the gorilla drums.[3] Mr.
Falkenstein observed he beat his breast with both fists:
"im Übermass des Wolbefindens und aus reiner Lust,"
getting up on the hinder feet. At the same time he clapped
his hands, and, turning himself round, began to dance in
such a jovial manner that the observer thought the ape
must be drunk. Yet he was not, and all his jumping
originated from a mere pleasure in doing it ("surplus of
vigour"). He was not taught to do so, and never did in
Europe, perhaps—as Falkenstein justly concludes—because his health failed. It is known that the gorilla,
when attacking his enemy, beats his breast in exactly the
same manner.

Gorillas are not at all the only dancing and drumming
species in the animal kingdom. The tetrao phasianellus

---

[1] On the difference of emotional and intellectual expression see my
essay, "Über die Bedeutung der Aphasie," in *Viertelj. f. Musikw.*, vii.,
Jahrg., i. Heft.

[2] Garner's above-mentioned observations distinctly point to power of
reflection in apes. The late female chimpanzee, Sally, in the Zoological
Gardens "knew the difference between three and five straws" (Morgan,
Anim. Sketch, p. 71). "Later on she was able to count up to ten, and to twenty
when with the guard alone." The Cays, which themselves possess plaintive
and joyful tones, learn how to distinguish various modifications of the voice
as well as of the features (Rengger, *l. c.*, pp. 51 and 55).

[3] Falkenstein, *l. c.*, ii. p. 152; confirmed by Du Chaillu and Koppenfels.

(North America) runs round and round in a circle,[1] the snipe drums with his tail, the tetrao umbellus and the kalij pheasant in the Himalayas drum with their wings.

Ostriches dance a waltz, they beat the ground, and then they revolve, at first slowly, gently beating time with their wings, but soon quicker and quicker, until at length they twirl round at a bewildering rate, sweeping round and round with breathless rapidity.[2] These manners of dancing much resemble the dances of some savage tribes.

With these facts to hand, we shall have to object to Darwin's view, that the original music was the bird's love-song, and that the agreeable feelings which naturally accompanied it were transmitted (through individual heredity) to further generations and even *species*, and that this accounts for the pleasure men have in music. I shall have to object to this theory from different standpoints, and first of all from a psychological one.

1. It is possible that male-birds of handsomer plumage are preferred by the hen-birds, but may we thence infer that birds understand painting? Similarly some male-birds may be preferred by the hens for the quality of their song; can we, therefore, say that they understand music? Is the bird's song a composition? Certainly not. But by music we always understand a musical composition, or at least its reproduction, that is to say, a consciously designed and constructed work of art. I am aware that there is no difference in kind between the bird's instinct and the human design; there is only a difference of degree, as between mind and instinct generally, but this degree must nevertheless be attained before we are justified in speaking of any group of sounds as music. Birds have no conscious intention of charming by the display of magnificent hues in such and such a manner, nor is it within their power

---

[1] Darwin, *l. c.*, ii. pp. 68, 74.   [2] Morgan, *Anim. Sket.*, p. 171.

to choose their colours any more than it is to change their songs, so as to make them correspond with their feelings. A corresponding change may actually have taken place in many cases, but are we sure that it was intended? Can we take it as a consciously-arranged composition? [1]

On the other hand, however, it may be asked whether the hen-birds, in distinguishing between different singers, do not show that they appreciate their singing to at least a limited degree. But even if it be admitted that they really appreciate *singing*, their discriminative taste for bird-minstrelsy could as little be called a feeling for music as their distinguishing one bird's plumage from another amounts to a feeling for painting. No doubt, every bird hears sounds and distinguishes the call of one bird among that of others, but it is one thing to hear a sound, another to recognise it as a melody. We usually say the hen-bird chooses the best singer, but which is the best singer? The audience in a concert-room do not agree which singer is the best, while we pretend to know exactly which bird sings the best and to think that the hen-bird knows it too and is certainly of the same opinion as ourselves! Not one of us knows whether the hens' choice among the cock-birds' singing is awarded on musical grounds, whether other motives do not prompt them to follow the males, and whether the coincidence between their action and a certain quality of song be only a matter of chance. To me it appears that birds are lacking in that act of reflection by which they might comprehend the time-ordered melody as a whole, and distinguish it from a certain number of incoherent notes. Birds do not keep time unless they reproduce invariably and mechanically the same short

---

[1] There was a time when the bee was called a good mathematician because of the admirable construction of the honeycomb, " whereas it is now generally admitted to be the result of the simple principle of economy of material applied to a primitive cylindrical cell " (Wallace, *Darwinism*, p. 336).

refrain at the same pitch, and I fear that in speaking of bird-music we impute too much of human psychological interest both to their declarations of love and to their appreciation of the so-called " song ".

As to that, some writers would seem to have a special mission to interpret the language of birds. Mr. Berg, for instance, assures us that, strictly speaking, all kinds of animals equipped with a sound-apparatus, including frogs and crickets, " must be considered as musical creatures, since they experience the same feelings in their concerts as music excites in us, and many of them pursue in music the same object as ourselves ". I must confess I envy Mr. Berg his ability of extracting correct information from frogs, crickets, and the like, as to their musical attainments, and I envy too the frog himself for his admirable knowledge of what causes pleasure in human beings, without which he would never have been able to compare his own feelings with ours, or to disclose that he takes the same pleasure in croaking as we in singing; we poor men sometimes do not know ourselves of what our pleasure in art consists. Darwin himself says (*l. c.*, p. 74) : " We must not judge by the standard of man's taste ". As we are men, however, and do not know other standards of taste, we had better not judge at all. Romanes again says (*Anim. Intell.*, p. 282) " that the standard of æsthetic taste differs in different species of birds as it does in different races of men ". If this is so we can never get to the bottom of birds' æsthetic taste, as we cannot ask them. It is as if we would say the magpie is covetous as it stole a sovereign ; it was a false one, it is true, but this shows that there are different standards of covetousness. In fact, however, the magpie was struck by the lustre, not by the money, as birds are affected by the sound without being inspired by the music. Indeed, not even in the relations of the sexes can the sense of beauty be said to play an important part in the animal kingdom, and it is this peculiar part of

Darwin's theory which has been altered in the most satisfactory way by Westermark (*l. c.*, pp. 240-252). Not different standards of beauty caused racial differences—as Darwin supposed—but racial differences were caused by different necessities to best suit the surroundings. These "outward manifestations of physical perfection" may have been taken later on in higher stages of mental development as beauty in the æsthetic sense. "Even if we grant, as we fairly may, that brightly coloured flowers, . . . in association with nectar, have been objects of appetence to insects, and that brilliant plumage, in association with sexual vigour, has been a factor in the preferential mating of birds; this is a very different thing from saying that either in the selection of flowers by insects, or in the selection of their mates by birds, a consciously æsthetic motive has been a determining cause " (L. Morgan, *Anim. Intell.*, p. 413). In my opinion the simple beating of a drum contains more " music " than all the sounds uttered by birds, and we owe our musical faculty to the time-sense rather than to our sense of hearing. Of course, in following the utterances of the animal kingdom down to a very primitive stage, we must go back as far as the bird's song, but we are not more or less justified in discerning in it the origin of music, than we should be in saying that all animals equipped with sound-apparatus speak English, the English language being just as peculiar an order of utterance—of which the peculiar origin is still *sub judice*— as is human music. The origin of language is not to be sought in the fact that *birds* call " cuckoo," cluck " go-back," or imitate our speech, but in *our* connecting certain things and ideas with certain sounds. It is true some animals do so too, but why then do we not at once call birds little poets, who sing the praises of universal love as they flit in the forest from bough to bough? We know now-a-days that even some kinds of fishes produce sounds: why are not they considered musical? There must be as great a difference between these sounds and our music as there is between a barking dog and a poet—a difference perhaps only of degree, but yet of so many degrees as to render us unable to call both by the same name, and this for the same reasons as prevent us from calling a fish an ape, although in the scale of animals the latter is evolved from the former. I cannot conclude this subject better than in Morgan's words : " I do not for one moment deny that in animals are to be found the perceptual *germs* of even the higher emotional states, but adequate terms must be to a large extent emptied of their meaning before they can become applicable to the emotional consciousness of brutes " (L. Morgan, *Anim. Intell.*, p. 414).

2. There is also biological evidence against Darwin's theory of our pleasure in music. The emission of sound such as we hear in nature does not develop correlatively with the evolution of the higher classes of animals.[1] It might indeed be possible with some little trouble to show, as Darwin did, that there is something akin to singing even amongst mammalia, but it will never be possible to show that this so-called singing of mammalia, if from a musical point of view it be worthy of notice at all, is really developed from birds' singing, with human song as its highest outcome. It is not even singing proper from a mere physiological point of view (as we have seen, p. 240). Birds' song is in many cases not at all confined to the love season,[2] and it is, to say the least, extremely doubtful that acquired modifications, such as those due to the accompanying feelings of the bird's song, are transmittable to the offspring and to further species (Weismann). But, even if all Darwin's hypothesis were correct, I have a further objection, taken from the character and develop-ment of the bird's song, which we will now take into consideration :—

[1] Compare Stumpf, *Musikpsych. in England, l. c.*, pp. 300-314.
[2] Spencer, " Orig. of Mus.," *Mind*, Oct., 1890.

"The young bird acquires his song by *traditional inheritance*," that is, each brood, endowed by physiological inheritance with the necessary organs for singing, learns, after long practice, by constantly hearing the song of its elders, "the melody *peculiar to that species*".[1] Thus the most important factor in acquiring a song is direct imitation;[2] it may happen that if the bird's tutors belong to another species, the bird learns the song of this other species, not of its own. Witchell in his careful investigation into this subject also confirms the above: "The songs of birds are not immediately acquired, but developed *in each individual* by practice and cultivation".[3] Thus the composer Spohr observed a species of cuckoo at Thierachern in Switzerland, which somehow acquired a third tone between the common two of the cuckoo's call (singing G, F, E).[4] The primitive sounds of birds are onomatopoetic, *e.g.*, sounds produced by eating, signify food,[5] and so probably many other pleasing sounds might be traced to a very material association without betraying an æsthetic sense in any way. This accounts for gregarious birds being garrulous, solitary species silent. Mr. Witchell further shows in examples that the call-note and the danger-cry have a common origin, namely, the cry of distress,[6] while a whole phrase is constructed by means of repetition of the alarm-cry, accompanied by rapid movement of the lungs similar to that which occurs during human laughter.[7]

Bearing in mind that the original cause of sounds being uttered was distress or alarm, and assuming that Darwin's presumption were true, the feeling which originally accompanied the emission of sound could consequently

---

[1] Clark, *l. c.*, p. 209.   [2] Morgan, *An. Int.*, p. 454.

[3] Witchell, *l. c.*, p. 240 ; so also is mimicry (p. 242); Witchell used the phonograph in getting the songs (p. 245).

[4] Spohr, *l. c.*, i. p. 257.   [5] Witchell, *l. c.*, p. 236.

[6] *Ibid.*, p. 234.   [7] *Ibid.*, p. 238.

not only accompany it in further stages of development but could also be transmitted to future generations. Thus making music ought to have the most awful consequences. Darwin does not seem to have taken into consideration that the bird's *love-song* means a comparatively high stage of its vocal utterances.

It is also improbable from a biological point of view that if anything be transmitted from one *generation* to the other, that it should at the same time be entirely transmitted from one *sex* to the other. " While among birds it is the male which generally sings, it is the female among men, who excels in voice and tries to attract the males." [1] To this is due—according to Haeckel—the general practice of, and perfection in, female singing in our "highly civilised " society.

3. There is finally a physiological evidence against the theory that human music should be the direct outcome of the bird's song. I still maintain that this is much more the case with human words than with human music. If the third frontal convolution in the bird's brain is stimulated by an electric current the bird begins to " sing ". Now this third frontal convolution is the *speech*-centre, on which our *musical* faculty does not at all depend. [2]

In former days we had a much simpler, yet similar theory, without heredity and development, according to which men learned music by direct imitation of the singing of birds. We have, however, never heard of an imitation of the *melody* in birds' song among savages. They imitate every bird's call, but not what we call the melody of the singing birds proper; wherefore, I presume, men do not acknowledge the song of birds as music before they are themselves well advanced in the art. Moreover, Australians have songs and music but scarcely any singing birds. " Feebly indeed, among Australia's birds, are represented

[1] Haeckel, *l. c.*, ii. p. 247.
[2] Compare my article on "Aphasia," *l. c..* p. 58, note 2.

the melodious notes which are freely poured forth by many of the species inhabiting countries north of the equator . . . no mavis has she to usher in the morning . . . no Philomel to break the stillness of the night . . . quietude, as regards the voice of birds, reigns supreme ; or if there be any exception to this rule it is the noisy screams of her parrots, honey-eaters, manura, reed-birds." [1]

Some time ago Prof. Weismann, in an essay full of interesting and important matter, declared that music arose " as a secondary effect of our sense of hearing not originally intended in nature ". It is perhaps a verbal contention to question whether we are justified in speaking of intention and of secondary effects in nature, but I do not think that our musical faculty is an effect of our sense of hearing, because the perception of particular tones and tunes plays a very low part, if any, in primitive music— certainly a much lower part than the rhythmical arrange- ment. It is perhaps for this reason, as Prof. Weismann endeavoured to show, that the sense of hearing in human beings was well developed before musical practice began, and was not developed by way of the latter.[2] I entirely agree with Prof. Weismann in his assertion that the same sense of hearing produces different musical effects accord- ing as there are in human beings different qualities of " soul ". My conclusion, however, is that, in an inquiry into the origin of music, it is this peculiar quality of

---

[1] J. Gould, *l. c.*, i. p. 2 ; Meinicke, *Austr.*, i. p. 85.

[2] Brehm in his *Thierleben* and Prof. Sully in an essay on " Animal Music " (*Cornhill Magazine*, 1879, ii. 605) came to the same conclusion. Stumpf (*Tonpsych.*, i. p. 344) also says : " The human ear has not improved in historical times ". Comp. Lubbock (*Times*, p. 597) : " The music of savages is rude and melancholy in comparison with ours : and thus, though the ear of man may not have appreciably altered, the pleasure which we may derive from it has been immensely increased ". Burney, however, says: " What is music ? An innocent luxury, unnecessary, indeed, to our existence, but a great improvement and gratification of the sense of hearing " (*Hist. of Mus.*, preface, p. xiii.).

"soul" which has to be examined, and not a certain condition of the sense of hearing. And this quality is the time-sense with the faculty of discerning in the strength, velocity, increase, and decrease of sounds produced by our "surplus vigour," forms corresponding to the flow of our feelings and ideas.

THE SPEECH-THEORY.

Another theory, according to which music arose from speech, seems to me to explain a correct observation in a wrong direction. We can see, in almost all the examples furnished by ethnology, that music is the expression of emotion. There is no doubt that emotion is one, though only one, of the sources of human language. Consequently we speak in faster or slower, louder or softer, higher or deeper tones, and with more or less variety of accent, for the same reasons as would influence us in musical expression. And since through speech the ideas which influence the form of our expression generally (to wit, its intensity, strength, rapidity, and modulation) acquire a definite verbal setting, we learn to connect certain ideas with certain forms of expression. By reason of this connection between our ideas and feelings and some form of expression we come more easily to associate them with any kind of music.

We need not push this theory too far. Music will certainly develop this form of expression, than which it has no other, in a different manner from speech, the only media of which are tones and their modulation, though the accompanying mode of diction is not to be neglected : it renders possible the composition of a poem, and qualifies music as a higher intellectual pleasure than any simple auditory impression could be. The characteristic feature, in my opinion, of Mr. Spencer's speech-theory is, that he first showed an intimate physiological connection between all our emotions and their expression, leading us to discover vestiges of music in declamation and conversely.   This it is which distinguishes it from all other speech-theories of the last century, which assumed the simple imitation of language ready-made (a notion long since refuted in the speech-controversy of that century, notably by Langere ; see Jullien, *La musique et la philosophie du XVIIIme siècle*).

Whereas Mr. Spencer, however, seems to think that musical modulation originates in the modulations of speech, I maintain that it arises directly from the rhythmical impulse.   It is true that modulation in the developed art of music is very often influenced by the modulations of speech, and it is remarkable that this influence occurs to a greater extent in modern music than in the older classical school (take Berlioz, Wagner, Beethoven in the 9th symphony, and compare, say, with Palestrina and Handel).   Herein may lie the source of that unanimity which I have noticed between the most zealous opponents and adherents of the speech-theory on the one point, *viz.*, that vestiges of declamation are to be met with in music, and that we ought, on the strength of this advance, to finish a controversy nearly a century old.   That it has become customary for our composers to have regard to the inflections of the speaking voice does indubitably facilitate the connection of ideas and feelings with music, even if it be purely instrumental ; but the fact has nothing to do with the question of the origin of music.   Even admitting the present reciprocity of influence in both music and speech, I doubt that such is the origin, and that for several reasons.

1. We find even in the most primitive state of culture a sort of recitative, side by side both with a kind of music, in which the rhythm alone plays a leading part, and with songs, the words of which are perfectly meaningless or at least cannot be understood by the tribe in question.   In such circumstances it is obviously impossible for the musical modulations to have taken rise from the spoken

modulations, since there is no genuine speech in the case at all. Among savages primitive vocal music reveals in many cases no connection with language, but is simply a succession of musical sounds sung by the voice. The recitative is a secondary form of poetical speech, the structure of which is influenced by music already invented, but it is by no means the original type of music. It is only made possible in stages where speech is so far advanced as to allow of connected sentences or stories.

2. Primitive music cannot have evolved from modulation of the voice in emotional speech, as the most primitive music is in so many cases no modulation of tone but merely a rhythmical movement in one tone, as, *e.g.*, in Tierra del Fuego, in Fiji Islands, and with some tribes of the North American Indians. Therefore, Mrs. Brown in her interesting book on *Musical Instruments* justly remarks: One of the two characteristic features of primitive music is the " decided prominence of the rhythmic as opposed to the melodic element "; the second is the " monotony which results from the fact that most of primitive songs are contained within a very narrow compass ".[1] " The sense of time seems to have been highly developed in man long before he had the faintest conception of what we call melody." [2]

3. Speech expressed in song does not develop at the same rate as speech itself; on the contrary, the intellectual importance of singing declines with the higher development of language   Examples of a word changing its meaning when spoken with a different vocal inflection are only to be met with in primitive language. Mr. Spencer in his recent essay says: " It may be that music uses distinct tones and speech indistinct, but the former might be developed from the latter ". If this were so, we should inevitably discern some traces of this development in its

---

[1] Brown, *l. c.*, p. 242.   [2] *Ibid.*, p. 243.

continual advance from a primitive stage up to perfectly
artistic songs, just as we are able to follow a parallel
development from the movements of a primitive, up to
those of a modern, dancer.

4. Music is an expression of emotion, speech the expression of thought. If we assume that music originates
in, and is developed from, speech, we must also assume
that emotion is developed from thought. It may be that
in the adult human organism particular emotions do arise
in this way, but it is not true of emotions generally. Moreover, many cases of aphasia prove that an expression cannot be emotional and intellectual at the same time, the one
kind of expression arising in and spreading through different
parts of the brain and nervous system from those occupied
by the other. It may be, however, that in a very primitive
stage of mental development thought and emotion have
not yet become clearly differentiated. To illustrate my
point, let us compare singing and speaking with drawing
and writing. Each member of these pairs constitutes at
the present day a distinct order of activities, though at
one time each pair wrought with the same materials,
writing being picture-drawing, just as singing and speaking may have used the same vocal sounds. Each, being
a specifically different mode of expression, developed its
material in course of time in a very diverse manner, till
musical tones and spoken sounds came to be as distinct
one from the other as a picture from a letter. Similarly
Mach says (*l. c.*, p. 125) that "music stands to speech as
the ornament to writing". There are indeed some primitive ornaments the appearance of which is such as to
render it impossible to distinguish them from primitive
written characters (compare Grosse, *l. c.*, pp. 403, 404).
Yet the psychical source is in both cases quite different.
Although writing a scientific book is entirely intellectual,
yet we may observe a good deal of emotional element in
the written characters of its MS.; and there was still more

of this element in the MSS. of ancient times.   Even early
prints betray this emotional influence.   Nevertheless, it
would be ridiculous to say that great painters write more
beautifully, and that people with prettier handwriting
possessing frequent emotional traces have more talent for
drawing.   No one would say, nor indeed has any one said,
that drawing originated in writing, or writing in drawing.
I think then that music and speech did not arise the one
from the other, but that both arose from (or together
with) an identical primitive stage in one of their common
elements.   Hence it happens that in inquiring into the
origin of music we necessarily come into contact with
primitive language, and in inquiring into the origin of
speech we come into contact with primitive music, or,
more correctly speaking, with the corresponding sounds.
Primitive human utterance, using sound-metaphors and
onomatopœia in order to make itself intelligible, may
resemble primitive musical tones ; nevertheless an early
separation of distinct tones and indistinct sounds seems
to have taken place, not as a transition from the one as
prior to the other as succeeding, but as a divergence from
a primitive state which is, strictly speaking, neither of the
two.   Sometimes, however, a kind of unity remains even
through later periods of civilisation, as ethnology can
show (*e.g.*, in Dahomey, Siam, China, Japan, Tierra del
Fuego) ; and, bearing this in mind, we cannot say, as has
been alleged by so many opponents of the speech-theory,
that there is no singing in speech in the world at all.
For this reason I should not agree with Gurney, who said
"that the six or eight wordless notes, which a child of
four will croon over to itself with never-ceasing delight,
are, both in themselves and in their emotional effect, as
truly and absolutely remote from speech as is the *Eroica*
symphony ".   They would be so indeed if they were purely
musical notes, but they are in fact neither music nor speech.
I have never heard an infant really sing—that is to say,

invent (though it may repeat) a song—before it could speak, while its crying is unfortunately a very familiar experience; and it is just this power of uttering, no matter what, that enables it in course of time to evolve a faculty both of singing and speaking.   Gurney's further remark—that music is a separate order, an adjustment of proportional elements, of which speech knows nothing—is inapplicable to all its elements, since music has one element in common with speech, *viz.*, sound-production. Look at the results of ethnological research.   It is as difficult to tell whether a primitive utterance is sufficiently developed to be called musical as it is to know whether it can properly be called language or not.   This is perhaps the reason why Darwin and Mr. Spencer do not agree on the question as to which comes first, music or language. " Spencer," said Darwin, " comes to an exactly opposite conclusion to that at which I have arrived.   He concludes, as Diderot did formerly,[1] that the cadences used in emotional speech afford the foundation from which music has been developed, whilst I conclude that musical notes and rhythm were first acquired by the male or female progenitors of mankind for the sake of charming the opposite sex.   Thus musical notes became firmly [I should rather say, possibly] associated with some of the strongest passions an animal is capable of feeling."   I think Darwin's mistake in the sentence here quoted lies in his speaking of " music," instead of musical *sounds, i.e.*, sounds which come to be used later in music.

Since the above was written for the first time in *Mind*

---

[1] This statement is not quite correct, as Diderot did not speak of the *origin* of music, but only of " *le modèle du chant* ".   " C'est la declamation, si le modèle est vivant et pensant, c'est la bruit, si le modèle est inanimé. Il faut considérer la déclamation comme une ligne et le chant une autre ligne qui serpenterait sur la première " (Diderot, *l. c.*, p. 198).   " Je ne voudrais *pas* assurer que celui qui récite bien chantera bien; mais je serais surpris que celui qui chante bien ne sût pas bien réciter " (*ibid.*, p. 199).

(July, 1891), Mr. Spencer published a reply in the same journal, Oct., 1891. To this I can only repeat what I said in my reply in Jan., 1892. Mr. Spencer takes objection that I should credit him with having said music arises from the intellect, whereas he had named the emotions as its origin. And in stating this he quotes his own words: "We may say that cadence, comprehending all variations of voice, is the commentary upon propositions of the intellect". Now, it was precisely to this that I took objection, namely, that the emotions leading to music (or as I put it more directly, music) should be held to arise as a commentary upon *intellectual* propositions; and I pointed to the physiological fact that emotion and intellect are associated with different parts of the brain and nervous system. The origin of emotions, and consequently of all their resulting products, must be independent of all propositions of the intellect.

With respect to his remark that it is not true to say speech is an expression of thought, I must again refer to those cases of aphasia where the patient retains the language of the emotions, the power of uttering single words, and of singing, when the power of speaking connectedly has long been lost. Emotions have unquestionably a language of their own ; from them *single words* may arise, but speech, so far as modern physiology and pathology can show, is an intellectual form of expression. Mr. Spencer concludes: " The whole argument of his essay is to show that it is from this emotional element of *speech (!)* that music is evolved ". Certainly ; but this emotional element, he says, grows up in proportion to the intellectual (*Essays*, p. 422), the changes of voice grow with the " more numerous *verbal* forms needed to convey our *ideas* ". It is the dependence which I call in question ; for the *growth* of the intellectual and emotional elements are, physiologically speaking, in no connection whatever.

Baker in his treatise on " Music of the North American Indians" came to the conclusion that of the two distinct forms of primitive music (rhythmical dance music and recitative) the former was the more ancient, and this for several reasons (*vide* p. 186).

There are besides some minor points in the speech-theory requiring perhaps further explanation. My experience has not shown me that people who have a singing element in their speaking voice are more musical than others. And even in their case it would be impossible as a rule to put down any given spoken accents in notes. Again, these accents are not objectively fixed, nor is speech an abstract organon separated from all concrete life. Every one utters the same idea in his own fashion, and speech is only the sensuously perceptible part of a great psychical process, differing in different individuals at different times. It may, therefore, be no easy matter merely to imitate the modulations of speech, nor would it aid us in being mutually more intelligible (though it might afford us a good deal of guess-work in ideas), nor could music (I mean the art as such) ever evolve a new language, because musical forms—that is to say, the intensity, strength, velocity, increase and decrease of tones—can be understood only in a relative sense. Mr. Walker tried as early as 1789 to put the so-called natural song of speech down to notes, which attempt—so frequently made since then— must necessarily be a failure. Walker is quite right in stating: Singing notes rest on one note, speaking ones slide up and down " without any perceptible rest ".[1] But this is precisely the reason why Mr. Walker's attempt to fix the notes of the " song " in speech is in itself a contradiction and practically a voluntary transformation. Such theories have been refuted a hundred times during centuries, but have nevertheless constantly arisen again.

[1] Walker, *l. c.*, p. 7.

It has very often been said that music represents only
the typical forms of feeling. Strictly speaking, however, it
is impossible to represent the type as such. Representation
is individualisation. On the other hand, it is equally impossible to express by musical methods all our particular
feelings. Can we evade this dilemma? I think so. The
musician is situated similarly to the anatomist, who gets
a small piece of bone and is able to tell exactly whether
it is a human bone or not. It is not of course the human
type as such that is represented by the bone, and no one
can tell to which individual the bone belonged, yet we
recognise in this small fraction of a particular man the
human type. So I too am not wrong, I hope, in asserting
that music reproduces such a small fraction of the forms
both of external and internal nature that we can recognise
in it at best the type, and not the specific details. Music
can rouse feeling, but it cannot cause *what* it is we
feel, this being the outcome of each individual psychical
organism.[1] Coincidence between the feelings of composer
and audience can be only a fortuitous, not a necessary,
result, because of the relative nature of musical forms.
Nor is it essential, from an artistic point of view, that they
should completely coincide, since in the cultivation and
exercise of music a man's intention is not so much to
make himself intelligible as to inspire his fellow-men.

Correlative to the decline in the importance of vocal
inflection as an intellectual factor in human communication, as language undergoes higher development, is the
suggestive power of specific ideas implanted in highly-
developed music by feelings and associations, differing in
different psychical organisms. And from those vague
associations, suggested in a primitive stage by rhythmical
movements, are developed the higher pleasures of melody.

I am well aware that celebrated composers and specula-

---

[1] In asserting this rule, some musical forms of a stereotyped character,
such as a funeral march or a waltz, cannot be taken into account.

tive "philosophers" have been opposed to the importance of rhythm in music, but I am also aware that our best possessions are not the theories, but the works of art, bequeathed us by the former, and that our best philosophy is not of the speculative order. Whatever enthusiastic musicians or "philosophers" may have said of a music of the future without rhythm, I always feel inclined to interpret their prophecies poetically rather than scientifically, and believe that what Gurney said on the other side will remain true: "Wherever rhythm is perceived with enjoyment there is implied a nascent stimulation of the dance-instinct, and, however much music 'ought to be' independent of time, I am afraid that in listening to it, with our present physical organisms, we shall retain a prejudice for rhythmical phenomena in preference to unrhythmical noumena".

With regard to the dance-instinct Lombroso gave the physiological explanation that the auditory nerve stands in so close connection with the spinal cord that we may say "dancing is a sort of reflective motion caused by music".[1] It may be well to remember that the famous Laura Bridgman perceived the rhythm, arrangement, and loudness of tones through vibrations of the soil. Another deaf, dumb, and blind girl, Helen Keller, was also fond of music: "Elle fut tellement enlevée par la cadence de la musique qu'on eut beaucoup de peine à l'empêcher de danser".[2]

TALES AND LEGENDS.

Hindus attribute the origin of music to divine agency. Brahma invented it in virtue of his active power, as the goddess of speech, Saraswati.[3] The Chinese have an

---

[1] Lombroso, *l. c.*, p. 145.   [2] Bélugon, *l. c.*, p. 176.

[3] Panchkari Banerjea, *l. c.*, p. 4. He also attributes the decline of music in India to the music masters or ostads: "Ignorant generally as they

ancient tradition according to which they obtained their musical *scale* from a miraculous bird.[1] According to the Japanese tradition the sun-goddess once retired into a cave when music was devised by the gods to lure her forth from the retreat. Hence the natives of the Indian Archipelago shout and beat gongs when an eclipse takes place.[2] The Javans say the first music of which they have an idea was produced by the accidental admission of the air into a bamboo tube which was left hanging on a tree. With regard to the music of gamelan, "that, say they, was procured from heaven, and we have a long story about it".[3] Unfortunately this story was never told.

The Asaba people (on the Niger) say that music was first brought into the country by a hunter named Orgardié, a native of Ibuzo, upon his return from an expedition in search of big game. There he heard music in the thick forest proceeding from a party of forest spirits that were approaching. He remembered the *steps of the dances* and the music of the songs sung, and upon his return to his village taught his countrymen this music, which was called Egu olo. From Ibuzo music was imported to Asaba land. It must be mentioned that every fresh dance or song is believed to have been first heard by hunters during their expeditions in the jungles.[4] It is interesting to see how they appreciate music in connection with dance, *i.e.*, from its rhythmical side, and how they take to it *after* the hunt, *i.e.*, when their energy, employed in the hunt (struggle for life) a few moments before, ceases to be employed and then finds another vent in the form of play.

---

are of the other branches of knowledge, as a rule, do not unreservedly teach their pupils. They fancy that should they teach all that they know, they would ere long be thrown into the shade by their pupils" (p. 26).

[1] Engel, *Myths*, etc., i. p. 75.   [2] Crawfurd, *l. c.*, i. p. 304.
[3] Raffles, *l. c.*, p. 472.   [4] Day, *Niger*, p. 274.

According to a myth of the Nahua Nations (North America) the god Tezcatlipoca sent for music from the Sun, and constructed a bridge of whales and turtles (symbols of strength) by which to convey it to the earth.[1] The messenger went towards the house of the Sun singing what he had to say. And the Sun heard the song, and he straightway warned his people and servants, saying: "See, now, that ye make no response to this chant, for whoever replies to it must be taken away by the singer". But the song was so exceedingly sweet that some of them could not but answer, and they were lured away, bearing with them the drum, teponaztli, and the kettle-drum, vevetl.[2] Remarkable from a psychological point of view is the story told by the Maidu tribes (North America): An old man had in his hand the sacred rattle, from which all others since have been modelled, and said to his friends: "Always when you sing have this rattle with you, and let it be made after the pattern which I now show you. The spirit of sweet music is in this rattle, and when it is shaken your songs will sound better."[3] Thus those tribes seem to have the same impression as we have, that accompanying noises facilitate the musical imagination. An Arabic legend says that Modhar, the camel driver, fell down from his seat and had his arm hurt. In his pains he repeatedly called: "Ya, yadah". His fine voice stirred up the camels, they ran more quickly, and from that time all the camel drivers sang. This is said to have been the first song in Arabia,[4] although it looks like a joke rather than a myth. The natives of Abyssinia have a tale on the origin of music according to which S. Yared was the author of music, inspired as he was by the Holy Spirit, which appeared to him in form of a pigeon, teaching him at the same

[1] Bancroft, *l. c.*, ii. p. 92.   [2] *Ibid.*, iii. p. 63.
[3] St. Powers, *l. c.*, p. 296.   [4] Christianowitsch, *l. c.*, p. 12.

time reading, writing, and music[1] A similar tale is that of the Armenians. Here Mesrop invented music in the year 364 B.C.,[2] while Syrian music, *i.e.*, church music, was invented by St. Ephrem, 370 B.C.[3] In ancient mythologies the invention of stringed instruments frequently has some connection with the sea or water generally, so has the god Nareda of the Hindus, Nereus of the ancient Greeks, the Scandinavian god Odin, and Wäinämöinen, in the old national epos of the Finns, constructed his instrument out of fish bones; many Swedish, Scotch, Norwegian, and Danish stories show the same connection.[4]

[1] Villoteau, *l. c.*, p. 135. [2] *Ibid.*, p. 161.
[3] *Ibid.*, p. 154, note 1. [4] Compare Engel, *Myths*, vol. i. p. 75.

CHAPTER X.

HEREDITY AND DEVELOPMENT.

SINCE Darwin's epoch-making researches the scientific world has scarcely been more occupied by any subject than the inquiry into how the immense progress from the primitive cell up to the human organism may be satisfactorily explained. For a time the doctrine of heredity seemed to have furnished the correct answer, until Mr. Fr. Galton and Mr. August Weismann tried to explain the laws of development in a new and peculiar way. Darwin, as is well known, assumed that all the changes brought upon an organism from without are at once despatched to the germ, and through it transmitted to further generations. Some slight modification of this theory was adduced by Mr. W. K. Brooks, who attempted to prove that only those parts of the body that were not in sound condition despatched small particles (gemmules) to the germ-cells. Now these gemmules are but a mere hypothesis, and so the question again arises how it is that the germ-cell can assume all the hereditary tendencies of the whole organism. Here Mr. Weismann tries to show that "the germ-cells are not derived at all, as far as their essential and characteristic substance is concerned, from the body of the individual, but they are derived directly from the parent germ-cell".[1] Therefore all heredity is brought about by the peculiar substance of the "germ-plasm" alone, which is preserved unchanged —in spite of ordinary changes of the somatic cells—for

[1] Weismann, *l. c.*, p. 170.

(263)

the formation of the germ-cells of the following generation. (Theory of the " continuity of the germ-plasm ".) Accordingly hereditary transmission can take place (1) either by such external influences as *directly* affect the reproductive cells, not only the somatic ones, or (2) by two different germ-plasms of different individuals being mixed together and combined by procreation. Consequently *acquired* characters are not transmitted to the next generation, for they are simply the reaction of the organism upon a certain stimulus from without. It is only the original predisposition which is transmitted, or, in other words, the character of the " germ-plasm " alone is transmitted.

At this result Mr. Galton has also arrived in another way,[1] by stating that all the changes the organism undergoes in consequence of external influences are not hereditary unless they directly affect the reproductive elements. As an example of the comparatively great independence of the mother's organism from the child's, he mentions the following interesting experiment : " If in an anatomical preparation the veins of the mother are injected with a coloured fluid, none of it enters the veins of the child ; and *vice versâ*. Again, not only is the unborn child a separate animal from its mother, that obtains its air and nourishment from her purely through soakage, but its constituent elements are of very much less recent growth than is popularly supposed." [2]

I could, of course, not attempt to settle the question as to the heredity of acquired characters, but I may look upon the subject from the point of view of a biographer and historian. Here, too, the difficulties seem to be little less than in biology. First of all we cannot exactly define the term " musical," at least not in a way practicable for scientific researches. Then in many cases we do not agree as to the greatness of a well-known composer,

---

[1] Galton, *Theory of Heredity*.　　[2] Galton, *Nat. Inh.*, pp. 15 and 16.

while at the same time a considerable amount of real talent has remained unobserved,[1] not having been able to put itself forward in the most favourable light. Finally we have the well-known musician families, all their members taking up music as a profession without leaving us the slightest clue as to their real musical abilities, especially if we are to judge centuries after. Therefore, I do not think that all the minute researches of M. Ribot[2] and Mr. Galton, excellent and interesting in themselves, will ever contribute to definitely settle the question of the heredity of acquired modifications.

There is the Bach family with fifty-seven composers, of whom only one became a first-rate composer, while all of them were professional musicians; Donizetti's brother, being a conductor of a military band is, unfortunately, no proof of his musical ability—as experience shows. Michael Haydn would probably have remained entirely unknown but for his celebrated brother Joseph. Meyerbeer's brother Michael was anxious to be taken for a poet; Mozart's sister and sons, Mendelssohn's grandfather were all in their way so moderately gifted as to make us presume similar talent might have occurred in numerous families, the artistic importance of which has never been taken into account. According to Mr. Galton's most complete researches,[3] of 120 musicians whose relations were traced, twenty-six, or one in five, had celebrated relations. Of musicians of first rank Mr. Galton mentions seven with musical relations: Bach, Beethoven, Handel, Haydn, Mendelssohn, Mozart, Spohr. I am afraid that the artistic merit of all these relations was so modest that it would never have been considered worthy of remark if it had happened in other families. In the end the works of

---

[1] "The taxation of a celebrity will always remain unsettled and subjective; even the science and history of art is subject to constant changes and new systematic treatment" (Hirth, *l. c.*, vol. ii. p. 529).

[2] *L'hérédité Psychologique.*   [3] Galton, *Hered. Gen.*, p. 329.

such composers with celebrated relations may be different
from those without such relations, but in consequence of the
mere external circumstance of their living in the artistic
atmosphere and not in consequence of an internal peculiar
gift. Mr. Royse, in his *Study of Genius*, justly remarks:
" Haydn's father was a wheelwright, and his mother a
cook—employments which, neither singly nor together,
would seem to favour the development of a concord of
sweet sounds. A drunken tenor singer was Beethoven's
father. Schubert's father and forefathers for several
generations were schoolmasters. Schumann's father
was a bookseller." [1] It is utterly impossible now further
to examine their mental capacity, and thus the biographical
way in the case of celebrated men leads to no satisfactory
result.

There is, however, still another question to decide,
whether the composer owes all he is able to do to external
influences, to favourable surroundings, or to his internal
gift. Speaking of internal and external influences, it is
very tempting to deal with the question in a mere abstract
way and to say: No influence is purely and absolutely
external, for to be effective it must be a thing in itself,
must be of some peculiar internal quality, and is therefore,
if viewed from another standpoint, an internal influence;
to possess any quality it must be effective upon its surroundings and might therefore be taken as an external
influence. The student of logic will easily avoid this
circle of ideas by saying that internal and external influences, within and without, are correlative terms dependent
upon each other, merely serving the purpose of marking
different parts of one and the same process which can
never be separated in two by a distinct line. [2]

---

[1] Royse. *l. c.*, p. 168.

[2] I find this view put forward in a very able manner in a philosophical
paper of Mach's (" Analys. d. Empfindungen," p. 141): " There is no cleft
between psychical and physical proceedings, nothing purely internal and

I am well aware that nothing is won by merely abstract considerations. Let us therefore refer to the concrete example of the whales so often mentioned by biologists. These whales, although living in the water, are originally derived from terrestrial mammalia, and this (1) either through a mere internal power to change, or (2) through external influences that met either (a) with a pre-existing though latent disposition (germ), or (b) changed even the germ without its having any such tendency.

Abrupt as it may be, I will, nevertheless, at once pass from the whale to the musician and will ask a similar question as to his musical ability. Does a man become a composer merely by his (internal) talent or by external influences (surroundings) which transform his mental tendencies entirely, or give to his pre-existing but hitherto latent disposition a certain direction? I am in favour of this last view. Examples from the history of music, not to speak of the experience of every-day life, will no doubt contribute to make the statement clearer. Richard Wagner is said to have conceived the idea of his "Flying Dutchman" on a sea voyage from Riga to Havre, under the direct impression he got while on board. May we therefore say that this opera of his owes its origin to a mere external influence? Certainly not, for thousands make the same voyage without ever composing anything like the "Flying Dutchman". Rossini is said to have only composed when in want of money. Now, millions are in the same position and yet they never compose a "Barbiere di Seviglia".[1] In both artists there must have been something that only needed the external stimulus to be brought

external, no sensation to which a 'thing as such' different and independent from the sensation would correspond". Mr. James in his *Psychology* seems to be in favour of this view ; similarly Dr. Grosse in his pamphlet on "Spencer's Doctrine of the Unknowable" (*l. c.*).

[1] Other examples of surroundings influencing the composer's fancy from the life of Handel, Haydn. Schubert, Beethoven, by Royse, *l. c.*, pp. 148, 152.

to light; and this is what we find in the artistic genius in general, the internal disposition and the external cause; but we can scarcely say where one ends and the other begins. And now it may be well to remind the reader that our abstract and merely logical consideration leads to the same result, that internal and external influences, within and without, are only different names for one and the same process which in reality cannot be separated into two distinct parts. The artist, it is true, does not owe his genius to ordinary influences of every-day life, not to schools, teachers, examinations, testimonials, etc., but nevertheless to his surroundings, although it may be difficult, not to say impossible, to trace the effect of his delicate susceptibility in every instance to the external cause. Therefore, I am afraid we shall never be able to say how much of the artistic genius is an acquired character, and how much an innate disposition. Consequently the question as to the heredity of acquired modifications becomes still more complicated, and direct evidence will probably never be available. On the other hand, there is strong evidence against its validity, for this theory does not explain, even in the slightest degree, the development in music; indeed, I consider it downright impossible that heredity of acquired modifications contributes anything to the development of music. Biologists will very likely consider this a surprising and sudden decision to come to, but I will ask them to consider the following historical fact :—

What an immense progress has not the opera made from the days of Bellini and Donizetti to Richard Wagner, or instrumental music from Haydn to Berlioz! To what degree of perfection has not piano playing been brought by Liszt, violin playing by Paganini! Yet their pupils far surpassed the old masters—and can this be said to be due to heredity? Before the accomplishments of one artist had been made intelligible to the people through heredity, or could have been imitated owing to hereditary transmission, we should have had to wait for another laurentian or silurian period in order to make the progress from Haydn to Mozart, or from Weber to Wagner. But all this advancement has been made within a few years, during the life-time of one and the same generation. This could only be possible when every progression in music was at once imitated and preserved objectively for later generations. This principle of *objective heredity* (as I should call it in short) alone explains the rapid progress in music during the last thirty to forty years. How could it otherwise have taken place ? Through elimination of the organisms that were unfavourable to musical talent, and through combination of those better adapted, or through individual heredity ? Time has been far too short to accomplish anything of the kind ; and yet the progress has taken place, and tradition as well as imitation will explain it, although they do not furnish any direct evidence.

In the same way I would explain moral development and the transmission of instincts. Those birds on the islands of the Indian Ocean, which saw men for the first time without being frightened at them, need not have acquired the instinct of flight by experience and transmitted it to the next generation.[1] Nor is it necessary to say that only those birds survived that already had this instinct originally, for if a sufficient number had it travellers would not have made the observations that the birds did not fear men. In my opinion a single terrifying experience of one bird taught the others that witnessed it, and their fear, acquired simply by reflexive and direct imitation, was again imitated by all other birds. If one bird flies away in terror the others follow ; if this happens often enough the habit is acquired for life-time, and as the old generation

[1] Examples by Guyau, *Educ. Hered.*, p. 98 ; Weismann, *Essays* (1st ed.), p. 92.

does not die out at once, and the new comes one by one, the tradition of flight is maintained quite apart from the life of single individuals. " Much of the mystery of instinct—to quote Mr. Wallace—arises from the persistent refusal to recognise the agency of imitation, memory, observation, and reason as often forming part of it. Yet there is ample evidence that such agency must be taken into account." [1]

With the fact in our mind that direct imitation and tradition brought about all progress in music, it still seems incomprehensible how the necessity for it might ever have existed. In the case of birds and their fear of men such a necessity for experience and progress is easily explained ; but what was the immediate object of music, what its necessary connection with every-day life ?

Among arts, music especially seems to have such scanty relations with the necessary conditions of life, that the question unconsciously prompts itself how the same could attain that climax of importance which it undoubtedly occupies to-day. To be sure one hears not unfrequently that all art, and music particularly, is a " luxus "; that we do not derive from it any profit or advantage, and that its development therefore cannot be explained by the same natural laws which otherwise govern the struggle for existence. But I fear that one is prone to look upon music too much from the abstract point of view of our time, and not to consider sufficiently the position which it still occupies with primitive man.

---

[1] Wallace, *Darwin*, p. 442. One of the most striking differences in the conception of instinct is that of Lewes and Spencer. While Lewes says that instinct is " lapsed intelligence," Spencer thinks that intelligence is merely " compound reflex action " (comp. Romanes, *Ment. Evol. Anim.*, p. 256). I think that the question cannot be decided as long as we speak of instinct and intelligence in general. Some peculiar instinct may arise every day on the basis of our intelligence, while peculiar intelligent ideas arise from instincts. Whether the majority of cases goes one way or the other, I do not know.

Above all, one must keep in mind that primitive music does not have any necessary connection with a higher training and evolution of the sense of hearing, and that the whole development of music, beginning from primeval times to the present period, has not changed the human ear in any respect. All attempts to establish a connection between music and the exercise of the organs of hearing must therefore be strictly excluded from our investigation. The oldest music we know of is no effect of the sense of hearing, but of the conception of time; it is primarily a rhythmic movement, divisible into bars, and only in later stages is it melody and harmony. We must consider music in the form in which it occurs among primitive men, *viz.*, in connection with dance and mimic representation (pantomime). This is at the same time the oldest manifestation of art we know of.

In regard to the origin of art (including music), Mr. Herbert Spencer's theory of the "surplus of vigour" is evidently the correct one, as far as it goes. Instead of the expression "surplus," another would possibly have been more concise; for it appears to me that the term "surplus" implies too much—an unnecessary surplus of energy which is supposed to occur among the higher animals and man. On this basis it is easy to consider all that is effected by this "surplus" as an unintentional by-effect, a thing to which I cannot make up my mind. But it is by no means an excess of energy that the higher animals possess, it is only just so much as is sufficient, not only to ward off, in the struggle for existence, the enemy when he approaches, but to annihilate him completely so that he is not able to come again. After this is done the energy lies latent and is not called into play for a time, and must then be applied in some way. When the gorilla advances against an attacking enemy he proudly delivers blows upon his breast.[1] Let us suppose

[1] Du Chaillu, *Equ. Afr.*, p. 71.

—a thing which will generally take place—that he comes forth victorious from the struggle for existence; his energy is then not employed, and with exactly the same blows with which he goes to the duel he entertains himself in his hours of leisure, jumping and dancing about in a circle and beating his breast rhythmically. All this takes place not because nature has given him too much, not because she has given him a surplus of energy for the struggle for existence, but because she has given him just sufficient to annihilate his enemies. I also believe that the lower animals not only have no surplus of power, but that they have distinctly too little; nevertheless they manage to squeeze through in life, but they must constantly be on the lookout and not consume all their energy in this effort, while the higher animal gets rid of its enemy and does not simply elude him. Among the lower animals this lack of power is usually recompensed by enormous fertility in order to ensure the propagation of the species. That energy, therefore, which finds employment in games and dances is not a surplus *for which our organism was originally not adapted;* the organism was adapted for the energy which is absolutely necessary in order to support ourselves perfectly. But *for this very reason* it at times finds no employment because it has already completely fulfilled its duty. For the struggle for existence even the higher animals have no surplus of energy; but with them a fight is a rarer occurrence than with the lower animals, and in consequence the state of *unapplied energy* is produced.

Primitive man is in this respect placed in exactly the same position as the higher animals. Thus the Apono (West of the Ashango, West Africa) have a war-dance called M'Muirri which is remarkable for the singular noises the dancers made, " yelling and beating their breasts with both hands, like the gorilla, and making a loud vibrating noise with their lips, resembling the word

muirri ".[1]   Moreover, as this dance is performed by several
men they are obliged to keep the rhythmical beats in
accordance with each other, because of the peculiar innate
tendency of rhythm for unification.[2]   Consequently people
are obliged to observe the rhythmical beats, and thus the
mechanical rhythmic beating is transformed into well-
arranged intentional beats kept in strict time.

In addition to any outward resemblance to the gorilla-
dance savage dances have often also a similar meaning.
The war is transmuted into a war-dance after the battle
is over; one and the same sound is war-cry and primitive
song; the swinging of the spear is their mode of fighting
and also of beating time; the same ponderous step is
attack and joyous dance.   Therefore, these dances are
not a surplus, a luxury, which primitive man allows himself, they are absolutely necessary to prepare for the hunt
or war, and afterwards to preserve and develop their
power.[3]   If daily life at times does not offer any occasion
for war the latter must be invented, and the one who
possesses this power of invention is in fact the artist.
Everywhere among primitive man the choral-dance plays
the part which we have here assigned to it.   In Australia
the war-dance is the preparation for war and its sequel;
the songs of the women goad on the men to battle; in
the South Sea Islands the songs of the savages are frequently the cause of war; in Madagascar it is even
customary for the women to sing and dance while the
men are out to war, because (as they themselves state
and believe) this strengthens the courage of the men.   For
the same reason the wives of the Gold Coast negroes

[1] Du Chaillu, *Ashango Land*, p. 272.

[2] *Cf.* Souriau, *l. c.*, p. 65, "*unification des rythmes*".

[3] " Art will be the perpetual revenge of those of our faculties which are
not employed.   One might conceive that art, that luxury of our imagination
would end by becoming a necessity for all, a sort of daily bread " (Guyau,
Esthetique, p. 11).

dance at home a fetish dance in imitation of battle to give their absent husbands strength and courage.[1] Describing a dance of the Fans, Du Chaillu says : One of the consequences of the dance will be that we are to have a great elephant hunt (*cf*. similar examples in chap. vii.).[2] The Kafirs, the finest warriors of Africa, sing and dance the war-dance with such great rhythmical precision that the whole tribe (several hundred in number, as travellers report) make the impression of a single huge machine working with mechanical precision. Among the Central American aborigines, Morgan tells us,[3] " any person was at liberty to organise a war-party and conduct an expedition wherever he pleased. He announced his project by giving a war-dance and inviting volunteers. If he succeeded in forming a company, which would consist of such persons as joined him in the dance, they departed *immediately*, while enthusiasm was at its height."

These examples go to show that the war-dance is a war-play, a preparation for common action. This is no less the case with pantomimic representations, the primitive drama, whose oldest form is the animal pantomime. These animal pantomimes (which are customary among the savages of all continents) betray such an extraordinary power of observation, and so great a familiarity with the character of animals, that they cannot possibly be without a favourable influence upon the participants in them. They keep those performing in them in constant practice, awaking interest in all the spectators in hunting, and give to them, one may say, an instructive example which may prove of use to them in case of need, especially since the talent of the savages in mimicking and acting is such an extraordinary one, that the animal pantomime is in truth a representation, correct in all details, of the actual hunt.

---

[1] Tylor, *Anthr.*, p. 298.   [2] Du Chaillu, *Equ. Afr.*, p. 81.

[3] Morgan, *Anc. Soc.*, pp. 117, 118.

Some time ago the London papers contained the report that it was customary among the street-arabs of the East End to play constable, magistrate, and criminal. No small indignation was expressed at this style of amusement, because (as was claimed) the children were in this way familiarised too much with the ingenuity of the police, the proceedings at court, the tricks of criminals, and the particulars of an exciting life in which revolt against the most necessary social restrictions played a very important part. In the same way in which these games are a school for crime the games of the savages are a preparation for savage life—war and hunting, *i.e.*, the struggle for existence. Dancing and play-acting, to quote Mr. Tylor, seem to savages " so real that they expect them to act on the world outside ".[1]

Up to this point the social importance of the primitive drama, the pantomime, will incur little opposition I think. But what has music got to do with all this? If these representations were the work of single actors as now-a-days, music might be missing, or it would only be of accessory importance. But in those representations the whole tribe takes a part, and this action *en masse* is only possible if it manifests itself in the well-arranged form of march and dance. The war-play as well as the animal pantomime are choral-dances of the whole tribe, and the precision with which they are executed is only possible if a high degree of natural rhythmic sense exists. [This time-sense is the psychological origin of music.] Primitive music in its actual aspects, with the rhythmical element strongly pronounced, is an organising power which holds together the participants in the dance and makes a common action possible. This custom of the whole tribe to act in common as *one body*, and the skill evinced in doing this, cannot be without influence in the

[1] Tylor, *Anthr.*, p. 296.

struggle for existence.   Just because primitive music is
so perfectly united with the wants of daily life, because it
has such practical aims, has it with such difficulty severed
itself from these wants, and so late developed into an
independent art.   In former times, however, it was in-
separably connected with the war- and hunting-play.   It
is to the warriors we owe the first rhythmical beating of
time ; to them we owe the first fixed melodies (signals) ;
to them the first choral song and the first orchestra (the
first orchestra was a military band), things which are only
too plain in the life of the African savages.   This primitive
music has in all respects the same function which the
drummers, trumpeters, and fife-players still have with the
army and with public processions.   Their music is in no
wise an effect of the sense of hearing in the musical sense
of the word, and in no way a luxury which might just as
well be wanting.   Attempt to arrange a march, a dance,
or a public procession without the organising force of
time (in the musical sense), and you will at once recognise
how great and important this force is, and how it may be
brought to serve practical ends.   The savages themselves
seem to be conscious of the importance which common
action has for their life, and there are even examples
where rhythmic precision in executing the dances stands
in a *direct* connection with the preservation of life.   Boas
relates of the Kwakiutl Indians (British Columbia) : [1] " As
chorus-singing is practised at all festivals, a good deal of
practice is necessary before an artistic effect can be reached.
The Kwakiutl are very particular in this respect, and any
mistake made by a singer or dancer is considered oppro-
brious.   On certain occasions the dancer who makes a
mistake *is killed ;* this custom reminds us of the ancient
Mexicans."   I think modern musicians will be glad of the
assurance that I am speaking of ancient times only.

[1] F. Boas, *l. c.,* p. 57.

However this may be, since the sense of time (always of course in the musical sense of the word), together with rhythmical movement, does alone make choral-dances and games possible, seeing that this sense of time is the beginning of music, while those games have their importance in the struggle for existence, it is clear how the same principle which we find all through nature is applicable to the development of musical talent. A tribe which does not practise common action, which does not prepare and preserve its energy by *war-games* will have less prospect of success in real battle. These games (choral-dances), however, are possible only in combination with primitive music, and this circumstance brings all musical ability within the scope of the law of natural selection.

I know well that the validity of Darwin's law has been denied for the domain of ethics and art (including, of course, music). This opposition has proceeded from men whose epoch-making importance in the field of natural science imposes upon me the duty of the greatest respect, while at the same time it necessitates my weighing my conclusions with the utmost scrupulousness. In the following I confine myself entirely to the domain of music, and I consider myself the more justified in doing this since the historical facts with which ethnology furnishes us could scarcely be taken into consideration sufficiently, a connected treatment of the same, not existing. Alfred Russell Wallace, in discussing the development of our musical faculties, has made use of the material as furnished by the *English Cyclopædia*, which in my opinion is not quite satisfactory. He says: " Among the lower savages music, as we understand it, hardly exists, though they all delight in rude musical sounds, as of drums, tom-toms, or gongs ; and they also sing in monotonous chants. Almost exactly as they advance in general intellect and in the arts of social life, their appreciation of music appears to rise in proportion ; and we find among them rude stringed instruments and whistles, till, in Java, we have regular bands of skilled performers, probably the successors of Hindoo musicians of the age before the Mohammedan Conquest. The Egyptians are believed to have been the earliest musicians, and from them the Jews and the Greeks no doubt derived their knowledge of the art, but it seems to be admitted that neither the latter nor the Romans knew anything of harmony or of the essential features of modern music." [1]

I believe that my whole book forms a contradiction to the above statements, and in consequence the conclusions would also have to be changed. In reference to the latter I would like to make one more remark. Wallace says: "The musical ability is undoubtedly, in its lower forms, less uncommon than the artistic or mathematical faculty, but it still differs essentially from the necessary or useful faculties in that it is almost entirely wanting in one-half even of civilised man". [2] To be sure musical activity is *to-day* distributed very unevenly among mankind; but originally it was not the same thing as to-day, in the climax of its development. In fact the whole tribe participates in the musical choral-dance and mimic representation among savages; we have never heard that certain individuals had to be excluded from it through lack of talent. If any one should prove awkward in these dances, some tribes, as we have heard, cut matters short by killing him. Purely musical composition also is much more general than to-day. "Among the Andamans every one composes songs. A man or woman would be thought very little of who could not do so. Even small children compose their own songs." [3] With primitive man music, and painting and sculpture probably as well, are not purely æsthetic occupations in the modern sense, they are

---

[1] Wallace, *Darwin*, pp. 467, 468.   [2] *Ibid.*, p. 471.
[3] Portman, *l. c.*, pp. 184, 185.

most intimately bound up with practical life-preserving and life-continuing activities,[1] and receive only gradually their present more abstract form. And therefore a law like that of " natural selection " has original validity here as well, while it is less easily comprehensible in connection with the music of the present time whose conditions of existence have become too complicated. But after we have recognised the full scope of the law, the spiritual life of man has been brought closer to that of the animals, and in regard to the continuity of both, I would like to add a few more words. Wallace has destroyed the bridge between the spiritual life of man and the animals; a deep cleft separates the two. Darwin attempted to construct the same by trying to trace a number of the psychological traits of man in the animal kingdom ; I fear that some of his adherents go too far in this, and that they approach too closely upon anthropomorphism. The hypothetic character of those arguments has been so successfully shown by Prof. Morgan that it is quite sufficient simply to refer to them ; but he has also shown that one is not on that account compelled to relinquish the connection between the spiritual life of man and the animals. It is therefore my opinion that it is much easier to show that primitive man still is, in reference to his mental state, an animal. For this view at least we have a more trustworthy collection of empiric facts than for the opinion that the animal is already man, or that there is no connection between the spiritual life of both. To furnish this proof for the whole domain of psychic activity will be one of the tasks of ethnology.

The sense of beauty, in the higher meaning of the

[1] I mention this because L. Morgan has said (*Anim. Life and Intell.*, p. 501): " Natural selection, which deals with practical life-preserving and life-continuing activities, has little to say to the æsthetic activities, music, painting, sculpture and the like ". If only music, painting, etc., were æsthetic activities among primitive man !

term, is an abstract sensation which animals do not
possess, just as little as primitive man; how it is nevertheless developed in man in the course of time, is a thing
amply illustrated by a mass of reliable observations.   For
this development the theory of Galton and Weismann
seems, in my eyes, to furnish the most satisfactory explanation, especially in the domain of music.   To be sure I
have not (as I have before mentioned) the impression that
music is to be considered an effect of the sense of hearing,
and that it is a secondary effect not originally intended by
nature; the further development, however, is, in my eyes,
only explicable as direct imitation and tradition.   Under
such conditions it is in no way unlikely (what Weismann
also presumed) that we civilised nations, and, for example,
the negroes, receive the same degree of musical ability by
birth and yet accomplish such different ends.   Quite apart
from the training of our individuality, they lack examples
and the social necessity of coming up to their level.
Neither of these can be artificially ingrafted upon their
social status, and therefore they are pretty well lost to
musical, and probably any other form of, culture.

The average child of civilised parents does not necessarily come into the world with a higher mental equipment
than the little savage, as Mr. Nisbet[1] thinks.   Nevertheless, it is not obliged to work out everything *de novo* because
it comes into *another* world, into a world with a settled
tradition.   Into this the child gradually grows, and out of
it its individuality is formed, while a negro boy will always
have the impression that the European world is something
strange to him, not made by his equal.   His very colour,
if not the general behaviour of his white "friends," will
soon convince him of this.   All mental progress seems to
be traceable in the object rather, while the individuals
have remained stationary.   More highly gifted individuals

[1] Nisbet, *l. c.*, p. viii.

are the outcome of sudden favourable combinations, not the climax of a continual line leading up to them.

When primitive music has advanced beyond the first purely rhythmical stage, when an invention of melody takes place which is retained in memory, it has often been observed that these short musical phrases impress just as much to-day as they do among the savages. The advantage we have over primitive man in regard to music is simply that we are able to work up, develop, any given theme, while the former spins out a theme, however short it may be, into a lengthy piece simply through endless repetitions. This art of working up a given theme must be acquired by each individual afresh; the capacity for it is not a whit greater in the present generation than during former times. To be sure it is probable that we learn quicker, but only because we have more numerous and better patterns, and because in our study we save ourselves the trouble of scholastic by-ways, in learning which past generations have, through want of experience, wasted unnecessary time and energy.

On the other hand, those of the savage tribes which are really musical comprehend our music, at least that of a simple character; that means, to the same degree that our peasants do. It is also astonishing how quickly Negro Hottentot and Malay orchestras grasp European dance music and play it immediately, by hearing, in the orchestra.

In the drawings done by savages one can trace exactly the same mistakes and peculiarities as with our children.[1] I do not doubt that this will in time be proved by ethnology more completely than I am able to do within the limits of this abstract. But I might mention that we are able

---

[1] With perfect justice Hirth (*l. c.*, vol. ii. p. 583) has expressly not traced the lack of perspective in the disposition of a child's drawing to atavism, but has designated it as a peculiarity of the spirit of the nursery. Examples of savage drawings in Andree, *Ethn. Par.*, p. 258 (Neue Folge, p. 56).

to observe the same in the compositions of children, or more properly in the musical invention of children, even up to the time of boyhood or girlhood, and all this in spite of the fact that the child unconsciously undergoes even in tender youth the influence of modern music.

The origin and development of painting seems also to come under the influence of natural selection. Thus the most important and most original products of Dyaks' painting are the bizarre decorations of their shields. They were bizarre and grotesque in order to frighten the enemy against whom they were held. (The ancient Greek painting of the Gorgo Medusa head originally had the same meaning, *viz.*, to frighten the deity.) The fantastic demons of the Dyaks were the result of a competition in the struggle for life, which sought to constantly increase by new decorations the dread of the defending shields. Other ornaments were originally signs of property, and thus the whole branch of ornamental art owed its origin to the struggle for life.[1]

We also have the best of reasons to suppose that among the "faculties" of the human mind the so-called musical faculty at least has not been heightened in course of time, and that all progress has simply been brought about by objective heredity. Long before this could take place the practice of music was so intimately connected with life-continuing and life-preserving activities that the law of natural selection held good even in the domain of music.

A mere psychological consideration of the case will lead us to a similar result. I venture to say that the old doctrine of separate powers, capabilities (Vermögen, as the German psychologists formerly used to call it) in the human mind has generally been abandoned by modern psychologists. There is no such thing as an independent

---

[1] Hein, *Techn. Künste d. Dayaks*, vi. 3, p. 203.

musical ability, or musical sense, distinctly separable from other faculties. If this is so, it is impossible to say that a special musical faculty is developed under a special law. The human mind is one whole, equally subject to one and the same natural influences. More than that, mind and body are one whole. Where is the physiologist or physicist who could draw a distinct line between a mere physical movement, a reflex action, and an intelligent will? Who can say up to what point the mere corporal faculty extends, and from where the mental one begins? How can we say then that our brain is subject to the natural law of natural selection and our ideas to supernatural or any other influence? How can we venture to apply to this one whole of human being different influences and say, for instance, that one part is developed under natural laws, another under supernatural, again another under direct divine agency? how can we say that the one is a primary effect, the other a secondary one, and that among all there is a special compartment somewhere in the brain carefully locked up and called the musical faculty, which is preserved under the particular care of—we do not know what?

As there is no special musical faculty (the term faculty has always been used like the term soul for the shortness of expression) we must again remember that we said it was not the musical talent alone which made the composer. The artist is the man whose total energy, interest, and labour, whose feelings and ambition are entirely given up to the one artistic object, whatever it may be. If this has happened we speak of a peculiar faculty for this object in a certain man, but this so-called "faculty" is nothing but the resulting tendency of our mind as a whole which turns in a certain direction under certain favourable circumstances. And so the "musical faculty" too is the end of a certain disposition of our mind, towards which all the so-called faculties tend, not a separate starting-point from which they arise. Of course, some organic structures may be more favourable to a certain end, under certain external circumstances, but we shall never be able to find a unique source for any artistic disposition. So it may happen that the mental disposition, say of a great politician, would have been much more favourable to artistic development, than that of many actual artists, had he been placed under the most appropriate external conditions. This would not be possible if there were such a thing as a peculiar artistic faculty. It is mental strength in general which characterises the great man of the future, and nobody knows in which direction it will concentrate itself at last. Thus the German poet Victor Scheffel intended to become a painter at first, until one day, quite accidentally, his talent for poetry was discovered by a lady friend and then turned to account by himself. The painter Fritz Uhde felt himself so entirely in the wrong place when he first frequented the painting academy in Dresden that he left it and became an officer. Only later on he took up his former profession again, recognising it, at the same time, as the most appropriate to his talent. Rousseau considered himself a composer only, and wrote his philosophical and educational works, merely occasionally, as an occupation of secondary importance. Had not his opera "Devin du Village" had such an immense success, he would probably have devoted himself entirely to philosophy, and we should not know anything of his compositions. And to what did he owe this success—to favourable circumstances or to the merits of the compositions? Merits? The present generation knows Rousseau as philosopher only, and I dare say there will be many people who never knew that Rousseau composed at all. Goethe once seriously thought of becoming a painter. Zelter, his contemporary, was destined to become a bricklayer like his father, and devoted himself to music comparatively late.

These examples tend to show that general strength and greatness of mind assumes that peculiar shape which in course of time proves itself as the most effective in the outside world and the most appropriate to the circumstances, or as the naturalist would say in plainer language, it assumes the form most *useful* to the individual. This view is not at all in opposition to the fact that great characters assert themselves in spite of their disregarding entirely all the surroundings they have to live in. Thus one may say Richard Wagner would have been more successful in the beginning of his career if he had written in the customary easy-going style of the Italian opera, and with the pomposity of Meyerbeer, in favour with the masses. Precisely so. In the beginning he would have been more successful, but he knew that musical development ought to turn in quite another direction which he pretended to foresee in the future ; and with regard to this future of music, which would then prove still more favourable to him than the success of the ordinary musician of his time, he wrote what he actually called " Zukunftsmusik ". In his earlier days, however, when his operas " Das Liebesverbot " and " Die Feen " had proved failures, he did write in accordance with the taste of the masses, like Meyerbeer, and brought out his " Rienzi ". But by this time there happened to be too many competitors in this domain, so he remained unnoticed, and as there was nothing to be hoped from the present he wrote for the future.

Thus it is just the example of Wagner which at first sight seems to tell against the theory of usefulness in art, but which at bottom is eloquent in favour of it. By this theory I do not mean to degrade the action of the artist. The word " use " can be taken in a very ideal sense. He who pretends to despise use is himself too low to conceive a higher meaning of it. If to some friendship is more useful than gain, if the law of usefulness has produced all the beauty in the world, the grandeur of the sky as well as the tender blossoms of the earth, then it will also be effective enough to form the highest artistic ideals the human mind is capable of.

Which artistic direction will be the most useful for a great mind to take is difficult to predict. It depends upon custom, countries, times, even upon the fashion. There have been centuries of poets, of painters, sculptors, architects, while we ourselves seem to live in the century of musicians, I mean of poetical, intelligent musicians of the pattern of Wagner. How such changes in artistic tendency are brought about, how they are felt at once by millions of people on different continents, and why they are responded to, I cannot say. But that they are most effective everybody seems to be aware of.

So much of the past. But how will future events shape themselves? This question has frequently been broached by musicians, especially when they found themselves face to face with a phenomenon so singular and unexpected as Wagner. In their complete surprise and passionate enthusiasm, which can easily be comprehended, they have confessed as their sincere opinion that in him not only music but the whole world in general had reached its climax. From this height all things were expected to decline, and nothing perfectly new could in their opinion be created. This truly Chinese view has, however, hindered the development of music on countless occasions, and has caused such severe struggles as have accompanied the appearance of original geniuses like Berlioz and Wagner. The less are *their* adherents in their turn justified in adopting the same principle, which in the case of the "conservatives" they justly censured. None but the uninitiated could arrive at the above conclusion (and they will probably continue to do so), for any one knowing the prospects of music in the future would already be half a composer; to *theoretically* expound what this future of music may be none, not even the artist, is able to do; the product of his genius, the work of art, alone can and will reveal it. Reasoning in regard to the future of art is futile, but imagination has for a period of five thousand years continued to produce new works of art, and there is no reason why all this should have come to an end in the year 1883. On the contrary, this assumption seems to my mind both narrow-minded and unfounded. Unfounded because there is no absolute standard of beauty, for we, with our purely subjective and individual conception of art, should never make the preposterous assertion that in this way and no other can art attain to absolute perfection. A work of art is made *for* us and is consequently subject to all changes *in* and *through* us.

An experience of my own has always been to me an appropriate example of how opinion may change in course of time. My teacher of counterpoint once took up Bach's mass in B minor and said : " In this work is comprehended all musical wisdom, beyond it we can never go ". From the point of view of musical labour and polish, or of the art exercised in execution, he was no doubt right. But there is still another point of view, that of colouring and emotional element, and this has found grander and more eloquent expression in Wagner than in any other composer. Incidentally I may mention that this constitutes, in my opinion, Wagner's supreme mastership. Nobody can say which point of view coming generations will take, for we are not the coming generation, and only in the divinely inspired artist will it be anticipated.

The above negative decision in regard to the future of art is not, however, free from a certain narrowness of view which has excluded the consideration of the long evolution of music, and especially of dramatic music. What a length of time has not elapsed since the first attempt to represent the events of chase and war before the assembled company in order to induce it to participate in common action. How long a time did not elapse before these primitive dances and animal pantomimes could have become customary, and before their old stereotyped form could at last lead to innovations and improvements. Let us not forget that those dances occurred among people who in every other respect have not advanced beyond the civilisation of the stone period. In comparison with them a dramatic festival as advanced and accomplished as the corrobberree or the kuri-dance in Australia represents an epoch in literature, an artistic advancement of centuries. And how simple, how childish this drama appears when compared with the ancient Indian drama, of which we are told that only in later stages was the customary song replaced by spoken words. The tropic glow, the fiery passion of a Sakuntala designate a height of perfection which again is separated by centuries from the epoch of the corrobberree. And still, what is this when compared with the drama of Pericles' time, or of the Roman theatre, both of which have so many characteristics in common with modern dramatic art. But this is the period with which in so many cases our historical investigations used to commence, while for the times preceding we had merely a geological interest. What changes had not occurred in the drama up to the Roman period, and what changes were still to come. Lost in the mental darkness of the middle ages, it nevertheless at last found the saving path from the grimacing, immoral derivations of the old mysteries to the bright splendour of the artistic stage, from mysterious choirs and disreputable cloister-alleys to the open and unreserved tribunal of the people, to those boards that represent the world, a free play, inspired as once before by love of mankind and taken from its varying fates. Now the first oratorios appeared, now the first operas were produced, small in the beginning and diffident, but soon centres of interest for the entire spiritual life of society. On their account parties were formed, on their account the whole of Paris was once roused to passionate enthusiasm and fierce hatred ; indeed, in the days of Gluck and Piccini even politics were forgotten for a time, so entirely absorbed were the parties in the musical questions of the day.

But these miracles know no limits. The stage is animated with new characters; the figure of stone appears in the gloom of night ; in dungeons deep a prisoner awaits the blessed hour of liberty; elves flit through the air; the spirit of the earth leaves with aching heart the deceitful love-phantom of human life; the Italian carnival crosses the stage in wanton revelry ; till at last the daughters of the Rhine rise from the depths of the holy river, Sigfried's horn resounds, and Walhall, the resplendent seat of the gods, shines in sublime grandeur.

This is for the present the last stage in the long line of evolution, more varied and more eloquent in the history of the musical drama than in any other domain of human accomplishments. A review of this domain of our mental activity betrays as much vital creative power as it reveals the prospect of new and glorious blossoms, and an insatiable desire on our part to enjoy them in their full splendour and their eternal youth.

Such at least is the conclusion to which the theoretical observer may come; to everything else the creative artist will return answer.

SUMMARY.

I. *A general view of primitive music in Africa, Australia, the South Sea Islands, Asia, and America.*

A general view of primitive music shows us that in the most primitive state the main constituent of music has always been rhythm, while melody has remained an accessory. At the same time music is associated with dancing, and in dance-music the idea is to excite the performer and to fatigue him, even to exhaustion. The musical dance-chorus is of a social character; music keeps the company together and enables them to act simultaneously.

II. *Singers and composers in primitive times (the human voice).*

There was a class of professional composers and singers in primitive times which was highly flattered and well rewarded for the services rendered to the public, but at the same time was very little esteemed from a social point of view. Its power and influence upon the masses was well known, and was very often made use of by the chiefs in their endeavours both to rule the people and to keep up their own reputation. The mode of singing all over the savage world is best characterised by the words, the louder it is the more beautiful, the strength of the voice and the physical perseverance of the performer being chiefly exhibited. Men and women sing at such a high pitch (the former frequently in falsetto) as to have given rise to the presumption that the human voice must formerly have been higher. This, however, cannot be proved by ethnological facts, and the high pitch is merely due to the great excitement with which savages sing. Women sing in many cases better and more frequently than the men; there are poets and composers amongst them.

III. *Instruments.*

The oldest instrument we know of is the pipe, specimens of which have been found among relics coëval with the Irish elk (*cervus alces*). It seems to have been originally an ornament consisting of the bone of a dead animal or a slain enemy perforated with a hole so as to be hung up by a string and worn. Similar bones are used

(291)

as musical instruments and played upon by Maoris and Indian
tribes.   The next oldest instrument appears to be the gong (or
sounding stone-plate).   The drum, in the comparatively elaborate
and enormous shape savages know, is by no means the most primitive instrument, as is commonly supposed, although drumming with
sticks or on stretched deer-skins, or the clapping of hands and stamping of feet, was evidently regarded as the simplest means to mark
the rhythm, and was, too, the earliest form of musical accompaniment.   Bowed instruments frequently occur among primitive tribes
all over the world, but it is difficult to decide whether European
instruments influenced their construction or not.   At any rate the
supposed Indian origin of bowed instruments has no better foundation
than any hypothetical African origin would have.   Other instruments,
such as tubes, trumpets, bells, castanets, rattles, the marimba, gourah,
and all sorts of stringed instruments (of savages only), have been
described, their chief peculiarities and distribution given.

The orchestra, especially the military band, seems to be a very
early institution, arising immediately from the social character of
primitive music.

IV. *The basis of our modern musical system.*

(*a*) *Scale.*   The supposition of the older music writers that the
pentatonic scale is the earliest known cannot be maintained in the
face of ethnological research.   Old Egyptian flutes dating from the
year 3000 B.C. (the bronze age) have a complete diatonic scale.   The
above-mentioned prehistoric pipes have the first four tones of the
diatonic scale, that is to say, the first of the equal halves of this
scale.   Diatonic intervals frequently occur on primitive instruments,
side by side with other instruments with the pentatonic or any
intervals.   From this we may conclude that Helmholtz's supposition,
that our present diatonic system is an artistic invention, the result
of musical speculation, does not hold good, since men of the bronze
age and of the reindeer period could hardly have invented a musical
system.   This system must have come about in a more natural way.

(*b*) *Harmony.*   As soon as music passes the mere rhythmical stage
the lowest races in the scale of man begin to sing in different parts,
in intervals as well as with a bass accompaniment (*e.g.*, Hottentots,
New Zealanders).   Many savages tune their instruments together in
harmonious chords and in accordance with their voices; indeed, the
quartette form frequently occurs in savage instrumental music.   Some
tribes easily put a second part to any European tune they hear for
the first time.   Thus harmony does not seem to be so new an invention

as is commonly supposed, nor is it confined to European races. These facts again considerably alter the position of harmony in our musical system, which might be as old as melody, especially considering the original poverty of the latter.

(c) *Major and minor key.* Both keys occur among primitive races, and do not seem to be in any causal connection with the mood and disposition of mind. The merriest people sing their merriest words in minor keys, and, as some tribes sing in harmony as well, minor *chords* occasionally occur. Thus it does not seem to be more difficult to sing in the minor key than in the major.

V. *Physical and psychical influence of music.*

Savages are highly susceptible to music, which excites them in the highest imaginable degree. Their songs sometimes even lead to war. In some cases music causes physical pain, and makes men sick and unfitted for work for days together. Savages know this power of sounds, and apply it—as they think—with success in cases of illness.

VI. *Poetry and music.*

Vocal music does not always imply poetry as well as music, but in many cases music only, meaningless words serving the purpose of articulation. The subjects are extremely simple, taken from events of every-day life, expressed in a few short sentences, and repeated over and over again for hours. More elaborate poetry is sometimes sung in a kind of recitative. Some tribes have a so-called "speech-song".

VII. *Dancing and music.*

Dancing and music are in fact one act of expression, not merely an occasional union like poetry and music. There is no dance without music. Such dances consist of all the movements necessary in the struggle for life (war-dance, hunting-dance). In deer-dances the imitations of the habits of animals are very striking, and always true to nature. Women are the most persistent dancers, and, as they are the better singers as well, *primitive* music owes its support to a great extent to women.

VIII. *Primitive drama (pantomime, opera).*

In addition to the above performances, songs are introduced which enable the performers to make a more complicated action clear to the audience. The subjects are comic as well as tragic, in the latter of which some tribes seem to take peculiar pleasure.

Dramatic or operatic performances are a national festival, in which very often different tribes—even enemies—take part, all rivalry being laid aside during the festival.

IX. *Origin of music.*

From the character of primitive music, as exhibited by the musical practice of savages, I venture to conclude that the origin of music is to be sought in a general desire for rhythmical exercise, and that the "time-sense" is the psychical source from which it arises. The rhythm through itself leads us to certain tones (and consequently tunes) by which rhythmical periods are better marked, and the whole movement becomes more distinct. I do not agree with Darwin's theory, for, although the production of tones may be traced as far back as to the bird's "song," yet we have no exact proof of the existence of so many complex psychical actions in animals, as the term "music" seems to imply. (In addition to this a description of the tone-production in the animal kingdom is given, with an investigation into the character of the adequate organs.) According to Mr. Spencer, music arises from the natural melody of emotional speech. Since, however, the most primitive music is no melody, but noise reduced to time, it can hardly be the direct offspring of emotional speech. The so-called "recitative," moreover, is not the earliest still less the *only* form of primitive music; it is the outcome of music united with poetry, where the language is sufficiently developed to allow of connected stories. Even in these cases the original chorus-dances occur side by side with the recitative. (For other reasons against Darwin's and Spencer's theory on the origin of music see the book.) A collection of the earliest tales on the origin of music follows as an appendix to this chapter.

X. *Heredity and development in music.*

Accepting Mr. Galton's and Weismann's theory of the non-heredity of acquired variations, I will try to explain the progress in music by tradition and imitation. This alone would seem to account for the rapid progress of music during the present century, and especially during the last thirty years, in which (considering the short time of one generation) no heredity, nor elimination, nor organic combination can possibly have taken place at all.

Primitive music is not at all an abstract art, but (taken in connection with dance and pantomime) is a part of the necessaries of life (war and hunting), for which it seems to prepare, or to maintain our strength and skill during time of peace. Primitive music, as it is (*i.e.*, keeping in time), is an organising power for the masses, the tie which enables the tribe to act as one body. It facilitates association in acting. Tribes which know how to keep time, which are accustomed to *play* at war and at hunting, associate more easily, act better in case of need, and, since association accounts for something in the struggle for life, such tribes are better prepared for it; for this purpose the musical faculty is developed and trained. Thus the law of natural selection holds good in explaining the origin and development of music.

AUTHORITIES QUOTED.

(The numbers in brackets refer to the page of this book where the work is quoted.)

AALST (T. A. van), Chinese Music, Shanghai, London, 1884 (16)

Adair (James), The History of the American Indians, London, 1775 (173)

Addison (Lancelot), An Account of West Barbary (printed Oxf., 1671), *Pinkert. Collect.*, vol. xv. (14, 129, 211)

Adelburg (A. von), Entgegnung auf Liszt's Des Bohémiens, Pest, 1859 (63)

Albertis (Luigi Maria), New Guinea, 2 vols., London, 1880 (28, 110)

Allen (Grant), Physiological Æsthetics, London, 1877 (233)

Allen (William Francis), Slave Songs of the United States. Edited by Allen, C. P. Ware, L. M. Garrison, New York, 1867 (61, 175)

Allgemeine Musikalische Zeitung, Leipzig

Ambros (August Wilhelm), Geschichte der Musik, 5 vols., Breslau, Leipzig, 1862-1882 (58)

American Journal of Psychology (The), edited by G. J. Hall, Baltimore

American Naturalist, Philadelphia

Amyot (Joseph), Mémoire sur la musique des Chinois, Paris, 1779 (16)

Anales del Ministerio de Fomento, Mexico, 1854 (138)

Anderson (John), Mandalay to Momien, London, 1876 (16)

Andersson (C. J.), Lake Ngami, London, 1886 (123, 124)

Andree (Richard), Das Amur Gebiet, Leipzig, 1867 (100, 120)

—— Ethnogr. Parallelen Stuttgart, 1878, Neue Folge, Leipzig, 1889 (84, 281)

Angas (G. F.), Polynesia, London, 1866 (87, 93, 204)

—— Savage Life and Scenes in Australia and New Zealand, 2 vols., London, 1847 (38, 83, 93, 101, 107, 217, 218, 223)

Angelo (Michael), Carli (Denis de), A Voyage to Congo, 1666, 1667, *Pinkert. Collect.*, xvi. (99, 107, 114, 117, 143)

Annalen des k. k. Naturhistorischen Hofmuseums, Wien

Antananarivo Annual and Madagascar Magazine (The), Antananarivo

Appun (Carl Friedrich), Unter den Tropen, 2 vols., Jena, 1871 (54)

Archæological Journal (The), London

Archiv für mikroskopische Anatomie, Bonn

Archiv für Ohrenheilkunde, Leipzig

Ashe (Thomas), Travels in America 1806, London, 1809 (48)

Astley (Thomas), A New General Collection of Voyages and Travels, 4 vols.,
　　London, 1745 (8, 16, 65, 86, 88, 104, 117, 118, 125)

Atkinson (T. W.), Travels in the Regions of the Upper and Lower Amoor,
　　London, 1860 (23)

Ausland (Das), Stuttgart Augsburg

Avezac (M. d'), Notice sur le pays et le Peuple de Yébous en Afrique, in
　　Mémoire de la Soc. Ethnol., tom. ii. pt. ii. p. 89 (99, 131)

Azara (Don Felix de), Reisen in dem südlichen Amerika, 1781-1801, in *Jour-
　　nal f. L. und S.*, p. 74, Bd. vi. (55)

BAKER (Sir S. W.), Ismailïa : A Narrative of the Exped. to Central Africa,
　　2nd edit., London, 1879 (9)

—— The Albert Nyanza, Great Basin of the Nile, and Explor. of the Nile
　　Sources, 2 vols., London, 1866 (189, 199)

Baker (Theodor), Über die Musik der Nordamerikanischen Wilden, Leipzig,
　　1882 (76, 92, 95, 96, 138, 142, 143, 151, 160, 161, 173, 186, 195)

Balfour (Edward), The Cyclopædia of India and Eastern and Southern Asia,
　　London, 1885 (142)

Balfour (Henry), The old British " Picborn " or " Hornpipe " and its Affinities,
　　in *Anth. Journ.*, vol. xx. p. 142 (98)

Bancroft (Hubert Howe), The Native Races of the Pacific States of North
　　America, 5 vols., New York and Cambridge, 1875-76 (47, 48, 49, 50,
　　75, 76, 83, 88, 93, 97, 103, 109, 111, 116, 117, 118, 138, 143, 146, 172,
　　208, 212, 213, 219, 226, 227, 261)

Barker-Webb (Ph.), Berthelot (Sabin), Histoire naturelle des Iles Canaries,
　　3 vols., Paris, 1835-49 (190)

Baron (S., native of Tonqueen), A Description of the Kingdom of Tonqueen,
　　Pinkert. Collect., vol. ix. (137, 207)

Barrow (John), An Account of Travels into the Interior of Southern Africa
　　in the years 1797-98, 2 vols., London, 1801-04 (121, 164)

Bartalus (Stephan), Die Zigeuner und ihr Verhältnis zu unserer Musik in
　　Ungar. Monatschrift Budapest, ii. Bd. 1st and 3rd Heft, Sept., 1868, p.
　　60 (63)

Barth (Heinrich), Reisen und Entdeckungen in Nord und Central Afrika
　　1849-55, 5 Bde., Gotha, 1857-58 (134)

Bastian (Adolf.), Indonesien, Berlin, 1884 (97, 102, 107, 122, 128)

—— Die Culturländer des alten Amerika, 2 vols., Berlin, 1878 (53)

—— Remarks on the Indo-Chinese Alphabets, in *Journal of the Roy. Asiat.
　　Soc.*, new series, vol. iii. part i., London, 1867 (185)

Bates (Henry Walter), The Naturalist on the River Amazon, 2 vols., London,
　　1863 (55, 56, 101, 122)

Baumann (Oskar), Usambara, Berlin, 1891 (71, 113, 127)

Beckler (Hermann D.), Corrobberri, in *Globus*, vol. xiii. pp. 82, 122 (37, 89,
　　209)

Beecham (John), Ashantee and the Gold Coast, London, 1841 (12, 92, 100,
　　114, 122, 133)

Beechey (Fred. Will.), Narrative of a Voyage to the Pacific and Behring Straits, 2 vols., London, 1831 (35, 191)

Beeckman (Daniel), Voyage to and from the Island of Borneo, in *Pinkert. Collect.*, vol. xi. (105)

Behr (H. F. von), Kriegsbilder aus dem Araberaufstand in Deutsch-Ostafrika, Leipzig, 1891 (11)

Bélugon (L.), Une nouvelle Laura Bridgman, in *Revue Philosoph.*, 1889, tom. 28 p. 175, transl. from 57th An. Rep. of the Perkins Inst. and Massachusetts School for the Blind, Sept., 1888 (259)

Berg (H., *Pseudonym ?*), Die Lust an der Musik, Berlin, 1879 (76, 244)

Berlioz (Hector), A travers chants, Paris, 1862 (17)

Bernau (Rev. John Henry), Missionary Labours in British Guiana, London, 1847 (94, 105, 129)

Berthelot (Sabin), Mémoire sur les Guanches, from part i. vol. i. of Iles Canaries, in *Mémoires de la Ethnolog.*, Paris, 1841, tom. i. p. 202 (190)

Bickmore (Albert S.), Travels in the East Indian Archipelago, London, 1868 (100, 105, 135, 192)

Billert, Japanische Musik, in *Reissm. Mend. Lexicon*, 5th vol. (16, 18)

Bird (William Hamilton), The Oriental Miscellany: being a Collection of the most Favourite Airs of Hindostan, Calcutta, 1789 (19)

Birdwood (Sir George Christopher M.), The Industrial Arts of India, 2 vols., 1880, South Kensington Mus. Art Handbook, London, 1884 (18, 19)

Boas (Franz), Chinook Songs, in *Journ. Amer. Folklore*, vol. i., 1888, p. 220 (72, 172)

—— On Certain Songs and Dances of the Kwakiutl of British Columbia, in *Journ. of Amer. Folklore*, vol. i., 1888, p. 49 (159, 276)

Bock (Carl), The Head-Hunters of Borneo, London, 1881 (128, 134, 192, 202, 207)

Bonwick (James), Daily Life and Origin of the Tasmanians, London, 1870 (40, 41, 76, 146, 201, 204, 212, 218, 224)

Bosman (William), A New and Accurate Description of the Coast of Guinea, *Pinkert. Collect.*, xvi. (100, 124)

Bouche (Pierre), Sept ans en Afrique occidentale, Paris, 1885 (12, 105, 106, 125)

Bowdich (Thomas Edw.), Mission from Cape Coast Castle to Ashantee, London, 1819 (92)

—— An Essay on the Ancient Egyptians, Abyssinians, and Ashantees, Paris, 1821 (141)

Bowring (Sir John), The Kingdom and People of Siam, 2 vols., London, 1857 (20, 70, 137, 142)

Boyle (Frederick), Adventures among the Dyaks of Borneo, London, 1865 (26, 218)

Brasseur de Bourbourg, Gramatica de la Lengua Quiché, in *Collect. des documents inédits*, vol. ii., Paris, 1862 (49, 227)

Breitenstein (Heinrich), Aus Borneo, in *Mittheilg. der geogr. Gesell. in Wien*, xxviii., 1885, pp. 193, 247 (25)

Brett (William Henry), The Indian Tribes of Guiana, London, 1868 (213, 220)

Bridges (Thomas), Manners and Customs of the Firelanders, in *A Voice of South America*, vol. xiii., 1866 (58)

Brooks (W. R.), The Law of Heredity, Baltimore, 1883 (263)

Brown (Mary Eugenia and Adams William), Musical Instruments and their Homes, New York, 1888 (13, 16, 18, 19, 20, 22, 87, 94, 120, 252)

Browne (James), Die Eingebornen Australiens, in *Petermann's Mittheilg.*, 1856, p. 443 (222)

Brüe, A Description of the River Sanaga, in *Astley Collect.*, ii. (13, 89, 125)

Brugsch (Heinrich), Reiseberichte aus Ægypten, Leipzig, 1855 (198)

Buchanan, afterwards Hamilton (Francis), An Account of the Kingdom of Nepal, Edinburgh, 1819 (19)

Buchner (Max.), Kunst und Witz der Neger, in *Das Ausland*, 1884, p. 13 (221)

—— Kamerun, Leipzig, 1887 (88, 112, 113, 176, 228)

—— Reise durch den stillen Ocean, Breslau, 1878 (72, 113, 202, 204)

Bulletins de la Société d'Anthropologie, Paris

Bulletin de la Société de Géographie, Paris

Burchell (W. T.), Travels in the Interior of Southern Africa, 2 vols., London, 1822-24 (1, 2, 3, 94, 104, 110, 119, 139, 163)

Burckhardt (John Lewis), Notes on Bedouins and Wahabys, edited by Sir W. Ouseley, London, 1830 (13, 129, 176)

Burney (Charles), A General History of Music, 4 vols., London, 1776-89 (249)

Burton (Richard Francis), First Footsteps in East Africa, London, 1856 (33)

—— Notes on the Dahoman, in *Memoirs Anthrop. Soc. of London*, 1863-64, vol. i. p. 313 (185)

—— A Mission to Gelele, 2 vols., London, 1864 (12, 133)

—— Explorations of the Highlands of the Brazil, London, 1869 (56)

—— The Lake Region of Central Africa, 2 vols., London, 1860 (11, 100, 106, 146)

Busch (Moritz), Wanderungen zwischen Hudson und Mississippi, 1851-52, 2 vols., Stuttgart, 1854 (61, 73)

Byam (George), Wild Life in the Interior of Central America, London, 1849 (239)

Cäcilia, Zeitschrift für die musikalische Welt, Mainz

Caillié (Réné), Journal d' un Voyage à Timboctou, 3 tom., Paris, 1880 (68, 124, 133, 204)

Cameron (Verney Lovett), Across Africa, London, 1885 (117, 133, 197 211)

Campbell (Archibald), A Voyage round the World, Edinburgh, 1816 (207)

Carli, *vide* Angelo

Catlin (George), Letters and Notes on the North American Indians, 2 vols., London, 1841 (45, 93, 103, 160, 175)

Century (The), New York and London

Challenger Expedition, *see* Murray (John)

Chamberlain (A. F.), Notes on the Mississagua Indians, in *Journ. Amer. Folklore*, vol. i., 1888, p. 150 (103, 194)

Chamisso (L. Carl Adalbert), Bemerkungen und Ansichten v. d. Naturforscher der Exped., in *Kotzebue Entdeckungen*, Bd. iii. (73, 74, 101, 192, 194, 198, 213, 224)

China Review (The), Hong Kong

Chinese Repository (The), Canton

Choris (M. Louis), Voyage pittoresque autour du Monde, Paris, 1822 (226)

Chorley (H. F.), The National Music of the World, edited by Hewlett, London, 1880 (156)

Christianowitsch (Alexandre), Esquisse historique de Musique Arabe, Cologne, 1863 (154, 261)

Christy (Edwin Pearce), Plantation Melodies, part v., New York, 1851-56 (61)

Christy (Henry), Lartet (E.), Reliquiæ Aquitanicæ, London, 1868 (81)

Chrysander (Friedrich), Über die altindische Opfermusik, in *Viertelj. f. Musikw.*, vol. i., 1885, p. 5 (19, 152)

Clavigero (Francisco Saverio), The History of Mexico, 2nd ed., 2 vols., London, 1807 (138, 195)

Clark (Xenos), Animal Music, its Nature and Origin, in *The Amer. Naturalist*, vol. xiii., April, 1879, No. iv. p. 209 (247)

Clément (Félix), Histoire de la Musique, Paris, 1885 (20, 22, 132)

Columbus [Colon] (Christoph), Bericht an den König Ferdinand und die Konigin Isabelle über Amerika, 3rd Reise, from Span., in *Journ. f. L. und Seereisen*, Bd. lxiv. p. 97 (166)

Commetant (Jean Pierre Oscar), La Musique, les Musiciens et les Instruments de Musique chez les différents peuples du monde, Paris, 1869 (14, 19, 52, 53, 57, 63)

Continental Monthly (The), edited by C. G. Leland, Boston and New York

Cook (James), An Account of a Voyage round the World in the Years 1768, 1770, 1771, first voyage, 3 vols., 1773 (89, 92, 114, 115, 204)

—— A Voyage towards the South Pole and round the World, 2 vols., second voyage, London, 1777 (46, 72, 93, 94, 97, 102, 207)

—— A Voyage to the Pacific Ocean, vols. i. and ii. by Cook, vol. iii. by King, third voyage, 3 vols., London, 1784 (172, 191)

Cornhill Magazine (The), London

Corry (Joseph), Observations upon the Windward Coast of Africa, London, 1807 (94, 118, 122, 188, 200)

Cranz (David), The History of Greenland, 2 vols., London, 1820, (60, 109, 166)

Crawfurd (John), History of the Indian Archipelago, 3 vols., Edinburgh, 1820 (24, 25, 86, 129, 155, 260)

—— A Sketch of the Geography of Borneo, *Journ. Royal Geogr. Soc.*, vol. xxiii. p. 69 (25)

Crotti (Primo), Musiconomia, o leggi fondamentali della scienza musicale spiegate, Parma, 1890 (236)

Curr (Edward M.), The Australian Race, London, 1887 (77, 223)

DALLAS (Robert Charles), The History of the Maroons, London, 1803 (10)

Daniel (Francisco Salvador), Essai sur l'origine et la transformation de quelques instruments, in *Revue Africaine*, tom. vii. p. 266 (136)

—— Fantaisie sur une flute double, in *Revue Africaine*, tom. x. pp. 382, 424 (96)

—— La Musique Arabe. (Printed separately and in *Revue Afr.*, tom. vi., vii., 1862-63.) Alger, 1879 (154)

Darwin (Charles), Descent of Man, 2nd edit., London, 1888 (156, 195, 199, 242, 244)

David (E.), Lussy (M.), Histoire de la notation musicale, Paris, 1882 (162)

Davies (James A.), Appendix to G. Grey's Polynesian Mythology, London, 1855 (154)

Davis (W. W. H.), El Gringo, New York, 1857 (97, 142)

Davy (John), An Account of the Interior of Ceylon, London, 1821 (21, 135, 136, 192)

Day (Charles Russell), The Music and Musical Instruments of Southern India and the Decan, London, 1891 (19, 142, 153)

—— Music and Musical Instruments, in Mockler-Ferryman's *Up the Niger* (76, 94, 100, 110, 112, 118, 120, 121, 141, 148, 151, 160, 260)

Day (Charles William), Five Years' Residence in the West Indies, 2 vols., London, 1852 (61)

Deutsche Rundschau, Berlin

Diderot (Denis), Le Neveu de Rameau, vol. ix. of the *Petite Bibliothèque de Luxe*, Paris, 1883 (255)

Dieffenbach, New Zealand and its Native Population, 2 vols., London, 1841 (175, 177)

Dobrizhoffer (Martinus), An Account of the Abipones, transl., London, 1822 (53, 54, 103, 204)

Doehne (Jacob Ludwig), Das Kafferland und seine Bewohner, Berlin, 1843 (167)

Domenech (Emanuel), Seven Years' Residence in the Great Deserts of North America, 2 vols., London, 1860 (212)

Donovan (J.), Music and Action, London, 1889 (208)

—— From Lyre to Muse, London, 1890 (236)

Dorsey (J. Owen), Ponka and Omaha Songs, in *Journ. of Amer. Folklore*, vol. ii., 1889, No. iv. p. 271 (72)

Doyle (Dr.), Sketches in Australia, in *Illustrated London News*, 3rd October, 1863, p. 353 (221)

Drury (Robert), Madagascar; or, Journal during Fifteen Years' Captivity, London, 1729 (102)

Du Chaillu (Paul B.), A Journey to Ashangoland, London, 1867 (108, 273)

—— Explorations and Adventures in Equatorial Africa, London, 1861 (106, 117, 166, 271, 274)

Dumont (d'Urville), Histoire Générale des Voyages, 4 vols., Paris, 1859 (93, 125)

Dwight's Journal of Music, 8th November, 1862 (61)

ECKERT (Franz), Japanische Leder, in *Mittheilg. der Gesellschf. f. Ostasien,* 20th Heft, June, 1880, pp. 422-428, and 23rd Heft, March, 1881, p. 131 (72)

Edwards (Amelia Blandford), A Thousand Miles up the Nile, 2nd edition, London, 1889 (199)

Edwards (Charles L.), Folklore of the Bahama Negroes, in *Amer. Journ. of Psychol.,* vol. ii., No. iv. (62, 147, 196)

Ellis (Alexander J.), On the Musical Scales of Various Nations, in *Journal of the Soc. of Arts,* vol. xxxiii., 27th March, 1885, pp. 485, 1102 (152, 153, 155)

—— On the History of Musical Pitch, in *Journal of the Soc. of Arts,* London, 5th March and 2nd April, 1880, pp. 293-336, vol. xxviii. (78)

Ellis (William), Narrative of a Tour through Hawaii, London, 1826 (75)

—— History of Madagascar, London, 1858 (14, 69, 71, 114, 122)

—— Polynesian Researches, 2 vols., London, 1829 (95, 102, 111, 180)

Elson (Louis C.), Curiosities of Music, Boston, 1880 (10, 108, 119, 136, 224)

Emerson (James), afterwards Tennent (Sir J. Em.), Ceylon, an Account of the Island, 5th edition, 2 vols., London, 1860 (21, 74, 100, 116, 237)

Engel (Carl), An Introduction to the Study of Nat. Music, London, 1866 (161, 162, 178)

—— Musical Myths and Facts, 2 vols., London, 1876 (168, 169, 260, 262)

—— The Music of the most Ancient Nations, London, 1864 (62, 85, 152, 160)

—— Researches into the Early History of the Violin Family, London, 1883 (130)

—— Descriptive Catalogue of the Musical Instruments in the South Kensington Museum, London, 1874 (81)

English Cyclopædia, conducted by Charles Knight

Erman (Georg Adolph.), Reise um die Erde, 1828-30, Berlin, 1835-41 (77, 123, 219)

Erskine (Capt. John), Journal of a Cruise among the Islands of the Western Pacific, London, 1853 (30, 88)

Etzel (Anton von), Grönland, in *Wiedenmann, Hauff, Reisen,* Lief. 44, Stuttgart, 1860 (60)

Evans (George William), A Description of Van Dieman's Land, London, 1822 (41)

Eyre (Edw. John), Journals of Expeditions of Discovery into Central Australia in 1840-1, 2 vols., London, 1845 (39, 88, 109, 136, 175, 191, 211)

FABER (Ernst), The Chinese Theory of Music, in *China Review,* vols. i. and ii., and *Notes and Queries on China,* vol. iv. (16)

Falkenstein (J.), *see* Guessfeldt

Falkner (Thomas), A Description of Patagonia, Hereford, 1774 (54, 169)

Fétis (François Joseph), A. Stradivari, Paris, 1856 (129)

—— Sur un nouveau mode de classification des races humaines d'apres leurs systémes musicaux, in *Bulletins de la Soc. d'Anthrop.,* t. ii., Série ii., Paris, 1867, p. 134 (64, 65)

Fétis (François Joseph), Histoire générale de la Musique, 5 vols., Paris,1869-76
     (17, 81, 82)
Fewkes (J. Walter), A Few Summer Ceremonials at Zuñi Pueblo, in *Journ.
     Amer. Ethn.*, vol. i. (125, 126, 161, 194)
—— A Contribution to Passamaquoddy Folklore, in *Journ. Amer. Folklore*,
     vol. iii., 1890, No. xi. p. 257 (172)
Field (Barron), Geographical Memoirs on New South Wales, London, 1825
     (41)
Finsch (Otto), Ethnologische Erfahrungen aus der Südsee, in *Natur. Hist.
     Hof. Museum.*, Vienna, Bd. iii. (74, 120, 126)
—— Reise nach West Sibirien im Jahre 1876, Berlin, 1879 (22)
Flegel (Edward Robert), Lose Blätter aus dem Tagebuche meiner Haussa-
     Freunde, Hamburg, 1885 (102)
Fleischer (Oskar), Land, Recherches sur l'histoir gamme arabe, in *Viertelj.
     Musikw*, vol. ii., 1886, p. 497 (154)
Fletscher (Alice C.), Leaves from my Omaha Note-book, in *Journ. Amer.
     Folklore*, vol. ii., 1889, No. vi. p. 225 (72)
Folklore Journal, vol. v., London
Folklore Society Publications, 1878-1885, The former Publications published
     under the title, *The Folklore Record*, London
Forbes (Henry O.), A Naturalist's Wanderings in the Eastern Archipelago,
     London, 1885 (73)
Forel (Auguste), Les Fourmis de la Suisse, Zürich, 1874 (237)
Forrest (Thomas), A Voyage to New Guinea and the Moluccas, London,
     1779 (28, 206)
Forster (Johann Georg Adam), A Voyage round the World, 1772-75, 2 vols.,
     London, 1777 (141, 148)
Forsyth (Capt. James), The Highlands of Central India, 2nd edition, London,
     1871 (96)
Fortier (Alcée), Customs and Superstitions in Louisiana, in *Journ. of Amer.
     Folklore*, vol. i., 1888, No. ii. p. 136 (126)
Foster (Henry), Narrative of a Voyage to the South Atlantic Ocean, 1828-
     30, 2 vols., from the private Journ. of W. H. B. Webster, London,
     1834 (77, 88, 185, 188)
Franklin (Sir John), Narrative of a Journey to the Polar Sea, London, 1823
     (196)
Freycinet (Louis de), Voyage autour du monde, 9 vols., Paris, 1824-44 (37,
     192)
Fritsch (Gustav), Drei Jahre in Süd-Afrika, Breslau, 1868 (90)
—— Die Eingeborenen Süd-Afrika's, Leipzig, 1872 (86, 90, 110, 119, 197)
Frœbel (Julius), Aus Amerika, 2 vols., Leipzig, 1857-58 (117)

GALAUP de la Pérouse (Jean François), A Voyage round the World in the
     Years 1785-1788, transl., 2nd edition, 3 vols., London, 1799 (46, 142)
Galton (Francis), A Theory of Heredity, in *Journ. Anthrop. Inst.*, vol. v.
     pp. 343-345 (264)

Galton (Francis), Natural Inheritance, London, 1889 (264)
—— Inquiries into Human Faculty and its Development, London, 1883 (238, 240)
—— Hereditary Genius, London, 1869 (265)
—— Narrative of an Explorer in Tropical South Africa, London, 1889 (5, 6, 124)
Garcilasso de la Vega, El Inca, *Hakluyt Society*, 2 vols., London, 1869-71 (51)
Gardiner (Allen Francis), Narrative of a Journey to the Zoolu Country, London, 1836 (71, 178)
Gardiner (William), The Music of Nature, London, 1832 (107)
Garner (R. L.), The Simian Tongue, in *New Review*, June, 1891, p. 555 (240)
Georgi (Johann Gottlieb), Beschreibung aller Nationen des Russischen Reichs, St. Petersburg, 1776 (23, 193, 203, 212)
Gerland (Georg), Über das Aussterben der Naturvölker, *see* also Waitz, Leipzig, 1868 (44)
Gill (William (Wyatt), Myths and Songs from the South Pacific, London, 1876 (193)
Gilman (Benjamin Ives), Zuñi Melodies, in *Journ. Amer. Ethn.*, vol. i. (150, 158)
—— On some Psychological Aspects of the Chinese Musical System, in *Philosoph. Review*, vol. i. 1, 2 (155)
Globus, edited by Karl Andree, Braunschweig
Goertz (Carl von), Reise um die Welt, 1844-47, Stuttgart, 1835 (77, 226)
Gould (John), Handbook to the Birds of Australia, 2 vols., London, 1865 (249)
Graah (W. A.), Narrative of an Expedition to Greenland, London, 1837 (75)
Graber (Vitus), Die chordotonalen Sinnesorgane und das Gehör der Insecten, in *Archiv Mikroscop. Anatomie*, Bd. xx., 1882, p. 506 (238, 239)
Graham (W. W.), Climbing the Himalayas, in *From the Equator to the Pole*, London, 1887 (22)
Grant (Colquhoun), Description of Vancouver Island, in *Journ. Lond. Geogr. Soc.*, vol. xxvii. p. 268 (172)
Grant (James Augustus), Speke (John Hanning), Lake Victoria, compiled by G. C. Swayne, London, 1868 (132)
Grant (James Augustus), A Walk across Africa, London, 1864 (9, 11, 68, 94, 99, 113, 115, 116, 121, 132, 152, 189)
Greenwood (J.), Curiosity of Savage Life, London, 1863 (179)
Grey (George), Journals of Two Expeditions of Discovery in N. W. and W. Australia, 2 vols., London, 1841 (68, 74, 109, 164, 165, 175, 177, 206)
—— Polynesian Mythology, London, 1855 (42, 43, 154)
Grosse (Ernst), Ethnologie und Æsthetik, in *Viertelj. für wissensch. Phil.* (1891), xv. 4 (253)
—— Herbert Spencer's Lehre von dem Unerkennbaren, Leipzig, 1890 (267)
Grout (Lewis), Zululand, Philadelphia, 1864 (176)
Grove (Sir George), A Dictionary of Music and Musicians, 4 vols., London, 1879-89

Guessfeldt (Paul), Falkenstein (Julius), Pechuël-Lœsche (Emil), Die Loango
   Expedition, Leipzig, 1879 (114, 182, 183, 239, 241)
Gurney (Edmund), Power of Sound, London, 1880 (255, 259)
Guyau (Jean Marie), Les Problémes de l'Esthétique contemporaine, Paris,
   1884 (234, 235, 236, 237)
—— Education and Heredity, transl., London, 1891 (269)

HAAFNER (J.), Reise längs der Küste Orixa und Koromandel in Indien, 1784
   (from the Dutch), in *Journ. of L. und S.*, Bd. vii. pp. 117, 147 (203)
Haddon (Alfred C.), The Ethnography of the Western Tribe of Torres
   Straits, in *Journ. Anthr. Inst.*, vol. xix. No. iii., 1890, p. 297 (104, 114)
Hæckel (Ernst Heinrich), Indische Reisebriefe, 2nd Aufl., Berlin, 1884 (22)
—— Generelle Morphologie der Organismen, 2 Bd., Berlin, 1866 (248)
Hahn (Theophilus), Die Nama-Hottentoten, in *Globus*, xii. p. 278 (141, 178)
Hall (Basil), Account of a Voyage to Corea and the Great Loo-Choo Islands,
   London, 1818 (58)
Hall (C. F.), Arctic Researches among Esquimaux, New York, 1865 (58)
Hamilton (Alexander), A New Account of the East Indies, in *Pinkerton
   Collect.*, vol. viii. (93, 107)
Hamilton (F.), *see* Buchanan
Harkness (H.), A Description of the Neilgherry Hills, London, 1832 (19)
Hart (George), The Violin and its Music, London, 1884 (130)
Hauser (Michael), Aus dem Wanderbuche eines österreichischen Virtuosen,
   edited by S. Hauser, 2 vols., Leipzig, 1859 (35)
Hein (Alois Raimund), Malerei und Technische Künste der Dayaks, in *Anal.
   K. K. Naturh. Hofmuseum*, Vienna, Bd. iv. (282)
—— Die bildenden Künste bei den Dayaks auf Borneo, Wien, 1890 (25, 93,
   110, 111, 128, 168, 207)
Helmholtz (Hermann L. v.), On the Sensation of Tone, 2nd edition, transl.
   by A. Ellis (German edition, 4th Aufl., 1877), London, 1885 (143, 150,
   153)
Herrara (Antonio de), The Voyage of Francisco de Orellana, A.D. 1540-41, in
   Markham's Exped. into the Valley of the Amazons (239)
Heuglin (Theodor von), Reise in das Gebiet des weissen Nil, Leipzig,
   Heidelberg, 1869 (118, 125, 205)
—— Die Tinne sche Expedition im Westlichen Nil-Quellgebiete, in *Ergän-
   zungsheft* 15 *zu Peterm. Mitth. Ergänzungsband*, iii., 1863-64 (15)
Hinrichs (Johann Christian), Entstehung der russischen Jagdmusik, St.
   Petersburg, 1796 (96)
Hipkins (A. J.), Cantor Lectures on Musical Instruments. Reprinted from
   the *Journ. of the Soc. of Arts*, 31st July, 7th and 14th August, London,
   1891 (121)
—— Musical Instruments, Historic, Rare and Unique, Edinburgh, 1888 (16,
   18, 20)
Hirth (Georg), Aufgaben der Kunstphysiologie, 2 vols., München, Leipzig,
   1891 (265, 281)

Holtz (von), Zwei japanische Lieder, in *Mittheilg. d. deutsch. Ges. f. Natur. and Völkerk. Ostasiens*, 3rd Heft, September, 1873 (72)

Holub (Emil), Seven Years in South Africa, 1872-79, 2 vols., London, 1881 (132)

Home (Henry, Lord Kames), Elements of Criticism, 8th edition, 2 vols., Edinburgh, 1807 (232)

Houtou de la Billardière (Jaques Julien), An Account of a Voyage in Search of La Pérouse, 1791-93, transl., 2 vols., London, 1800 (31, 32)

Howitt (A. W.), Songs and Songmakers of some Australian Tribes, in *Anthr. Journ.*, vol. xvi. p. 327 (38, 39, 68, 146, 217)

Humboldt (F. H. Alexander von), Bonpland (Aimé), Reise in die Æqua-torialgegenden des neuen Continents, 1799-1804, 6 parts, Stuttgart, 1815-32 (90, 91, 210)

Hunter (John), An Historical Journal of the Transactions at Port Jackson and Norfolk Islands, London, 1793 (168)

Hupfeld, Das zwiefache Grundgesetz d. Rhythmus und Accent, in *Zeitschr. d. deutsch. morgl. Gesell.*, vi. p. 170 (235)

ILLUSTRATED London News, London

Im Thurn (Everard F.), Among the Indians of Guiana, London, 1883 (83, 86, 96, 101, 124, 196, 220)

International Oriental Congress, Actes du sixième Congrès International des Orientalistes tenu en 1883 à Leide, Leide, 1884

Irwin (Eyles), Chinese Musick, examples, in *Oriental Collect.*, i. p. 343

—— Chinese Tunes, examples, in *Oriental Collect.*, ii. p. 148

Ives (Joseph C.), Report upon the Colorado River, in *36th Cong. 1st Sess. House Ex. Doc.* 90, Washington, 1861 (97)

JACKSON (James Grey), An Account of Timbuctoo and Housa (from oral communications by El Hage Abd. Salam Shabeeny), London, 1820 (200)

Jagor (F.), Andamanesen oder Mincopies, in *Zeitschr. f. Ethn.*, 1877, vol. ix. (24, 75, 87)

—— Travels in the Philippines, transl., London, 1875 (57)

James (William), The Principles of Psychology, 2 vols., New York, 1890 (267)

Jewitt (John R.), A Narrative of J. R. J. during a Captivity of nearly Three Years among the Savages of Nootka Sound, Wakefield, 1816 (83, 88, 93, 103, 172)

Johnston (H. H.), The River Congo, from its Mouth to Bolobo, London, 1884 (101, 117, 125)

Joinville, On the Religion and Manners of the People of Ceylon, in *Asiatick Researches*, vol. vii., 1801, pp. 399, 438 (20, 21, 152)

Jones (Edward), Lyric Airs, London, 1804 (41)

Jones (William), On the Musical Modes of the Hindus, also 6th vol. of his Select Works, London, 1784 (18)

Joseph Charles Louis (Archduke of Austria), Czigány nyelvtan románo csibákero Sziklaribe, in *Magyar Tudományos Akademia*, 1888 (63)

Journal für die neuesten Land und Seereisen, Berlin, 1808-36

Journal of American Ethnology and Archæology, edited by J. Walter Fewkes, Boston, New York

Journal of American Folklore (The), Boston

Journal of the American Oriental Society, Boston, New York and London

Journal of the Ethnological Society of London, London

Journal of the Gipsy Lore Society, Edinburgh

Journal of the Royal Asiatic Society of Great Britain and Ireland, London

Journal of the Royal Geographical Society, London

Journal of the Indian Archipelago and Eastern Asia, Singapore

Journal of the Ceylon Branch of the Royal Asiatic Society, Colombo

Journal of the Society of Arts, London

Jukes (Joseph Beete), Narrative of the Surveying Voyage of H.M.S. *Fly*, 2 vols., London, 1847 (110, 135, 204)

Jullien (Adolphe), La Musique et la Philosophie du xviii. me siècle, Paris, 1873 (251)

KAINES (Joseph), On some of the Racial Aspects of Music, in *Anthrop. Journ.*, vol. i., 1872, p. xxviii. (149)

Keating (W. H.), Narrative of an Expedition to the Source of St. Peter's River, 2 vols., Philadelphia, 1824 (172, 220)

Kennan (George), Tent Life in Siberia, London, 1873 (122, 180)

Keppel (Hon. Henry), Expedition to Borneo, 3rd edition, 2 vols., London, 1847 (192)

Kerst (S. Gottfried), Über brazilianische Zustände der Gegenwart, in *Journ. f. L. u. S.*, lxxi. pp. 303-4 (133)

Kiesewetter (Rafael Georg), Die Musik der Araber, Pref. by Hammer-Purgstall, Leipzig, 1842 (183)

King (P. Parker), and Fitz-Roy (R.), Narrative of the Surveying Voyages of the *Adventure* and *Beagle*, 3 vols., London, 1839 (35)

Kœnig (Arthur), Beiträge zur Psych. und Phys. der Sinnesorgane. Helmholtz als Festgruss, Hamburg, Leipzig, 1891

Kohl (Johann Georg), Kitschi-Gami oder Erzählungen vom Obern See, 2 vols., Bremen, 1859 (160)

Kolbe (Peter), Caput Bonæ Spei Hodiernum, Nürnberg, 1719 (138)

Kosegarten (J. G. L.), Die moslemischen Schriftsteller über die Theorie der Musik, in *Zeitschr. f. d. Kunde d. Morgenl.*, Bd. v. p. 137 (154)

Kotzebue (O. von), A Voyage of Discovery into the South Sea and Behring Straits, 3 vols., London, 1821 (36)

Krapf (Johann Ludwig), Travels during an Eighteen Years' Residence in Eastern Africa (German edition, Stuttgart, 1858), London, 1860 (167)

Kraus (Alexandre), Ethnographie Musicale, La Musique au Japon, 2nd edition, Florence, 1879 (17)

Krebs (C. A.), Kurzer Bericht über die Kurilischen Inseln (geheime See Exped. de Capitain Billings), in *Journ. f. L. und S.*, Bd. xvii. p. 355 (219)

Krusenstern (Adam Johann von), Reise um die Welt in den Jahren, 1803-1806, Bd. iii., St. Petersburg, 1810-11 (36, 105, 202)

Kueffner (Joseph), Siebold (Ph. von), Japanische Weisen gesammelt von Ph. Fr. von S., Leiden, 1836 (17)

LABILLARDIÈRE, *see* Houtou

Laing (Alexander Gordon), Travels in Western Africa, London, 1825 (67, 198)

Land (J. P. N.), Recherches zur l'histoire de la gamme Arabe, in *Actes du 6em Congr. Intern. des Orient.*, part ii. sect. i. p. 37, Leide, 1885 (154)

—— Groneman (J.), De Gamĕlan te Jogjakarta, in *K. Akad. van Wetenschappen. Verh. Afd. Letterk.*, Deel 19, Amsterdam, 1890 (24, 25, 142)

Landa (Diego de), Relation des choses de Yucatan, in *Collection de documents dans les langues indigenes*, vol. iii., Paris, 1864 (138, 213)

Lander (Richard), Records of Captain Clapperton's Last Expedition to Africa, 2 vols., London, 1830 (71, 89, 178, 179, 182, 187, 189, 190, 197, 217)

Lander (Richard and John), Journal of an Expedition to Explore the Course and Termination of the Niger, 3 vols., London, 1832 (197)

Landois (Hermann), Die Ton und Stimmapparate der Insecten, Leipzig, 1867 (239)

Lang (Andrew), Myth, Ritual, and Religion, 2 vols., London, 1887 (125, 198)

—— Custom and Myth, 2nd edition, London, 1885 (125)

Langsdorf (Georg Henrich v.) Voyages and Travels in Various Parts of the World, 1803-07, transl., 2 vols., London, 1813-14 (36, 47, 71, 75, 146, 154, 171, 179, 202, 210, 212, 219)

La Pérouse, *see* Galaup

Lartet (S.), *vide* Christy

Lassen (Christian), Indische Alterthumskunde, 4 Bde., Bonn, Leipzig, 1847-62 (18, 184)

Lay (G. Tradescant), The Chinese as They Are, London, 1841 (25)

Leems (Knud), An Account of the Laplanders of Finmark, in *Pink. Collect.*, vol. i. p. 376 (22, 88)

Le Mesurier (C. J. R.), The Veddas of Ceylon, in *Journ. of the Ceylon Br. of the R. As. Soc.*, vol. ix. No. xxxii. p. 336, 1887 (70)

Lempriere (William), A Tour from Gibraltar to Morocco, *Pinkert. Collect.* xv. (13, 129)

Lenoir de Lafage (Juste Adrien), Histoire Générale de la Musique, 2 vols. and Atlas, Paris, 1844 (14, 16, 19)

Lenz (Oskar), Skizzen aus Westafrika, Berlin, 1878 (8, 9, 10, 105, 106, 107, 124, 167, 216)

—— Timbuktu, 2 Bde., Leipzig, 1884 (67)

Lesseps (Ferdinand Marie de), Travels in Kamtschatka, 1878-88, 2 vols. (from the French), London, 1790 (176, 219)

Lewin (T. H.), Wild Races of South-Eastern India, London, 1870 (95, 96, 97, 225)

Lewis (M. G.), Journal of a Residence among the Negroes in the West Indies, London, 1845 (168)

Lichtenstein (Dr. Martin H. C.), Travels in Southern Africa, 1803-1806, transl., 2 vols., London, 1812-15 (33, 119, 133, 151)

Liebich (Richard), Die Zigeuner, 3 Abth., Leipzig, 1863 (63, 131)

Linnæus (Carl), Lachesis Lapponica, publ. by J. E. Smith, 2 vols., London, 1811 (88)

Lisyansky (Yury Fedorovich), A Voyage round the World, 1803-06, London, 1814 (47)

Liszt (Ferencz), Des Bohémiens en Hongrie, Paris, 1859 (62)

Livingstone (David), Missionary Travels and Researches in South Africa, London, 1857 (6, 114, 115, 118, 143, 189)

Lloyd (G. T.), Thirty-three Years in Tasmania and Victoria, London, 1862 (39)

Lobo (Jerome, Portuguese Jesuit), A Voyage to Abyssinia, from the French, *Pinkert. Collect.*, vol. xv. (13, 75)

Lockwood (Rev. S.), A Singing Hesperomys, in *Amer. Naturalist*, vol. v., 1871, p. 761 (239)

Lombroso (Cesare), Klinische Beiträge zur Psychiatrie, Leipzig, 1869 (259)

Long (C. Chaillé), Central Africa, Naked Truths of Naked People, London, 1876 (99, 109, 189, 205)

Long (Stephen H.), Account of an Expedition to the Rocky Mountains, 2 vols., Philadelphia, 1823 (203, 219)

Longman's Magazine

Low (James), History of Tennasserim, in *Journ. of the Roy. Asiatic Soc.*, vol. iv., 1837, p. 47 (22)

Lubbock (Sir John), Pre-Historic Times, 5th edition, London, 1890 (93, 201, 202, 249)

—— The Origin of Civilisation, 5th edition, London, 1889 (35, 198)

—— Ants, Bees, and Wasps, *Int. Sc. Series*, vol. xl., London, 1882 (237)

—— On the Senses, Instincts, and Intelligence of Animals, *Intern. Sc. Series*, vol. lxv., London, 1889 (237)

Lumholtz (Carl), Among Cannibals, transl. from the Danish, London, 1889 (70, 109, 147, 171, 175, 222)

Lunn (Charles), The Philosophy of Voice, 6th edition, London, 1888 (240)

Lux (A. E.), Von Loando nach Kimbundu, Wien, 1880 (201)

Lyell (Charles), The Geological Evidence of the Antiquity of Man, 4th edition, London, 1873 (81)

Lyon (George Francis), A Narrative of Travels in Northern Africa, 1818-20, London, 1821 (71, 114, 129, 179, 204, 220)

MacCann (William), Two Thousand Miles' Ride through the Argentine Provinces, 2 vols., London, 1853 (169)

Macdonald (Rev. J.), On Manners and Customs of South African Tribes, in *Anthr. Journ.*, vol. xx. p. 142 (167)

Mach (Ernst), Analyse der Empfindungen, Jena, 1886 (253, 266)

Macmillan's Magazine

Magyar (Laszli), Reisen in Süd-Africa, transl., Pest, Leipzig, 1859 (94, 116, 117, 167, 200)

Malcom (Howard), Travels in South-Eastern Asia, 2 vols., Boston, 1839 (22, 33, 137)

Man (E. H.), The Aboriginal Inhabitants of the Andaman Islands, in *Anthr. Journ.*, vol. xii. p. 388 (24, 69, 136, 174)

Mariner (William Martin), An Account of the Tonga Islands, in *Quarterly Review*, vol. xvii. No. xxxiii. p. 33, 1817 (32, 86)

—— An Account of the Tonga Islands, compiled by J. Martin, 2nd edition, 2 vols., London, 1818 (31, 32)

Markham (C. R.), Expeditions into the Valley of the Amazons, *Hakluyt Society*, 1859, *see* Herrara

Marknengo-Cesaresco, Negro Songs from Barbadoes, in *The Folklore Journ.*, vol. v. p. 5, 1887 (62)

Marryat (Frank S.), Borneo and the Indian Archipelago, London, 1848 (26, 105)

Marsden (William), The History of Sumatra, London, 1811 (136, 146, 154, 182, 225)

Martin (W. C. L.), General Introduction to the Nat. Hist of Mammalia, London, 1841 (156)

Martius (Carl Ph. von), Beiträge zur Ethnographie und Sprachenkunde Amerikas, Leipzig, 1867 (44, 183)

—— Spix (Johann Baptist), Travels in Brazil, 1817-1820, 2 vols., transl., London, 1824 (56, 227)

Mauch (Carl), C. Mauch's Reisen in Süd-Afrika, 1865-1872, in *Petermann's Mitth. Ergänzungsbd.* 8, *Ergänzungsheft*, No. xxxvii., 1874 (9, 92, 100, 108, 116, 189)

Mayne (C. R.), Four Years in British Columbia and Vancouver Island, London, 1862 (169)

Meinicke (Carl E.), Die Insel Pitcairn, Prenzlau, 1858 (34)

—— Die Inseln des stillen Oceans, 2 vols., Leipzig, 1875-76 (29, 31, 35, 36, 41, 87, 191, 201, 209, 213, 218)

—— Das Festland Australien, 2 th., Prenzlau, 1837 (249)

Melville (Hermann), Narrative of a Four Months' Residence among the Natives of the Marquesas Islands, London, 1846 (115)

Mémoires de la Société Ethnologique, Paris

Merck (Dr. Karl Heinrich), Nachrichten von den Tschuktschen (from a MS.), in *Journal f. L. und S.*, Bd. xvii. (110, 213, 219)

Merolla da Sorrento (Jerom, Missioner in the year 1682), A Voyage to Congo (from the Ital.), *Pinkert. Collect.*, xvi. (99, 107, 117, 118, 121, 143)

Metz (Rev. Franz), Tribes Inhabiting the Neilgherry Hills, 2nd edition, Mangalore, 1864 (19, 170)

Meyer (A. B.), Publicationen des K. Ethnologisch. Museums in Dresden, 9 vols., Leipzig, 1881-90 (19, 25, 95, 97, 116, 120, 123, 191)

Michaelis (C. F.), Ueber die Musik einiger wilden Völker, in *Allgem. musikalische Zeitung*, Nos. xxx. xxxi. pp. 509, 525, Leipzig, 1814 (76, 119)

Miklukha Maklay, Die Papuas auf New Guinea, in *Das Ausland*, 1874, p. 845 (97, 110, 210)

Mind, London

Mittheilungen der Anthropologischen Gesellschaft, Wien

Mittheilungen der k. k. geographischen Gesellschaft, Wien

Mittheilungen der deutschen Gesellschaft für Natur-und Völkerkunde, Berlin, Yokohama

Mockler-Ferryman (A. F.), Up the Niger, with Appendix by C. R. Day, London, 1892

Moffat (Robert), Missionary Labours and Scenes in Southern Africa, 11th thousand, London, 1846 (119)

Mohr (Edward), Nach den Victoriafällen des Zambesi, 2 Bd., Leipzig, 1875 (5, 67)

Molina (Giovanni Ignazio Abbé Don), History of Chili, transl., 2 vols., London, 1809 (169)

Moloney (Sir Alfred), Notes on Yoruba and the Colony and Protectorate of Lagos, in *Proceed. R. Geogr. S.*, new series, vol. xii., 1890, p. 596 (112)

Monts de, Nova Francia, containing Canada and Louisiana, in *Oxford Collection*, ii. 796 (172)

Moodie (John W. D.), Ten Years in South Africa, 2 vols., London, 1835 (119, 140)

Morgan (C. Lloyd), Animal Life and Intelligence, London, 1890-91 (245, 246, 247, 279)

—— Animal Sketches, London, 1891 (241, 242)

Morgan (Lewis H.), Ancient Society, London, 1877 (247)

—— League of the Ho-dé-no-san-nee, or Iroquois, Rochester, 1851 (52, 173, 194, 210)

Müller (Wilhelm Christian), Versuch einer Æsthetik der Tonkunst, Leipzig, 1830 (150)

Müller (Dr.), Einige Notizen ueber die japanesische Musik, in *Mittheil. d. deutsch. Ges. f. Ostasien*, 6 Heft, 6th Decem., 1874, pp. 13-32 (17)

Müller (Friedrich), Allgemeine Ethnographie, 2 Aufl., Wien, 1879 (87)

Munzinger (Werner), Ostafrikanische Studien, Schaffhausen, 1864 (181)

Murray (Boyles), Pitcairn, in *Nautical Magazine*, 1834, p. 543 (34)

Murray (Hugh), Wilson (L. John Marius), The African Continent, London, 1853 (67)

Murray (John), Thomson (Sir C. Wyville), Report on the Scient. Res. of the Voyage of H.M.S. *Challenger*, under command of G. S. Nares and F. F. Thomson, 2 vols., London, 1882-1885 (97, 107)

Murray-Ansley (Mrs. J. C.), Some Accounts on Primitive Dances in Africa, Asia, and Europe, in *Folklore Journal*, 1887, vol. v. p. 251 (193, 207, 210, 213)

Music Herald, New York

Musikalisches Wochenblatt, Leipzig

Musters (George Charvarth), At Home with the Patagonians, London, 1873
(54, 127, 135, 195)

NACHTIGAL (Gustav), Sahara and Sudan, 2 vols., Berlin, 1879-81 (116, 205)

Nansen (Fridtjof), The First Crossing of Greenland, 2 vols., London, 1890 (59)

Nautical Magazine, London

Nebel (Carl), Voyage dans Mexique, Paris, 1836 (49, 138)

Nell (Louis), An Introductory Paper on the Investigation on Singhalese
Music, in *Journal of the Ceylon Branch, Roy. As. Soc.*, 1856-58, p. 200
(22, 152)

New Review, edited by A. Grove, London

Niebuhr (Carsten), Reisebeschreibung nach Arabien, und andern umliegen-
den Ländern, 3 vols., 3 Bd. by J. N. Gloyer u. J. Olshausen, Kopen-
hagen, 1774-1837 (162, 203)

Nisbet (J. F.) Marriage and Heredity, London, 1889 (280)

Notes and Queries on China and Japan, Hong Kong

OLDFIELD (Augustus), On the Aborigines of Australia, in *Transaction of the
London Ethnolog. Society*, new series, vol. iii., 1865, p. 215 (171, 191,
211)

Oriental Collections, edited by Sir W. Ouseley, London, 1797-1799

Ouseley (W.), Anecdotes of Indian Musick, in *Oriental Collect.*, vol. i. p. 70
(18, 19)

Oxford Collection of Voyages and Travels, compiled from the Library of
the Earl of Oxford, 2 vols., London, 1745

PALGRAVE (William Gifford), Narrative of a Year's Journey through Arabia,
2 vols., London, Cambridge, 1865 (23)

Panchkari Banerjea (Pānchkadi Vandyopādhyāya), History of Hindu Music,
Bhowanipore, 1880 (259)

Park (Mungo), Travels in the Interior District of Africa, *Pinkert. Collect.*,
vol. xvi. (92, 99, 107, 117, 121, 124)

Parker (Samuel), Journal of an Exploring Tour beyond the Rocky Mountains, Ithaca, 1838 (172)

Parkyns (Mansfield), Life in Abyssinia, 2 vols., London, 1853 (240)

Parry (C. H.), Dance Rhythm, in *Grove's Dict.*, iv. p. 605 (236)

Parry (William Edward), Journal of a Voyage for the Discovery of a North-
west Passage, London, 1821-24 (59)

Pechuël-Lœsche, *see* Guessfeldt

Pennant (Thomas), Tour in Scotland, in *Pinkert. Collect.*, vol. iii. (120)

Pennell (Elizabeth Robins), A Gipsy Piper, in *Journ. Gipsy Lore Soc.*, ii. p.
266 (98)

Peron (M.), Historical Relation of a Voyage to the Southern Islands, *Pinkert.
Collect.*, vol xi. (165)

Pérouse, *see* Galaup

Perrin du Lac, Reise in den beiden Louisianen, 1801-1803, in *Journ. f. L. u. S.*, i. pp. 60, 89 (193, 219)

Peschel (Oskar Ferdinand), Völkerkunde, 2nd edition, Leipzig, 1875 (37)

Petermann, Über die Musik der Armenier, in *Zeitschrift der deutschen morgenländ. Gesellschaft*, vol. v., Leipzig, 1851 (87, 183)

Petermann (Dr. A.), Mittheilungen aus Justus Perthes Geograph. Anstalt., Gotha, 1879

Petherick (J.), Egypt, the Sudan, and Central Africa, London, Edinburgh, 1861 (87, 178)

Pfeiffer (Ida Laura), The Latest Travels of I. P., inclusive Madagascar, transl., London, 1861 (15, 75, 167, 201)

—— A Lady's Second Voyage round the World, 2 vols., London, 1855 (26, 224, 228)

—— A Lady's Travels round the World, London, 1852 (17)

Philosophical Review, edited by J. G. Schurman, Boston, Massachusetts

Philosophical Transactions of the Royal Society of London

Pigafetta, Voyage round the World, first voyage 1519-1522, *Pinkert. Collect.*, xi. (27, 115, 128)

Pinkerton (John), A General Collection of Voyages and Travels, 17 vols., London, 1808

Ploss (Hermann Heinrich), Das Kind, 2 vols., Stuttgart, 1876 (169, 178, 179)

—— Das Weib in der Natur und Völkerkunde, 2nd Aufl., edited by M. Bartels, 2 vols., Leipzig, 1887 (169)

Pogge (Paul), Im Reiche des Muata Jamwo, in *Beiträge zur Entdeckungs-gesch. Afrikas*, 3rd Heft, Berlin, 1880 (109, 117, 122, 131)

Pont-Gravé du, *see* Monts

Poole (Francis), Queen Charlotte Islands, London, 1872 (176)

Portman (M. V.), Andamanese Music, in *Journ. Roy. As. Soc.*, new series, vol. xx. p. 181, London, 1888 (75, 76, 87, 142, 152, 174, 181, 278)

Powell (Wilfred), Wanderings in a Wild Country, London, 1883 (95, 97, 120, 125)

Powers (Stephen), Tribes of California, in *Contributions to North American Ethnology*, vol. iii., Washington, 1877 (45, 47, 48, 72, 261)

Prescott (William H.), History of the Conquest of Mexico, London, 1878 (49, 138)

—— History of the Conquest of Peru, 3 vols., London, 1878 (53)

Preyer (William), Über die Grenzen der Tonwarnehmung, in *Physiol. Abhandl.*, Jena, 1876 (237)

—— Über den Ursprung des Zahlbegriffs aus dem Tonsinn, in Kœnig, *Beiträge* (237)

Price (Julius M.), Across Mongolia, in *Illustr. London News*, 14th Nov., 1889, vol. xcix. (23)

Proceedings of the Royal Geographical Society, London

Proceedings of the Royal Society, London

Proyart (Abbé), History of Loango, Kakongo, and other Kingdoms of Africa, *Pinkert. Collect.*, xvi. (89, 167)

QUANDT (C.), Nachrichten von Surinam, in *Journal f. L. und S.*, Bd. v. p. 1 (196)
Quarterly Review (The), London

RAFFLES (Thomas Stamford), The History of Java, London, 1817 (24, 84, 135, 225, 260)
Rameau (Jean Philippe), Traité d l'Harmonie, Paris, 1722 (145)
Ratzel (Friedrich), Völkerkunde, 3 vols., Leipzig, 1885-88 (33, 59, 87, 88, 117, 122, 124, 126, 127, 132-134, 146, 178, 189, 209)
Reade (W. Winwood), The African Sketch-book, 2 vols., London, 1873 (166)
—— Savage Africa, London, 1863 (216)
Reissmann (Mendel), Musikalisches Conversations Lexicon, 11 vols., 2nd edition, Berlin, 1880-81 (17)
Rengger (Johann Rudolph), Naturgeschichte der Saügethiere von Paraguay, Basel, 1830 (241)
Revue Africaine, Journal des travaux de la Société Historique Algérienne, 1871-80, Alger, Paris, Constantine
Revue Philosophique de la France et de l'Etranger, dirigée par Th. Ribot, Paris
Ribot (Théodule), L'hérédité psychologique, 2me éd., Paris, 1882 (265)
Richard, History of Tonquin, in *Pinkert. Collect.*, vol. ix., transl. (137, 207)
Richardson (Rev. J.), Malagazy, "Tonon-Kira" and Hymnology, in the *Antananarivo Annual and Madagascar Magazine*, No. ii., Christmas, 1876, p. 23 (14)
Riebeck (Emil), Die Hügelstamme von Chittagong, Berlin, 1885 (122)
—— Die Sammlung des Herrn, Dr. E. R., xxi. Tafeln., Berlin, 1884 (122)
Rink (H. I.), Tales and Traditions of the Eskimo, Edinburgh, London, 1875 (60)
Rochon (Alexis Marie), Voyage à Madagascar et aux Indes Orientales (German edition, 1792), Paris, 1791 (113, 206)
Romanes (George John), Animal Intelligence, *Intern. Sc. Ser.*, vol. xli., London, 1882 (244)
—— Mental Evolution in Animals, with a posth. Essay on Instinct by C· Darwin, London, 1883 (270)
Romilly (H. H.), The Western Pacific and New Guinea, London, 1887 (31)
Rosenberg (C. B. H. von), Reistochten naar de Geelvinkbaai op Nieuw-Guinea, in *Inst. voor de Taal-Land-en Volkenkunde van Nederl. Indie*, 1875 (102, 192)
Rousseau (Jean), Traité de la Viole, Paris, 1687 (129)
Rowbotham (John Frederick), A History of Music, 3 vols., London, 1885-87 (127)
Royse (N. K.), A Study of Genius, Chicago, New York, 1891 (266, 267)

Rühlmann (J.), Die Geschichte der Bogeninstrumente, Braunschweig, 1882 (130)

SABINE (Edward), Die Eskimos auf der Westküste von Grönland, in *Journ. f. L. und Seereisa*, xxxiii. (58)

Sainte-Croix (Fel. Renonard de), Reise nach Ostindien, 1803, in *Journal f. L. u. S.*, Bd. xi. and xii. (207)

Saint John (Sir Spenser), Life in the Forests of the Far East, 2nd edition, 2 vols., London, 1863 (122, 134, 218)

Salvado (Radesindo), Voyage en Australia, transl. from the Italian, Paris, Wassy, 1861(39, 88) ✻

Sampson (John), English Gipsy Songs and Rhymes, in *Journ. of the Gipsy Lore Soc.*, ii. p. 80 (63)

Sartorius (Christian Carl), Zustand der Musik in Mexiko, in *Cäcilia*, vol. vii., Mainz, 1828, p. 199 (50, 94)

Saurindramohana Thakura, Hindu Music, Calcutta, 1875 (for private circulation only) (142)

Schadenberg (Dr. Alexander), Über die Negritos der Philippinen, in *Zeitschr. f. Ethn.*, 1880, vol. xii. p. 145 (180)

Schauenburg (Edward), Reisen in Central Afrika von M. Park bis auf E. Vogel, 3 vols., Lahr, 1859-67 (8, 112)

Schefferus (Joannes), The History of Lapland, transl. from the Latin, Oxford, 1674 (74, 110)

Schelling (Dr. O.), Musik und Tanz der Papuas, in *Globus*, vol. lvi. No. vi. p. 81 (70, 73, 93, 97, 102, 171, 210, 218)

Scherzer (Carl von), Aus dem tropischen Amerika. Ein Skizzenbuch, Leipzig, 1864 (138)

Scheube (Dr. B.), Die Ainos, in *Mittheilungen d. deutsch. Ges. f. Ostasien*, Bd. iii., 26 Heft, Feb., 1882, and Bd. iii., 22 Heft, Dec., 1880, p. 44 (23, 87)

Schlagintweit (Robert von), Californien, Cöln, 1871 (228)

Schomburgk (Robert), On the Natives in Guiana, in *Journal of the Ethnol. Soc. London*, vol. i., 1848, pp. 253, 273 (95, 173)

Schoolcraft (Henry Rowe), Historical and Statistical Information Respecting the Indian Tribes of the U.S.A., 2 vols., Philadelphia, 1851-60 (135, 161, 207, 212)

Schröder (Joh. Joach), Thesaurus linguæ Armenicæ, Amsterdam, 1711 (183)

Schulz (Aurel), Reise nach Madagaskar, in *Zeitschr. f. Ethn.*, vol. xii. p. 192 (122)

Schulze (Captain), Über Ceram und seine Bewohner, in *Zeitschr. f. Ethn.*, vol. ix. (27)

Schürmann (C. W.), Teichelmann (G. C.), Outlines of a Grammar of the Aboriginal Language of South Australia, Adelaide, 1840 (167)

—— The Port Lincoln Tribe, in Woods' *The Nat. Tribes of Australia* (159, 163, 209)

Schütt (Otto H.), Reisen im südwestlichen Becken des Congo, in *Beiträge zur Entdeckungsg. Africas*, Heft iv., Berlin, 1881 (69)

Schwatka (Frederick), Among the Apaches, in *Century Magazine*, May, 1887, vol. xxxiv. p. 41, New York (46, 73, 128)

Schweinfurth (Georg), The Heart of Africa, 3rd edition, 2 vols., London, 1878 (7, 9, 68, 91, 99, 127, 131)

Seemann (Berthold), Narrative of the Voyage of Herald, 1845-1851, 2 vols., London, 1853

Shaw (Thomas), Travels, or Observations Relating to Barbary and the Levant, Oxford, 1738 (13, 129)

Shooter (Joseph), The Kafirs of Natal and the Zulu Country, London, 1857 (77, 123, 167)

Shortland (Edward), Traditions and Superstitions of the New Zealanders, London, 1854 (43)

Shortt (John), The Hill Tribes of the Neilgherries, in *Transact. of the Ethnol. Soc.*, new series, vol. vii. p. 230, London, 1869 (20, 207)

—— An Account of the Supposed Aborigines of Southern India, in *ibid.*, vol. iii. p. 373, 1865

Sibree (Rev. James, Junior), Children Songs and Games of the Malagasy, in *Folklore Journal*, vol i. p. 97, 1883 (14)

Siebold (Heinrich v.), Ethnologische Studien über die Aino, in *Zeitschr. f. Ethnol.*, vol. xiii. suppl. 2, p. 48, 1881 (87, 163, 176)

Siebold (Ph. Fr. von), *see* Kueffner

Simmel (Georg), Psychologische und ethnologische Studien über Musik, in *Zeitschrift für Völkerpsychologie*, vol. xiii., 1882 (73, 237)

Smith (Edmond Renel), The Araucanians, New York, 1855 (120)

Smith (Eli), A Treatise on Arab Music, chiefly from a work by Mikhâil Meshâkah, transl. from the Arabic by E. S., in *Journ. American Orient. Soc.*, vol. i. No. iii. p. 171, 1847 (the whole vol. publ. 1849) (154)

Smith (Captain John), The General History of Virginia, New England, and the Summer Isles, *Pinkert. Collect.*, vol. xiii. (103)

Smyth (R. Brough), The Aborigines of Victoria, London, 1878 (190, 206, 217)

Snow (William Parker), A Two Years' Cruise off Tierra del Fuego, 2 vols., London, 1857 (58)

Souriau (Paul), L'Esthétique du monœment, Paris, 1889 (273)

Soyaux (Herman), Aus West Africa, Leipzig, 1879 (13, 62, 100, 111, 117, 123, 126, 127, 140, 146)

Spaulding (H. G.), Under the Palmetto, in the *Continental Monthly* for August, 1863 (61)

Speke (J. H.), *see* Grant

Spencer (Herbert), On the Origin and Function of Music, 1st, *Fraser's Magazine*, vol. lvi. p. 396, October, 1857, 2nd, *Mind*, October, 1890 (239, 246)

—— Essays, 3 vols., London, 1891 (256)

Spix (J. B.), *see* Martius

Spohr (Louis), Selbstbiographie, Cassel, Göttingen, 1860-61 (150, 247)

Sproat (Gilbert Malcolm), Scenes and Studies of Savage Life, London, 1868 (45, 166, 172, 227)

Stainer (Sir John), Music in its Relation to the Intellect and the Emotions, London, 1892 (231)

Stainer (Sir John), Mackie (S. J.), Great Paul, 1882 (106)

Stanley (Henry H. Morton), Coamissie and Magdala, London, 1874 (14)

—— In Darkest Africa, 2 vols., London, 1890 (11)

Stavorinus, Account of Java and Batavia, transl. from the Dutch, in *Pinkert. Collect.*, vol. xi. (105)

Stearns (R. E. C.), Music in Nature, in *American Naturalist*, 1890 (30)

Stedmann (J. G.), Narrative of an Expedition against the Negroes of Surimam, 2 vols., London, 1806 (83, 93, 96)

Steinen (Carl von den), Durch Central-Brazilien, Leipzig, 1886 (56, 57, 93)

Stephens (John L.), Incidents of Travel in Yucatan, 2 vols., London, 1843 (103)

Stevenson (W. B.), A Narrative of Twenty Years' Residence in South America, 3 vols., London, 1825 (195)

Stumpf (Carl), Lieder der Bellakula Indianer, in *Viertelj. f. Musikw.*, vol. ii. p. 405, 1886 (143, 151, 152, 153, 159)

—— Musikpsychologie in England, in *Vierteljahrs. Musikw.*, 3t Heft, 1885 (246)

—— Tonpsychologie, 2 vols., Leipzig, 1883-90 (78, 79, 249)

Sturt (Capt. Chas. H.), Narrative of an Expedition into Central Australia, 1844-46, 2 vols., London, 1849 (222)

Sully (James), Outlines of Psychology, 2nd edition, London, 1885 (231, 232)

—— Animal Music, in *Cornhill Magazine*, vol. xli. (249)

Symes (Michael), Embassy to Ava, in *Pinkert. Collect.*, vol. ix. p. 426 (16, 17, 22, 137)

Taplin (George), The Narrinyeri, in Woods' *The Nat. Tribes of Australia* (171, 186, 201)

Taylor (Rev. Richard Cowling), Te Ika a Mami, London, 1870 (41, 94, 177, 201, 213, 229)

Tennent, *vide* Emerson

Thewrewk de Ponor (Emil), The Origin of the Hungarian Music, in *Journ. Gipsy Lore Soc.*, vol. i. p. 313, 1889 (63)

Thomson (Joseph), To the Central African Lakes and Back, 2 vols., London, 1881 (182, 216)

—— In the Heart of Africa, London, 1887 (78)

Thunberg (C. P.), An Account of the Cape of Good Hope, in *Pinkert. Collect.*, xvi. (3, 110, 121)

Tombe (Charles François) Voyage aux Indes Orientales, 2 vols., Paris, 1811 (128, 224)

Topinard (Paul), L'Anthropologie, in *Bibliothèque des sciences contemp.*, vol. iii., Paris (65)

—— Etude sur les races indigènes de l'Australia, Paris, 1872 (38, 146, 177)

Torquemada (Juan de), Ia (IIIa) Parte de los veynte y un libros rituales y Monarchia Indiana, 3 vols., Sevilla, 1615 (49, 138)

Torrance (G. W.), Music of the Australian Aborigines, in *Anthropol. Journal*, vol. xvi. p. 335 (146)

Townsend (John K.), Narrative of a Journey across the Rocky Mountains to the Columbia River, Philadelphia, 1839 (172)

Traill (Thomas Stewart), On a Peruvian Musical Instrument, in *Transact. of the Roy. Soc. of Edinburgh*, vol. xx. p. 121 (96, 152)

Transactions of the Royal Society of Edinburgh, Edinburgh

Transactions of the Ethnological Society, London

Tromp (H.), Dajaken-Gedichte, in *Globus*, vol. liii. No. xiv. p. 218, 1888 (25)

Tschudi, Peru, Reiseskizzen aus den Jahren 1838-42 2 vols., St. Gallen, 1846 (50)

Tuckey (Capt. James H.), Narrative of an Expedition to the River Zaire (Congo) in 1816, London, 1818 (7, 101, 104, 121, 178)

Turner (George), Samoa, preface by E. B. Tylor, London, 1884 (86, 97, 146, 175, 202, 213)

—— Nineteen Years in Polynesia, London, 1861 (97, 175, 180, 202, 213)

Turner (W. Y.), On the Ethnology of the Motu, in *Anthrop. Journ.*, vol. vii. p. 482 (28)

Turpin, History of Siam, in *Pinkert. Collect.*, vol. ix., transl. from the French, 2 vols., Paris, 1771 (20, 70)

Tylor (E. B.), The Bow as Origin of Stringed Instruments, in *Nature*, vol. xlv. p. 184, Dez., 1891 (126)

—— Anthropology, London, 1881 (274, 275)

—— The Study of Customs, in *Macmillan's Magazine*, May, 1882, London (92)

—— Primitive Culture, 2 vols., London, 1871 (80, 173, 185)

—— Researches into the Early History of Mankind, 3rd edition, London, 1878 (161)

UNGARISCHE Monatschrift für Politik, Pest

Upham (Edward), The Mahávansi, transl. from the Singhalese, 3 vols., London, 1833 (21)

Upton (G. P.), Woman in Music, Boston, 1880 (208)

Urville (d'), *see* Dumont

VALLE (Pietro delle), Travels in Persia, in *Pinkert. Collect.*, vol. ix. (71)

Veth (Pieter Jan), Java, 3 vols., Haarlem, 1875-82 (24, 135)

Vierteljahrsschrift für Musikwissenschaft, edited by Spitta and Chrysander, Leipzig

Vierteljahrsschrift für wissenschaftliche Philosophie, Leipzig

Villoteau (Guillaume André), De l'état actuel de l'art musical en Egypte, part iv. of the work: *Description de l'Egypte*, Paris, 1812 (189, 262)

Virchow (Rudolf), The Veddas of Ceylon, in *Journ. of the Ceylon Br. Roy. As. Soc.*, vol. ix. No. xxxiii. p. 349, 1887 (22)

Vogt (Carl), Zoologische Briefe, 2 Bde., Frankfort a. M., 1851 (237)

Voice for South America (A), London

WAGENER (Dr. G.), Bemerkungen über die Theorie der Chinesischen Musik, in *Mittheilungen d. deutsch. Gesell. f. Ostasien*, 12 Heft, pp. 42-61, Mai, 1877 (16, 84, 157)

Wagner (Richard), Gesammelte Schriften und Dichtungen, 10 Bde., Leipzig, 1871-83 (187, 214)

Waitz (Theodor), Anthropologie der Naturvölker, 6 vols., Leipzig, 1859-72 (vol. v. part ii. and vol. vi. by Gerland) (6, 12, 37, 38, 53, 59, 74, 75, 87, 92, 116, 127, 165, 212)

Walker (John), The Melody of Speaking, London, 1789 (257)

Wallace (Alfred Russell), A Narrative of Travels on the Amazon and Rio Negro, 1st edition, London, 1853, 2nd edition, 1889 (56, 75, 93, 101, 103)

—— The Malay Archipelago, 10th edition, London, 1890 (29)

—— Darwinism, London, 1889 (243, 270, 278)

Wallaschek (Richard), Über die Bedeutung der Aphasie für den musikalischen Ausdruck, in *Viertelj. f. Musikwissenschaft*, vii. Heft i., Jahrg., 1891 (241, 248)

—— Das musikalische Gedächtnis bei Katalepsie, im Traum, in der Hypnose, in *Viertelj. f. Musikw.*, viii. Heft iii., Jahrg., 1892 (57)

Weber (Ernst von), Vier Jahre in Afrika, 1871-1873, 2 Thl., Leipzig, 1878 (4, 5)

Webster (W. H. B.), *see* H. Foster

Weddell (H. Algernon), Voyage dans le Nord de la Bolivie, Paris, 1853 (52)

Weismann (August), Essays upon Heredity and Kindred Biological Problems, transl., Oxford, 1889, 2nd edition, 1891 (263, 269)

—— Gedanken über Musik bei Thieren und beim Menschen, in *Deutsche Rundschau*, 1 Heft, 1890 (249)

Westermarck (Edward), The History of Human Marriage, London, 1891 (245)

Westphal (Rudolf), Die Musik des griechischen Alterthumes, Leipzig, 1883 (144)

Whymper (Frederick), Travel and Adventure in the Territory of Alaska, London, 1868 (47)

Wied-Neuwied (Maximilian A. Ph. Prinz zu), Reise nach Brazilien, 1815-1817, abstract in *Journ. f. L. und Seereisen*, xxxv., 2 Bde., Frankfort a. M., 1820-21 (73)

—— Reisen in das innere Nord-America, 1832-1834, abstract in *Journ. f. L. und S.*, vol. xli., 2 Bde., Coblenz, 1839-41 (55, 93, 103, 168)

Wilkes (Ch.), Narrative of the United States Explor. Exped. during 1838-42, 5 vols., London, 1845 (29, 30, 32, 34, 37, 53, 57, 58, 62, 73, 76, 86, 95, 101, 141, 168, 186)

Wilkinson (Sir John Gardner), Ancient Egyptians, new edition, 3 vols., London, 1878 (125, 152, 221)

Willard (N. Augustus), A Treatise on the Music of Hindostan, Calcutta, 1834 (144)

Williams (Thomas), Calvert (James), Fiji and the Fijians, and Missionary Labours among the Cannibals, London, 1870 (29, 30, 95, 97, 101, 109, 120, 141, 146, 186)

Williams (Wells), The Middle Kingdom, 2 vols., New York, 1883 (16, 17, 155)

Wilson (Daniel), Pre-Historic Man, 3rd edition, London, 1876 (29, 81, 82)

Wissmann (Hermann v.), Unter deutscher Flagge quer durch Afrika, 1880-83, Berlin, 1889 (104, 115)

—— My Second Journey through Equatorial Africa in 1886-87 (German edition, 1890), London, 1891 (117)

Witchell (Charles A.), The Evolution of Bird-Song, in The Zoologist, 3rd ser., vol. xiv. No. clxiii., July, 1890 (247)

Wood (Rev. J. G.), The Natural History of Man, 2 vols., London, 1868-70 (1, 4, 8, 9, 29, 42, 58)

Woods (J. D.), The Native Tribes of South Australia, Adelaide, 1879

Wyatt, see Gill

YULE (Henry), A Narrative of the Mission to the Court of Ava in 1855, London, 1858 (137)

ZEDTWITZ (Freiherr von), Japanesische Musikstücke, in Mittheilg. d. deutsch. Gesell. f. Ostasien, Bd. iv. Heft xxxiii., Aug., 1885, p. 128, Heft xxxii., Mar., 1885, p. 107 (17)

Zeitschrift der deutschen morgenländischen Gesellschaft, Leipzig

Zeitschrift für die Kunde des Morgenlandes, Bonn, ed. by Lassen

Zeitschrift für Ethnologie, Berlin

Zeitschrift für Völkerpsychologie, edited by Lazarus und Steinthal, Berlin

Zimmermann (W. F. A., pseud., i.e., W. F. Volliner), Die Inseln des indischen und stillen Meeres, Berlin, 1863-65 (27, 29, 30, 90, 141)

Zimmermann (Robert), Æsthetik, 2 vols., Wien, 1858-65 (232)

Zöllner (Heinrich), Einiges über sudanesische Musik, in Musikalisches Wochenblatt, 1885, vol. xvi. No. xxxvii. p. 446 (76, 159)

Zoologist (The), edited by J. E. Harting, London

Zwaardemaker (H.), Der Verlust an hohen Tönen mit zunehmendem Alter, in Archiv f. Ohrenheilk, Bd. xxxii., 1891, pp. 53-56 (240)

INDEX.

(323)

ABERDEEN UNIVERSITY PRESS.

N⁰ 1.

I.

II.

N⁰ 2.

N⁰ 3.

Nº 4.

Nº 5.

(Beckler.)

(Wilkes.)

Larghetto.

(Freycinet.)

№ 6. The Bride's Complaint. (♭♭ = ¼ flat, x = ¼ sharp)

№ 7.

№ 8. An Eskimo Lament.

Fine.

Da Capo al Fine.

№ 9.

№ 10.

Slow

№ 11. Andante.

Vivace. 1.

2.

Presto.

Allegro.

№ 12. Song of the Huchinom.

Nᵒ 18.

Nᵒ 19.

Nᵒ 20.

The Company.

The Dancers.

Water-Drum.

Nᵒ 21.

Note. The rising from *e* to *g*, and sinking again from *g* to *e* ought to be expressed by quarter tones. At every pause (◠) the singers are silent for some seconds, and then begin again, the voices rising by degrees from *e* to *g*.

№ 25.

Printed by Breitkopf and Härtel, Leipzig.